C0-ATG-475

# From Alienation to Addiction

# U.S. History in International Perspective

## Editors: Peter N. Stearns and Thomas W. Zeiler

EDITORIAL ADVISORY BOARD

Donna Gabaccia, University of Minnesota
James Gump, University of San Diego
Dirk Hoerder, Arizona State University, Universität Bremen
Peter Kolchin, University of Delaware
Robe Kroes, University of Amsterdam and University of Utrecht

NOW AVAILABLE

*Revolutions in Sorrow: The American Experience of Death in Global Perspective,* by Peter N. Stearns

*From Alienation to Addiction: Modern American Work in Global Historical Perspective,* by Peter N. Stearns

FORTHCOMING

*Diverse Nations: Explorations in the History of Racial and Ethnic Pluralism,* by George M. Fredrickson

*Comparing American Slavery: The U.S. "Peculiar Institution" in International Perspective,* by Enrico Dal Lago

# From Alienation to Addiction

## Modern American Work
## in Global Historical Perspective

### Peter N. Stearns

Paradigm Publishers
Boulder • London

HD
8066
.S69
2008

All rights reserved. No part of the publication may be transmitted or reproduced in any media or form, including electronic, mechanical, photocopy, recording, or informational storage and retrieval systems, without the express written consent of the publisher.

Copyright © 2008 Paradigm Publishers

Published in the United States by Paradigm Publishers, 3360 Mitchell Lane, Suite E, Boulder, CO 80301 USA.

Paradigm Publishers is the trade name of Birkenkamp & Company, LLC, Dean Birkenkamp, President and Publisher.

Library of Congress Cataloging-in-Publication Data

Stearns, Peter N.
    From alienation to addiction : modern American work in global historical perspective / Peter N. Stearns.
        p. cm. — (U.S. history in international perspective)
    Includes bibliographical references and index.
    ISBN-13: 978-1-59451-504-0 (hardcover : alk. paper)
    1. Labor—United States—History.   2. Work—United States—History.
    3. Working class—United States—History.   4. Work ethic—United States—History.
    5. Industrialization.   I. Title.
HD8066.S69 2008
331.0973—dc22
                                                                    2007044220

Printed and bound in the United States of America on acid free paper that meets the standards of the American National Standard for Permanence of Paper for Printed Library Materials.

Designed and Typeset by Straight Creek Bookmakers.

12  11  10  09  08    1  2  3  4  5

177824952

For Donna Kidd, with much love and many thanks

# Contents

# Acknowledgments

Veronica Fletcher provided reliable and imaginative research assistance for this book. I am grateful to many students at several institutions over the years, including George Mason University, for their interest in this topic. Donna Kidd provided useful suggestions as well. Leslie Lomas, as Paradigm editor, deserves my thanks for supporting this project. Annette Tallant and Laura Bell oversaw the preparation of the manuscript. I am grateful to the two anonymous readers for their good suggestions as well as their positive response.

# Series Preface

## U.S. History in International Perspective

This series offers a new approach to key topics in American history by connecting them with developments in other parts of the world and with larger global processes. Its goal is to present national patterns in mutual interaction with wider trends.

The United States has functioned in international context throughout its history. It was shaped by people who came from other countries. It drew political and cultural inspiration from other places as well. Soon, the nation began to contribute a variety of influences to other parts of the world, from new trade patterns to the impact of successful political institutions.

It is increasingly clear, however, that the field of U.S. history has not usually captured this perspective. National developments have been treated as significant but relatively isolated events. Distinctive American characteristics—sometimes systematized into a larger pattern called American exceptionalism—have been assumed but not tested through real comparison. Even the nation's growing role in world affairs has sometimes taken a back seat to domestic concerns. This kind of narrowness is inaccurate and unnecessary; it feeds a parochialism that is out of keeping with the global presence of the United States. A nation cannot be understood without placement in the perspective of other nations and transnational factors.

At a time when international developments play an increasing and incontestable role in any nation's affairs, the need for a new approach to national history becomes inescapable. This certainly applies to the United States. Calls for "internationalizing" the U.S. history survey course reflect this realization. The calls are welcome, but we need to translate them into accessible treatments of key topics in U.S. history—from obvious diplomatic and military initiatives to less obvious themes that in fact involve global interactions as well, themes that go deeply into the nation's social and cultural experience.

The project of internationalizing American history involves drawing a variety of connections. This series will compare American developments to patterns elsewhere to see what is really distinctive, and why, and what is more widely shared. Influences from other places, from technological innovations to human rights standards, factor in as well. The U.S. impact on other parts of the world, whether in the form of new work systems, consumer culture, or outright military intervention, constitutes a third kind of interconnection.

The result—and the central goal of this series—is to see American history in a revealing new light, as part of a network of global interactions. Wider world history gains from this approach as well, as comparisons are sharpened by the active inclusion of the United States, and American influences and involvements are probed more carefully.

Overall, a global window on the domestic interiors of U.S. history complicates conventional understandings, challenges established analyses, and brings fresh insights. A nation inextricably bound up with developments in every part of the world, shaping much of contemporary world history as well, demands a global framework. This series, as it explores a variety of topics and vantage points, aims to fill this need.

# CHAPTER 1

# Introduction: Analyzing Work as an Experience

An American manager had his own comparative work story, early in the twenty-first century. He was accustomed to national work patterns, which for his occupational bracket put a premium on visibly long hours. So he often stayed at the office into early evening, along with a number of colleagues, assuming that his supervisors would take notice. Then he took a position with a British company in London. But when he tried to apply his customary patterns, he discovered that both peers and supervisors found him odd—why would anyone stay late? Was this a sign of some revealing inefficiency on his part that he could not get things done during the normal day? He finally resolved his dilemma in part by claiming that he worked a bit late to avoid the worst of London traffic—this, but not an extra measure of devotion to work itself, was an acceptable excuse. But there was no question that he had encountered a bit of a culture gap where basic work habits were concerned.

His experience relates closely to larger patterns. Compared to most people in industrialized societies, Americans today work quite hard, at least by several measurements. A full 30 percent of all Americans do not take all the days off and sick days assigned to them annually, in use-it-or-lose-it programs; and while there are many reasons for this, a sense of the importance of work, and sometimes an inability to imagine anything more interesting, contributes strongly. Most strikingly, American vacation time is noticeably more limited than what is available in Western Europe or Japan. The Japanese, long and correctly regarded as a work-focused people, passed American vacation levels a few years back. Many Americans, with a week or two of annual leave, contrast vividly with, say, German workers, who enjoy five weeks a year at least. In 2005, 14 percent of all employed Americans said they had not taken more than a few days off in two years. Not surprisingly, given these patterns, American vacation time has increased very little in the past few decades, again a contrast with other industrial societies. Does the vacation differential and its result, more work during the average American year, reflect greater work devotion, meaner employers, or other factors? Does American culture, as some authorities have argued, encourage a particularly vigorous kind of work addiction?

In the 1970s, considerable discussion developed in the United States about work addiction—the term "workaholic" was coined. Various authorities bemoaned excessive work, particularly on the part of some males, and the damage this did to health and to family life. The discussion was revealing, and we will return to it. Equally revealing, however, was the extent to which it failed to alter many work habits, though surely some individuals were affected. In 2006, 56 percent of the top earners in the nation were working seventy hours or more per week, an increase over the hours during the previous decade. What some experts called "extreme jobs" demanded massive work commitments from many brokers, high-powered lawyers, and top managers, virtually as a price of admission to the fields. Equally interesting was the fact that most of the individuals involved claimed to love their work and their commitment. Of course, this was a minority phenomenon in the United States, not a typical pattern. But it revealed the extent to which something that might legitimately be called an addiction could not really be seen as a disease in the context of American measurements of social value.

There are other contemporary contrasts around the valuation of work. Many countries have government ministries devoted to leisure and free time, well beyond the focus of mere tourist bureaus; a project of this sort would seem frivolous in the United States, too personal but also too unimportant for government attention. Americans have also demonstrated in recent years how uncomfortable they are with programs that support healthy adults outside the labor force, cutting back on welfare payments by insisting on efforts to find work. Retirement is another intriguing area. Americans retire fairly readily, which obviously has to be factored into the work equation; but they are particularly likely, once retired, to claim that they are "busier than ever"—which, if true, means they can't really stop working or if, as is often the case, not really true, suggests how embarrassing it is not to seem to be working hard. Work seems to have a value and, for many, a focus in the United States that differs from the culture and experience of many other societies.

Of course, the United States hardly presents a uniform approach to work. Many groups have varied expectations and encounters where work is concerned. Women and men have reduced their work differentials in recent decades (as in other industrial societies), but there are still significant gender divides. Social class and rural/urban contrasts must be factored in. Children and work form a complex equation in many modern societies, and Americans, somewhat ironically, may be particularly edgy about overburdening their offspring. The elderly are another distinct work category, of growing importance in most industrial societies. Here, too, retirement patterns present many similarities with behaviors in other industrial societies, and some common challenges as well. It is important not to press differentiations too far.

Nevertheless, there are some American features attached to work and its symbolic importance, even as the nation participates in many common global trends. The nation's distinctiveness needs to be carefully explored, but it must also be explained. It's logical to assume that some particular qualities began to be associated with work earlier in the nation's past. The Puritan ethic, for example, had implications for work as a sign of God's grace. More prosaically, the demands of a frontier existence could create habits that would outlast the frontier itself, and possibly spread more widely. Recent historical research has highlighted how painful failures at work were during the nineteenth century, in a society that used work so readily as a measure of personal worth. It was in the nineteenth century also that the United States contributed to the world a dramatic increase in work regimentation—a sign of a willingness to impose work, if not on oneself, at least on others.

The basic proposition, then, is simple: many Americans have a somewhat unusual approach to work today; this results not merely from contemporary conditions but also from historical conditioning; and American distinctiveness has at times had wider consequences in the world as well.

Here, indeed, we need to place a fundamental comparative marker: while American work commitments have some intriguingly distinctive features, the basic American trajectory offers more similarities than differences with other industrial societies. The march toward modern work forms is the main point in the global work history of the past two centuries—although it should be carefully noted that many societies are only partially engaged in this march even today. The transformation of work—in the United States, but also in Western Europe, Japan and the Pacific Rim, and increasingly elsewhere—is the key focus even in comparative context, and most of this book will deal with these changes, their complexities, their advantages and disadvantages. American variants deserve attention as well, but only within this larger story. And the changes, crossing important political and cultural boundaries, have often been dramatic.

The comparative challenge—aimed at explaining, among other things, why Americans work so hard or at least want to think they work so hard—is only part of the story. The United States has also been engaged, along with many other parts of the world, in some very basic changes in what work is all about, changes that were initially associated with the Industrial Revolution but have amplified further as industrial economies themselves continue to evolve.

• Most modern urban people see their days divided between definite work periods and separate time for leisure and family (sleep and commuting also factor in of course); premodern work did not involve these sharp distinctions during the ordinary day. The whole notion of associating work so closely with clock time, a related change, required some painful adjustments. One of the unstated but quite real purposes of modern schooling is to teach the link between work and clock, so subtly that most students do not realize they're being trained.

• It's common to envisage premodern people working harder than modern people do, but we will see that the actual comparison is quite complicated. In terms of what, in modern language, we would describe as vacation days, premoderns often had moderns beat: many agricultural societies took as many as eighty to ninety special days off for festivals, easily dwarfing the formal vacation time available even in the more generous modern economies.

• Both premodern and modern work may require management of one's emotions. Many premodern workers had to show deference and obedience as part of serving others. But modern work often involves more elaborate staging—for example, injunctions to smile when dealing with customers, regardless of how one is actually feeling or how annoying the customers may be.

• The sheer number of job categories increases greatly as industrial economies develop and evolve. This partly reflects more detailed attention from census-taking bureaucracies. But it also suggests that the range of work categories, from very menial to highly trained, expands in modern societies. And it definitely captures increased specialization: premodern work, even manual labor, often involved various stages of production; much modern work cuts down the number of tasks in favor of precise, repetitious activities.

• A familiar contrast, though a fundamental one: almost all children were assumed to be workers in premodern society, whereas in modern societies child labor becomes a source of anxiety. How would this transition affect the way adults prepare for their own decades of work?

• Premodern work rarely involved complex equipment and normally depended on the power and speed supplied by humans and animals. Modern work is obviously vastly different. This raises a number of questions about changes in the meaning of work to those who serve the machines. In the 1830s a French factory owner placed a garland of flowers on the machine that had been most productive in the previous week. Quite apart from the high probability that the flowers wilted quickly, the sense of priorities this conveyed, in the balance between humans and technologies, was intriguing.

• Premodern work often involved physical dangers—from animal hooves, from excessive strain. Many weavers, who pushed part of their looms with their chests, developed characteristic chest concavities that could lead to illness later in life. Physical danger did not vanish from modern work, and mass accidents became more common. But modern work also added complaints about nervous strain, even nervous disease, which reflected new elements in the work equation.

These are just a few of a long list of fundamental changes in the work experience, associated with the rise, not only of industrial technologies and factories, but also of more modern offices and stores where emotion management might take on new contours. Not surprisingly, a key development with modern work involved new protest targets associated with work itself, rather than subsistence or landownership or slavery as in more traditional settings. A fundamental question, easy to raise though very hard to answer, is whether the huge changes in work over the past two centuries have worsened or improved this inescapable human experience.

For, along with the idea of new kinds of addiction to work, modern work conditions may also generate a real sense of alienation—a sense that work becomes so demanding and yet so meaningless that it is almost impossible to tolerate. Different kinds of alienation show up in modern work settings. We will see signs of alienation even in the United States, though the nation's professed devotion to work may make expression of alienation somewhat more difficult than is the case elsewhere.

This book tackles change and comparison alike, both generating key analytical issues about large slices of the quality of human life and both involving questions about alienation and addiction. The United States participated strongly in the movement toward more modern work experiences, as it imported industrial procedures from Western Europe and then rapidly expanded on the new forms. By the later nineteenth century, American industrial leaders were introducing further work innovations that would quickly have a global impact. Change continued through the following century, as industrial work was further refined and adapted to the growing array of service jobs and to new technologies such as computerization. But as it participated in, and often helped shape, basic modern forms of work, the United States also added its own flavor, building on a distinctive valuation of work that may have begun well before the industrial era. On the whole, as we will see, while both alienation and work addiction emerged in all modern societies, the American context made addiction slightly easier or more blatant than elsewhere, while complicating the expression of alienation compared to societies where work received slightly less glowing blessings. Contemporary Americans who take pride in avoiding long vacations, or who feel they have little alternative to work, reflect a particular blend of national and more broadly modern impulses.

*   *   *

Work is a fundamental feature of the human experience. Sigmund Freud once argued that the true measures of life were the quality of one's work, one's play, and one's love—and the latter two often depend on the first to a considerable degree. Work is so basic, so widely assumed, that it might be tempting to assume it has little history or little regional variety—it just is. But historians in recent decades have helped make it very clear that work is a considerable variable within societies, across societies, and across time. The arrival of modern work was a real jolt to many people accustomed to premodern standards, and it can be argued that, only two centuries into the modern experience, we're still adjusting to the new forms in many ways. History helps us measure where we are in the process of change and adjustment.

At the same time, work is also an oddly contested condition. Some children, not yet exposed to serious work, wish that they could avoid the encounter. Many adults, seeking retirement, cannot wait to escape the condition. Yet people without work often feel disoriented, and there are many value systems, including the dominant systems in the United States, that place great value on the capacity not just to work but to work hard. The Bible's Old Testament argued that work was a penalty for human sin, that before sin humans acquired what they needed without work. But many groups, including Christians, Muslims, and Jews who refer to the Old Testament, believe that work has religious meaning, a vital discipline for humankind and even a sign of God's grace. Again, history can help sort out the various and contradictory meanings of work and how contemporary American experience fits into this contested terrain.

The result can contribute not only to social understanding but also to personal meaning. Any society implicitly encourages people to fit into established work norms—this is as true in premodern as in modern conditions. But the result can discourage individual consideration of what work values best serve personal goals. Modern society offers several options, from true work addiction—which seems to suit some people well, though at some potential cost—to more casual engagement, to outright distaste. Thinking about work historically, and in comparative context, helps us grasp not only where the options came from and what they involve collectively, but also what they suggest about individual choices.

\* \* \*

This book, exploring the nature of modern and American work, divides into several time periods. The next chapter deals with traditional work patterns, including some changes in the eighteenth century; the ensuing chapter treats American traditions in the colonial period. Two chapters then take up the emergence of modern industrial work, first globally, then comparatively in the United States, from the late eighteenth until the mid-twentieth century. Chapter 6 then deals with special features of the modern workforce, from the onset of industrialization into the 1950s and 1960s. Chapters 7 and 8 take up recent trends of the past half century, globally and in American contexts.

Premodern work, our starting point, is a tricky concept, and obviously a very broad one. Hunting and gathering activities, nomadic efforts, and agricultural labor are quite different, but they are all premodern. Within agricultural societies, conditions vary greatly from upper to lower class, from rural to urban, and (often) from slave to technically free. Even a brief survey of premodern work needs to take both fundamental change and variety into account. The unifying characteristics of premodern work rest largely on the fact that, despite variations, it was never modern: it never, for example, depended on powered equipment the way modern work does.

Premodern work is a vital topic, however, despite its complexity, for three reasons. First, it provides a baseline from which modern changes can be measured. We can appreciate the strangeness and enormity of the transformations of work in factories and offices only when we really know how these jobs differed from what had long predominated. Second, premodern work long persisted. Even as we spend many following chapters dealing with changes away from premodern conditions, it is essential to remember that most people, even in the United States, continued to work in premodern settings well into the twentieth century (though of course these might change somewhat in response to the rise of some modern industry or other shifts such as the abolition of slavery—premodern work was never changeless). The world as a whole became half urban only in 2006—and many urban people continue to operate in an essentially premodern fashion. Premodern work, particularly but not exclusively in agriculture, has a massive constituency still, though it is increasingly on the defensive. Finally, even as modern work gains ground, premodern elements persist, in the values people apply and in habits they seek to defend. This complexity, as well, can only be grasped if we understand fundamental features of premodern work in the first place.

# CHAPTER 2

# Work in Premodern Societies

All historians of work would agree that many aspects of contemporary work are unnatural. For example, paying so much attention to coordinating and pacing work by the clock is a crucial modern innovation, only a couple of centuries old. There's nothing natural about it. But it is not too easy to determine what "natural" work consists of—partly because human beings have long proved fairly adaptable to different work regimes depending on the environment.

Hunting and gathering societies, the earliest type of human economy, do offer some suggestions about work and human nature. When societies depended on hunting for meat (normally a male task) and gathering seeds and berries (a woman's task, which often, however, generated more usable calories in food than more-ballyhooed hunting did), two or three characteristics predominated. First, on average, work in the sense of seeking food did not take up much time. It's been estimated that in surviving hunting and gathering societies, people spend only about two and a half hours a day in actual work—though this does not count child care, local politics, or other chores. Much time is available for what we would call play or leisure activities. Second, though more for men than for women, work tended to be sporadic, coming in bursts in which a day or more might be spent in intense labor, followed by longer periods of downtime. Work is obviously essential to survival in these societies, but it defines a smaller part of daily life than might be imagined. Children's association with work is also limited. Boys were not included in hunting until they reached their teens, and often a formal ceremony and testing period marked this transition to work. Children were also not useful as gatherers—contemporary studies show that mothers who take their kids on gathering expeditions are less productive than those who make other arrangements; children get in the way. Childhood was not, as a result, usually associated with very specific work obligations. Older people were certainly expected to help out as they could; even with diminished capacities, they could often help process nuts and seeds.

The traditional work patterns most relevant to modern human history derive, not from hunting and gathering societies, which began to be replaced over ten thousand years ago, but from agricultural economies, in which the bulk of the population usually consists of peasant farmers. Without question, transitions to agriculture involved significant changes in the nature of work. Most obviously, the amount of work required on a daily basis increased significantly. Agriculture offered the opportunity of assuring more-regular food supplies and supporting a larger population than had been possible with hunting and gathering, but there was no free ride. Agricultural work was, to be sure, seasonal, with specific conditions depending on climate. Many peasants worked far less in winter months, and, where food was in short supply (as in parts of preindustrial Ireland), they might actually sleep a great deal, semi-hibernating in order to conserve energy. But from planting onward, work was extensive, its boundaries determined mainly by available sunlight.

Childhood also became more closely associated with work than had been the case before. Many children were expected to begin some work contributions by age five. By their early teens many children worked hard enough that they were actually more than covering the costs of their upkeep. Many agricultural families depended on the labor of virtually all their members, in the house and on land around the house; there were often few other contributors available. Older children and young adults were expected to continue their work for the family economy, either not marrying until they could afford a household of their own—the unusual family pattern that developed in Western Europe by the early modern centuries—or more commonly marrying but continuing to operate as part of an extended family and extended household, the common pattern in eastern Europe, the Middle East, and Asia, where sons would bring new wives back to their family property.

Rural families also, however, frequently shipped teenage children to other families for some years of work, usually expecting that they would later come back home. There were several purposes here, and historians continue to discuss the key priorities involved. Most obviously, some families would go through a period when they had more young workers at home than they could fully utilize, particularly if their landholdings were modest. It only made sense to ship a few elsewhere, to childless families, for example (and up to 20 percent of all rural families would be incapable, for biological reasons, of conceiving children), or to families with larger landholdings and therefore more labor needs, or to older families who needed and could afford extra help. Sometimes, additional training was also a goal, and children were sent off to more-formal apprenticeship programs. But some historians have also speculated that parents might welcome a chance to send kids off for a few years when they were at a particularly difficult age, requiring strict discipline that parents themselves would rather not have to administer directly. Certainly, many work exchanges of children found the children saddled with poor living conditions and harsh treatment, including physical blows to encourage more diligent labor.

Gender divisions were always closely associated with agricultural work, though they were somewhat more contrived than in hunting and gathering societies.

Agriculture initially must have seemed very close to women's traditional work, since it involved the same kinds of products that gathering had emphasized. Many men surely found being tied to the land a somewhat unmasculine require-ment, compared to the presumed glories of hunting or nomadic herding or (as in the American West as recently as 150 years ago), ranching. But in most socie-ties women were soon squeezed out of the primary responsibilities for growing staple crops of grains. They might assist in planting and harvesting; they might take over if their husbands were absent, ailing, or dead—for they were perfectly capable of the kinds of work required. But they were rarely seen as having the primary production responsibilities in the family. This may have been an essential trade-off for involving men with agriculture: they had to be seen as central if they were to participate at all. But changing birthrates also created new constraints for women in agricultural work. With food supplies expanding, compared to hunting and gathering, and with children more necessary in the labor force, most adult women spent a considerable amount of time between their late teens and early forties pregnant or caring for very small children, in households that would typi-cally experience six to eight births and sometimes more. This limited the time available for work in the fields.

Women's labor was vital in this new system but tended to be seen as supple-mentary. Women cared for household and food preparation. Along with relevant children, they typically tended any vegetable plots near the house, and they often cared for family livestock like poultry. They made the family's clothing. Often, they were responsible for bringing water from the well, though interestingly there were some cases in which this was regarded as a man's job.

While gender identity in work was strongly emphasized, men and women shared many work features in agriculture. Their work was varied, with lots of dif-ferent tasks and relatively low levels of specialization. Most of the waking day was spent on work obligations, except on festival occasions (when, however, women, because of food-preparation responsibilities, might get much less of a break than men did). Considerable physical energy had to be expended, for key tasks were manual and demanding.

Old age was, inevitably, something of a variable at work. While no systematic retirement existed in agriculture, many people found their physical capacities diminishing (of course, some adults did not survive to old age at all) and had to arrange for some accommodations. In extended households, the elderly could still do some work while benefiting from the labor of younger members. European-style families, by the sixteenth century, presented a greater problem. Many older people tried to limit their adult children's access to marriage, to retain their labor. Often, couples deliberately had a child in their early forties—called a *Wunschkind*, or wished-for child, in German—to provide care when they aged. Some older people tried to use contracts to exchange part of their land, as early inheritance, to an adult child in return for agreed-upon provisions of food. But generational tensions about work and care could be considerable. Most traditional societies saw some older people, incapable of working enough to support themselves but lacking family assistance, resort to begging or enter charitable institutions—like hospitals—where they would wait to die.

While work in agricultural societies presented some standard issues and features, there were variations and changes over time as well. When first introduced, agriculture normally provided an exclusive focus for family labor, barring some occasional hunting at particular seasons. With time, however, some agricultural families began to introduce manufacturing work beyond the needs of the families themselves. This domestic manufacturing, conducted with simple equipment in peasant households, often involved the production of thread or cloth (including silks in China) or simple metal products like nails. Women might be heavily involved, for example in spinning and sometimes in weaving. Children worked as assistants in what was, like agricultural work, a family-based endeavor. Domestic manufacturing could bring in a bit of money, particularly desirable when the family's landholdings were meager. Workers sometimes received orders from urban merchants directly, sometimes took their work to town for sale more directly. But home manufacturing extended work demands as well. Considerable physical strength might be needed to activate the equipment. Some weavers, who pushed part of the handlooms with their chest, developed permanent deformities. Many domestic manufacturing workers also labored in excessive dampness, not only because of the conditions of their homes but also of the need to protect textile products from brittleness.

Some rural manufacturing, whether for sale or for family use, was conducted in group settings, mixing labor with community socializing. French peasants often conducted *veillées,* or evening gatherings, where by lamplight a group would work together, exchanging conversation, perhaps even songs, and sometimes dining together as well. These occasions drove home the extent to which traditional rural work often—by more-modern standards—mixed experiences, combining sheer labor with family and with social enjoyment.

Traditional rural work, whether manufacturing or agricultural, also usually involved a fairly relaxed pace. It extended over many hours and, in that sense, could seem grueling. And there were occasions, when a harvest needed to be completed or an order for manufactured goods was pressing, when work intensity could not be avoided. Generally, however, work was compatible with some chatting, with frequent breaks, and even with some naps. There was no sharp distinction, during the day, between what modern observers would label work and nonwork.

*   *   *

Long before modern times, many societies also developed elaborate categories of urban work, centered particularly around skilled craft manufacturing. There were, to be sure, a few cases, like Russia, where rural populations so predominated that urban work sectors were not clearly developed. In the Asian civilizations, in the Middle East/North Africa, in Western Europe and elsewhere, however, proud traditions of craft labor were well established before the challenge of industrialization.

Craft workers carefully distinguished themselves from rural labor (though they might recruit rural youths into apprenticeship programs). They tended to look down on country people, regarding their work as more mindless, certainly less skilled and artistic, than their own. In retrospect, however, we can also see that urban crafts embodied some of the same features as rural labor did, at least in contradistinction to more-modern work forms.

Traditions of craft work, finally, would contrast particularly vividly with many modern norms. It is of course important to remember that craft workers were always in a minority in premodern societies, even the most urbanized—most workers were always rural, and even in the cities there were unskilled transportation workers, construction assistants, and other groups quite different from the craft workers. But craft values were unusually well articulated, and they overlapped to some extent with premodern work goals more generally. The distinction from what developed later, with industrialization, provided vivid opportunities for conflict and tension, as workers compared the values they inherited, directly or indirectly, from craft traditions with what they now saw around them.

Craft production was centered on workers' skills. While some assisting equipment might be essential—obviously, furnaces in the case of metallurgical work or glass manufacture—hand tools were essential, from butchering meat to producing fine jewelry. The skills involved required training, and because of their complexity they also protected many artisans from too much open competition. They also provided a sense of creativity and direct engagement with the finished product. Typically, a whole series of operations had to be conducted before the product was complete—from cutting boards to assembling and finishing furniture, to take another example. There was no elaborate division of labor. Arguably, not only a feeling of participation but also a real engagement of interest was involved in most craft work.

As with agriculture, artisans typically worked long hours, depending of course on available light. But their pace was rarely intense. Some crafts had a certain seasonal quality: printers, for example, had to work unusually hard toward the end of the calendar year, when many official reports had to be turned out, whereas the intensity slackened during the summer. Typically, however, artisans could mix chatter and singing with the work they did. Lulls in the day might even offer a chance for a nap. A few specialties, like construction, established a tradition of taking a drink or two for relaxation before the workday began. Crafts that involved work in intense heat, like blacksmithing and baking, frequently saw workers drink alcohol recurrently during the day. Many European crafts took Sunday off for religious purposes but then followed with an informal Monday off as well. The French called this "holy Monday," sacred because it provided leisure time free from religious obligations.

Most artisans worked in small shops, which provided social bonds that reinforced the work experience. Many artisans lived in the same shop, sharing meals.
Families were directly engaged: wives often ran the business side of the operation,
selling the goods (in some cases, they were more likely to be literate than their
husbands, because such skills were commercially useful); children provided assistance, as in cleaning up scraps or carrying in raw materials. As in rural work,
the link between family and production was very close.

The social qualities of artisanal work were enhanced by the fact that, in most
cities, artisans in many crafts clustered in the same neighborhood. Many cities
thus had leather goods sections, or a district for the silver crafts. The arrangement
may seem irrational by modern standards, for it limited opportunities to exploit
a wider customer base by fanning out. But as we will see, the purpose of artisanal
work was not to maximize earnings but to participate in a rich experience, and
the opportunity to work alongside many similar craftsmen added to the social
qualities involved, while making it possible to share information about artistic
innovations. Again there were echoes of the rural experience in the absence of
boundary lines between social life and labor.

More formally than with rural work, however, the life of an artisan was divided
into stages. Apprenticeship was the first phase, after the sheer assistance period of
earlier childhood. Apprenticeships often started in the early teens and, depending
on skill levels required, could last up to seven years. Even relatively simple branches,
like lace making, demanded a full year of training. Apprenticeships ended with
a test of skill, creating a "master" work that could demonstrate full competence.
The trained worker then transitioned to journeyman status, capable of a full range
of production activities but still honing the skill. Many young journeymen, not
only in Europe but also in places like Japan, would travel for a few years from city
to city—the Germans called these the "wander years"—in order to gain additional
experience and have some fun, while working a few months in a particular shop
at each stop. In principle, after a variable period of service as journeyman, the
artisan would rise to own his own shop, becoming a full-fledged master artisan:
this might occur through marriage to a master's daughter, through inheritance
from an artisanal father, or through purchase. When the system worked well,
mobility within the lifetime was part of the artisan's work experience, in a process
that was more clearly defined than in the agricultural sector.

Craftsmen in many countries solidified and defended their work values through
organized guilds. Guilds developed during the Middle Ages in western and central
Europe. They arose also in Middle Eastern cities and in Japan. Their purposes
were several, but they all revolved around maintaining the key characteristics of
artisanal work. Guilds regulated the number of apprentices and the nature of apprenticeship, to make sure that skill levels remained high and that the crafts were
not overwhelmed with excess numbers that would drive down the value of labor
and individual earnings. Guilds also sought to make sure that masters did not
exploit apprentice labor by focusing entirely on assistance tasks like transporting

goods and materials, but rather provided solid training. The key point was keeping skill at the center of craft work.

Guilds also sought to limit the number of apprentices and journeymen an individual master could take, to prevent too much inequality within the craft and to make sure that personal relationships continued to combine with the work experience. This measure also restrained the temptation to drive workers too hard in order to maximize earnings; since there were boundaries to how far the shop could expand, there were boundaries as well to the pressures to maximize output.

Guilds actively worked to discourage technological innovations. The guilds vigorously defended traditional methods—the core of artisanal skill—against any attempt to introduce labor-saving devices. In fact, while small changes could and did occur in branches such as metallurgy before the modern centuries, there was a great deal of continuity in artisanal methods across the centuries. Here was an obvious contrast with the principles that would come to define work in the industrial age.

In return for defense of artisanal work values, guilds also sought to protect consumers against shoddy quality. Assurance that artisans had the requisite skills, and guild pride in artistry, provided some real guarantees—and this in turn became part of the artisan's self-definition.

Guilds also promoted representation of artisanal work in the wider urban society. Many guilds wielded real political power. They participated collectively in many urban ceremonies, marching as groups with distinctive uniforms and symbols. Here again was a way to demonstrate and to inculcate pride in the work done and to establish that work was really at the core of the individual's identity. Many guilds also organized collective leisure activities. Japanese guilds, for example, sponsored trips, and guilds in many places arranged feasts and drinking sessions; many provided assistance in illness or later age, reducing the insecurities that might otherwise be associated with work.

It is important not to overidealize the artisan tradition and its expression in guilds. In the first place, guilds deliberately limited output and retarded change— these were direct results of the core mission. They could in this sense frustrate an imaginative or ambitious worker. No society would ever be able to industrialize with a full guild apparatus in place in its cities. Guilds had declined in Britain by the eighteenth century. They were abolished in France and neighboring regions during the French Revolution—the key legislation, the Le Chapelier Act, was passed in 1791. Guilds would be largely abolished in central Germany by 1848, though they later revived, in part, as more purely social units. Guilds declined in Japan by the 1890s. Modern work and guild work could not easily coexist, and while many losses resulted for the workers involved, there were important gains as well.

Even before modern times, guilds worked imperfectly even in their own terms. In the first place, many urban workers were not in guilds. Transport workers and those in other unskilled categories had a very different work experience and structure, with much more uncertainty even about basic employment from day to day. Craftsmen themselves might not be in guilds: for no apparent reason, certain cities might not develop guilds in crafts that in other cities were well organized. They might share some features of the craft work experience, but with much less protection and prestige. Typically, the workers in these situations would face more competition, because access to the trade was not guarded, and inferior working conditions and living standards. A few trades, though skilled, were virtually never organized as guilds. This was particularly true of crafts in which women predominated, though there were occasionally a few female guilds. In many European crafts, women had actually been forced out of key fields during the sixteenth and seventeenth centuries. This meant that they either worked as part of a family group, where, as we have seen, their services could be essential, or operated alone, usually in a low-paying craft like lace making, where long hours of strenuous work were necessary to provide a meager subsistence.

Where guilds did operate, their principles might break down. Protection of apprentices was unreliable in many cases, and many apprentices were overworked and undertrained, and subjected to disciplinary beatings in the process. Also common was a process where the number of journeymen outstripped any opportunity to rise to a position of master. This not only voided the desired mobility, it also encouraged the masters to treat journeymen as inferior employees, even separating themselves at work and in social interactions. Guilds might turn, in the masters' hands, to devices to protect the masters and to confine access to ownership to the masters' own offspring. Journeymen were not always passive in these circumstances, for they were fully aware of craft principles and might try to restore the balance through their own organizations, which could resemble what later became known as trade unions. Strikes by disgruntled journeymen against masters whose behavior was too arbitrary or greedy dotted the European experience from the sixteenth century onward. Still, many journeymen could be desperately poor and suffer long periods of unemployment. Many found it impossible to marry, because they had no hope of secure work. And no amount of guild protection could save many artisans from some of the disadvantages of intense physical labor. Many skilled weavers, for example, were deformed by pushing looms with their chests, just as in the domestic manufacturing system. Many housepainters and printers suffered from lead poisoning.

Artisanal work life must be seen as a combination of distinctive and powerful principles and a host of pressures and problems. And while artisans on the whole would greet more modern work conditions with great suspicion and considerable outright protest, because of the defiance of older principles, a few would welcome new opportunities to escape the drawbacks and inconsistencies of the customary regime.

*    *    *

To a modern eye, preindustrial work, whether agricultural or artisanal, offered some common elements. Craft workers felt vastly superior to rural peasants;

ideas about country bumpkins are not modern inventions, and there were very real differences in skill levels and, with guilds, institutional contexts. Still, some themes were broadly shared.

Most preindustrial work was fairly diverse, involving a variety of tasks or production stages during a working day or week. Most work occurred in a familial setting, often literally in or around the household. Even people who were not literally family, like unmarried journeymen or farm laborers, were embraced in the household, frequently sharing meals and other social contacts. Most work proceeded at a fairly restrained pace. There might be periods of intense activity, like harvest time or (for coal miners) a production surge to prepare for the onset of winter. But more normally work could be combined with socialization and rest. Aside from outright days off, there was little daily distinction between work and leisure, for what modern people would regard as recreational elements were mixed in with the work process.

Many historians believe that premodern work also facilitated a sense of pride and personal contribution. Certainly, the guilds encouraged this kind of stake by emphasizing tests of skill and by publicly manifesting the power of the craft. Rural workers might, however, gain a somewhat similar sense, even amid many very prosaic and strenuous tasks, as they sponsored production from planting to harvest. This aspect of preindustrial work is not easy to pin down, and there is a danger of undue nostalgia. Many anxieties accompanied the process: What if a harvest failed, as occurred in most regions to some degree about every seven years? What if demand dropped and journeymen had to be thrown out of work? The sheer physical strain and, sometimes, outright danger of preindustrial work must be factored in as well. But the opportunity for some satisfaction might remain.

Most preindustrial work also offered a promise of rising toward a position of self-management, though within the confines of community norms and traditions. A peasant could legitimately hope, over time, to rise from assistance work within the family to outright ownership or at least greater voice in family councils. Artisans ideally often had a shot at master status by early middle age. To be sure, there were many potential barriers. Some agricultural laborers never had an opportunity for landownership, if only because their inheritance prospects were clouded by the claims of other siblings or by their parents' own poverty. We have seen that many journeymen never made it. But lots of workers could legitimately hope that periods of working under the direction of others, including parents, would yield to opportunities to plan their own workday. Most preindustrial work hierarchies were not too rigid in any event, at least after childhood. Preindustrial values did not encourage thoughts of social mobility in the modern sense. Though individuals did rise in society, and there were individual stories of peasant boys who made it to the ranks of the wealthy—like Dick Whittington, ultimately a lord mayor of London despite humble rural beginnings in the late Middle Ages—preindustrial culture emphasized the importance of remaining in one's social place and not assuming that work would be rewarded by some massive change in station. This said, it was also true that many people could legitimately expect some positive evolution in work status over a lifetime, within the assigned social place.

The situation for women workers was somewhat more complicated. Married women would always work in the shadow of their husband's control over the household (or the control of his own older male relatives, in the case of extended families). And single women faced a very difficult prospect because of limited work opportunities; often, they would have to accept a dependent position in someone else's household. But, for married women, male direction was usually fairly unspecific. The clear division of labor allowed fathers and husbands to assume that women would take care of a set of tasks on their own: not only management of children and the household, but also vegetable farming and care for the stock. This meant in turn that married women, at least as they grew older and had younger women in the household under their direction, could gain some sense of personal control over the workday, though again guided by custom and community expectations.

Many of the patterns of preindustrial work even described many slave rhythms in the premodern world, at least before the sixteenth century. Slavery was a well-established labor system in many societies before modern times. Greece and Rome relied heavily on slave labor in the classical period; so did Middle Eastern society under Arab rule and also sub-Saharan Africa. Russia had about 10 percent of its population in slavery until the midseventeenth century, when the practice began to fade. Slavery was far less common in East and South Asia from the classical period onward, though some domestic servants were held as slaves. Slaves performed all sorts of functions in most of the societies where they were widespread. Some served under harsh work conditions, doing dangerous jobs and operating under the whips of harsh taskmasters. Galley slaves who rowed the Greek and Roman ships in the Mediterranean, and also slaves who worked gold or silver mines in the classical period, endured unusually severe work that often shortened their lives. But most slaves, working as domestic servants, tutors for children, government bureaucrats and even soldiers, and agricultural laborers, had patterns of work not very different from the rest of the population in terms of pace, variety, and so on. Of course they had a very different legal status; they could be sold, unless (as was not uncommon) their masters granted their freedom or they earned enough money to purchase it. But the work attached to slavery was not, for the most part, really distinctive. This helps explain why some people sold their children into slavery or sought slavery themselves, hoping for more secure material conditions from their owner in return for loss of freedom; the trade-off in work itself was not always very great. Of course there was less hope for the acquisition of control over one's routine, though some slaves worked in considerable independence on condition of turning part of their earnings over to their owners. But for many slaves, this was the main difference where work was involved; the other basic rhythms were similar to those in premodern societies more generally.

Preindustrial work, finally, was informed by a deep sense of tradition. Most workers believed that their basic work values and methods were hallowed by the ages, and they were not entirely wrong. To be sure, change occurred. By the eighteenth century, for example, European peasants began to deal with new crops, like the potato. Chinese peasants had frequently participated in improvements in methods and seeds, for example in rice cultivation, and they too had adapted to new crops. The spread of domestic manufacturing, in Song China or in eighteenth-century Europe, was a very real change for peasant work life, even when some participation in agriculture continued. On the artisanal side, whole new crafts might spring into being, like printing in sixteenth-century Europe. But change was usually folded into a larger sense of continuity. Printers, though very proud of their literacy and special skills, quickly informed their craft with a sense of customary values, and broadly speaking, they did import the work patterns and guild institutions already developed in the older sectors, grafting onto printing a legitimate claim to tradition. Tradition, even if partly imagined, could add a sense of pride. Fathers could often expect their sons to duplicate their own work lives when they inherited the land or the craft master's shop. Women could see the same future for their daughters. This sense of family continuity could easily enhance a sense of pride and value in the work.

Tradition was double-edged, of course. It also could limit horizons and prompt resistance to changes that might have eased work burdens or created new opportunities. Certainly, the deep sense of work traditions would pose real challenges when work began to encounter more fundamental transformation with industrialization—challenges for those trying to orchestrate the changes, challenges for those on whom the changes were imposed. For, whatever one's assessment of the balance sheet of preindustrial work, there is no question that the traditions formed would long serve as the standard by which ordinary people would assess change—and often find it undesirable.

*   *   *

Basic work patterns were of course modified by regional cultural and social systems, including, of course, the extent to which slavery or other forms of coercive labor were present. We must be wary of overgeneralization. Several cultures (in much of Islam, but also in Hinduism) placed restrictions on women's activities outside the home, though these bore more fully on the upper classes than on others. These limitations would obviously affect work patterns, particularly when work might entail marketing efforts. In North Africa and other regions, until recently much food marketing was done by rural women, who though Muslim were less affected by gender restrictions, while urban women did not work in public settings. In another variant, agricultural traditions in parts of sub-Saharan Africa gave larger productive roles to women in the fields than was common elsewhere. Male labor was important also, as against some stereotypes that African agriculture was really female-dominated; only in the twentieth century, when many men went off to cities and mines, did women's role expand greatly. Still, the premodern pattern had some distinctive features. Certainly, different regions had different levels of artisanal and domestic manufacturing activities, with highly developed commercial societies like China and, by the early modern period, Western Europe, quite different from places like Russia.

*   *   *

Agricultural societies in general were not dominated by what in modern times would be called a work ethic. Members of the elite might in fact work very hard, but they tended to emphasize goals other than work when they communicated to the wider society. Aristocracies, most obviously, did not define their high status on the basis of superior work habits. They might point to military prowess, or political wisdom, or a cultivated lifestyle, or some combination of the three; but work was not an explicit component. Other cultural values pointed away from work at least to some degree. Most obviously, the major religions urged attention to spiritual advancement and attainments in the next life, not work for its own sake.

Work could be fit into the dominant cultures, of course. In China, Confucianists urged that the duty of ordinary people was to work productively, and in return for this performance and appropriate deference they could expect benevolent treatment from their superiors. Hindu belief, urging fulfillment of tasks appropriate to each caste, in essence urged many people to work according to their station. Many pious organizations used work as a framework for spiritual exercise. In Western Europe, the Benedictine Rule for monks, introduced in Italy in the sixth century, urged a careful regimen of work, along with ritual and prayer, to make sure the brothers remained tied to a discipline rather than opening themselves to dangerous flights of fancy. Some historians have seen in Western monasticism an unusual commitment to work routines that might affect the rest of society. Later, in Protestantism, the capacity to work hard was sometimes taken as a sign of God's grace.

Still, hard work in its own right did not sit at the top of the value system in premodern societies. This hardly distracted from most people's need to commit to the work systems of agriculture and the crafts on a daily basis. But the dominant value system was reflected in the common priority given to popular festivals as opportunities to let up on work and enjoy a day or a few days of alternative revelry or religious dedication in which work demands could be forgotten. Along with premodern work routines, this implicit nonwork priority would also be challenged by more modern systems, when the festival tradition eroded and many people became uncomfortable, even disoriented, when remaining holidays pulled them away from the regimen of work.

*   *   *

The most explicit challenges to premodern work traditions opened with the Industrial Revolution at the end of the eighteenth century. But historians are discovering that, even a few centuries earlier, changes were brewing in work patterns in many societies around the world. These changes foreshadowed some of the industrial developments, and they also generated new kinds of criticisms of groups that based their lives on values other than work.

Two factors pushed for some intensification of work in several regions. The most general was the heightening of global commerce, including the growing use of silver from the Americas. New opportunities for sales prompted many estate owners, mine owners, and manufacturers to press their workers to work harder. Individual peasant or artisan families might need to intensify their work as well, either to take advantage of new sales opportunities or to earn money to pay rising taxes. China, for example, required in the seventeenth century that taxes be paid in silver, and this put serious pressure on many ordinary people to expand output. Along with commercialization came population growth in several places, including China and some other parts of Asia. Many families had to work harder in order to support an unexpectedly large number of children surviving into adulthood.

New work pressures showed in several dimensions, though it is difficult to be terribly precise. The use of child labor, and the expectations for children at work, probably increased in many places in the seventeenth and eighteenth centuries. Older people often found it harder to ease up in their work. Traditionally, as we have seen, though formal retirement systems did not exist, many older peasants and artisans would gradually reduce their efforts as their health conditions changed, counting on support from other family members. This pattern may now have been disrupted, forcing some older people to work well beyond their expectations or normal capacities in order to obtain the means to survive. Most obviously, the new slave systems established in the Americas, and increasingly harsh serfdom in the Americas and in Russia, saw land- and mine owners attempt to increase the work pace and output of their laborers well beyond the standards common in more traditional slavery. Finally, some new technologies were introduced that, though still involving manual equipment, were designed to speed up production—for example, in European textiles, a new spinning wheel in the seventeenth century freed one hand of the women workers, who could then operate two machines, increasing output at a time of growing demand for thread.

None of this yet involved fundamental innovation in work patterns, as opposed to attempts to wrest more production from traditional techniques and habits. It did suggest, however, a building pressure to change, a pressure that would generate more radical experiments in the management of labor from the later eighteenth century onward.

One other change, perhaps related, was also interesting. In Western Europe, Enlightenment intellectuals in the eighteenth century, particularly in the prerevolutionary ideological buildup in France, began to attack the aristocracy on grounds that aristocrats did no work. Members of the rest of society, they argued, should have equal legal rights and political power because they, or at least the bourgeoisie, did society's work. Attacks on the aristocracy were hardly new: peasants in many societies had periodically protested aristocratic corruption or ownership of land that peasants thought belonged to them. But the charge of idleness, and the attendant claim that work should be the criterion for social participation, was a new twist. Here again, something new was in the air, in this case involving novel values that could in the long run inform actual experience as well.

*   *   *

Premodern work, both before and during the changes in the seventeenth and eighteenth centuries, offers several faces. No polls exist to tell us what people thought about their work lives, or what they wanted others to believe they thought. It is important not to be nostalgic. Much preindustrial work was physically demanding, and it took a toll on many backs and limbs. Many preindustrial workers faced a lifetime of constraint, forced as slaves or servants or laborers always to work for someone else. Almost everyone, in childhood and youth, would anticipate a period of being bossed around. Most modern people in industrial societies would probably not fancy many aspects of preindustrial work—we know that because they shun jobs, like migratory farm labor, that maintain many of the less-attractive aspects of this work. But for many premodern workers, there were also important values and meanings in work. Some of these were being challenged by the new pressures of the early modern period; many would be further tested by industrialization—and some, perhaps, lost outright. There was a crucial, if mixed and complicated, legacy for future evaluations, once work began to change quite rapidly.

# Further Reading

## On Peasant Work

Emmanuel Le Roy Ladurie, *The Peasants of Languedoc* (Urbana: University of Illinois Press, 1974); Thomas Sheppard, *Lourmarin in the Eighteenth Century: A Study of a French Village* (Baltimore: Johns Hopkins University Press, 1971). See also Fernand Braudel, *Capitalism and Material Life, 1400–1800* (New York: HarperCollins, 1974).

## On Urban Workers

Catharina Lis, *Social Change and the Laboring Poor: Antwerp, 1770–1860* (New Haven: Yale University Press, 1986); Peter Laslett, *The World We Have Lost*, offers a nostalgic view (London: Routledge, 1965).

## On Artisans

James Farr, *Artisans in Europe, 1350–1914* (Cambridge: Cambridge University Press, 2000); Merry Wiesner, *Working Women in Renaissance Germany* (New Brunswick, NJ: Rutgers University Press, 1986); Daryl Hafer, ed., *European Women and Preindustrial Craft* (Bloomington: Indiana University Press, 1995); David Herlihy, *Opera Muliebria: Women and Work in Medieval Europe* (Philadelphia: Temple University Press, 1990); Barbara Hannawalt, ed., *Women and Work in Preindustrial Europe* (Bloomington: Indiana University Press, 1986); Geoffrey

Crossick and Heinz-Gerhard Haupt, *Shopkeepers and Master Artisans in Nineteenth-Century Europe* (New York: Routledge Kegan & Paul, 1986).

## On Work Changes in Preindustrial Europe

Peter Kriedte, Hans Medick, and J. M. Schlumbohm, *Industrialization before Industrialization* (Cambridge: Cambridge University Press, 1981); and Maths Isacson and Lars Magnusson, *Protoindustrialization in Scandinavia* (New York: Berg, 1987).

## On Economic Developments in China Relevant to Work Patterns

Kenneth Pomeranz, *The Great Divergence: China, Europe and the Making of the Modern World Economy* (Berkeley: University of California Press, 2000).

## Studies of Rural Work

Although focused on current issues, the following studies help provide some historical perspective, particularly on gender issues.

Peter Lawrence and Colin Thirtle, eds., *Africa and Asia in Comparative Economic Perspective* (New York: Palgrave, 2001); David Ludden, *An Agrarian History of South Asia* (Cambridge: Cambridge University Press, 1999); Thomas Smith, *The Agrarian Origins of Modern Japan* (Stanford: Stanford University Press, 1959); Jean Allman, Susan Geiger, and Nakanyike Musisi, eds., *Women in African Colonial Histories* (Bloomington: Indiana University Press, 2002); Gracia Clark, ed., *At Work in Economic Life* (Walnut Creek, CA: Altamira Press, 2003); Deborah Bryceson, *Women Wielding the Hoe: Lessons from Rural Africa for Feminist Theory and Development Practice* (Oxford: Berg, 1995); Thomas Leinbach, ed., *The Indonesian Rural Economy* (Seattle: University of Washington Press, 2004); Ruth Dixon, *Rural Women at Work: Strategies for Development in South Asia* (Baltimore: Johns Hopkins University Press, 1979).

# CHAPTER 3

# Work and the American Tradition

Right off the top, American work, during the two centuries of British colonial experience, differed from patterns in Europe and many other premodern societies in two key respects. Both distinctions were admittedly rather general, not tied closely to daily jobs, but both could condition wider attitudes and reactions.

First, no aristocracy developed in British colonial America. Southern planters might offer examples of genteel living, particularly by the eighteenth century, though like many European aristocrats they often worked very hard in fact. But there was no dominant model of status and prestige associated with leisure or lifestyle pursuits, as there was in Europe from at least the Renaissance onward. It might as a result prove harder to criticize value systems based primarily on work and the achievements of work than was the case across the Atlantic. Boston intellectuals—the so-called Boston Brahmins—could fuss about too much mindless and money-grubbing effort during the first decades of industrialization in the nineteenth century, and again Southern leaders, eager to defend slavery as a "special" institution, also criticized undue materialism during the same period, but they had no really elaborate alternative to offer to a lifetime built around work.

Second, no organized guilds developed in the United States. Craft groups certainly emerged, though few could claim the artistic excellence of the most refined artisanry in Europe; colonial America did not yet generate rich art, and the wealthy imported their fine products from the Old Country. Many urban workers could define special skills, and apprenticeship programs and other features associated with carpentry, printing, and the like certainly emerged. But there were no outright guilds, which meant that the most systematic articulation and defense of traditional work values were not present in the American context. American craftsmen in the nineteenth century would form special kinds of unions, built around skill and bent on protecting some elements of older customs including apprenticeship; here, their patterns resembled those we will see in Europe and elsewhere. But there was simply no direct tradition to refer to in terms, for example, of the production of a masterpiece for admission into the fellowship of journeymen. Even in the eighteenth century relations between a shop owner and workers and apprentices emphasized greater hierarchy, rather than a shared community of skill and work. There was no protected wandering period for young adults during which organizations would help them find work as they moved from one community to the next; American craftsmen might move around in search of better opportunities, but they were essentially on their own.

These first points—the lack of features characteristic in older preindustrial settings—are obviously negative, in the sense of denoting an absence of two common preindustrial conditions. They suggest reasons that innovations in work systems and work values in the United States might later go farther, faster than in other societies—and we will see that this was indeed the case.

At the same time, these distinctions in context should not obscure the many similarities between traditional American work and its counterparts elsewhere. American farmers, like European peasants, accomplished a wide range of tasks, often involving hard manual labor. Many American families sent adolescents to work in other families, both rural and urban; as in Europe, the intention was to distribute children more effectively, to pass on disciplinary problems for a touchy age group, and in some cases to improve training opportunities. Again as in Europe, the result could be mixed. Many apprentices, for example, were ill-used, even by relatives; Benjamin Franklin, as a printer's apprentice in Boston, was beaten so often by his brother that he simply decamped to Philadelphia. Franklin was unusually articulate, but his experiences and reactions were undoubtedly widely shared: "Tho' a Brother, he considered himself as my Master, and me as his Apprentice; and accordingly expected the same Services from me as he would from another; while I thought he demean'd me too much in some he requir'd of me.... But my Brother was passionate and had often beaten me, which I took extreamly amiss; and thinking my Apprenticeship very tedious, I was continually wishing for some Opportunity of shortening it."[1] The link between most children and work was just as tight in the colonies as in other premodern societies. And the list of similarities could easily be extended.

Three features stand out, however, as offering American variants or partial variants on common patterns, in addition to the absence of some traditional institutions and values common elsewhere. American agriculture was different from that in Afro-Eurasia (though quite similar to conditions in Canada and Australia a bit later on). American slavery differed greatly from more traditional forms, though it must be compared with characteristics in other parts of the Americas. Finally, building on the more general impact of Protestantism on Western work culture, a "Puritan" work ethic, though concentrated in New England, might have wider implications in what was, after all, a formative period for American values.

*    *    *

The first comparative feature, impossible to explore conclusively but definitely suggestive, involves degrees of difficulty in agricultural work when colonial American farmers are compared with European or Asian peasants.

It is clear that American farm families worked very hard. A young boy on a New England farm in 1805 described how, on consecutive days at the end of a cold winter, he helped build a barn, cut wood, drained maple syrup, built a bridge (with some other people in the village), cut some remaining grass for hay, and repaired sleds; the boy reported one day off in a two-week span, when he roamed in the woods while looking for timber to make barrels and scouted good places to set animal traps. This was a full schedule in what might normally be seen as an off-season for farmers. A woman's diary, again in New England, is full of references to constant work—sewing, cooking, washing—with equally constant references to being tired (literally 50 percent of the entries refer to fatigue amid the endless list of chores). A Long Island wife sounded a similar note in 1768: "It has been a tiresome day it is now Bed time and I have not had won minutts rest; full of fretting discontent dirty and miserabel both yesterday and today" (spelling as in the original).[2]

The question is, of course, whether these kinds of references were at all unusual in an agricultural setting. At some point in the colonial period, many American farm families had to clear land of dense trees and rocks, to prepare it for planting—while also often constructing the first home, water wells, and farm buildings. This burst of work would have been unusually demanding. In contrast, in most of Europe and Asia, the frontier period had long since passed, and these extraordinary demands were no longer present. More to the point, in terms of longer-run routines, most American farms were larger than peasant holdings, sometimes running up to two hundred acres or more compared to typical European allotments that were usually under twenty-five acres. Furthermore, except to an extent in New England, American farms tended to be separate, rather than clustered around a village settlement. All this reflected the vast resources of the new land, which could be converted to unusual prosperity, but it may have taken an unusual amount of work to cash in. By the later nineteenth century, of course, American farmers would take a lead in adopting new equipment, which would ease the task of running large farms. But until 1850, manual labor was the unavoidable basis for planting and harvesting a large acreage. Community resources could come into play occasionally; groups of families would gather to raise a barn or build a bridge, often mixing feasting and socializing with the work itself. But on a daily basis, family labor, supplemented at most by a hired hand or two, was the only labor available. Colonial American families did have higher birthrates than their European counterparts—a reflection of greater resources in land, which could feed a larger brood, but also of the need for children to make the family economy work. But the demands on individual children in the American context may have been unusually great, preparing a lifetime of commitment to work and little else besides. It is revealing that, in mainly Protestant America, the number of festival occasions was far lower than in most traditional societies.

Farm families in other places might, of course, put in more intensive labor in some respects, precisely because their holdings were small. Rice cultivation in

Asia, for example, required intense daily work in weeding and regulating water levels in the paddies, as well as planting and harvesting. Smallholdings in Europe might require great attention as well, simply to eke out a precarious food supply; and of course many families combined farmwork with manufacturing and other activities. American farmers, often better fed than rural people elsewhere, may not have encountered distinctive strain in work. It is vital to remember also that the long working days American farmers reported were typical of rural work generally, where there were no clear distinctions, other than sleep, between work and any other activities in the daily routine and when a family commitment to work was both assumed and essential.

It is possible, however, that conditions in American agriculture induced a somewhat more single-minded commitment to work than was true elsewhere, a commitment important at the time and influential later on, when the nature of work would change with industrialization. Labor shortages amid abundant resources would certainly be a recurrent theme in American work history. In the colonial period, such shortages encouraged not only hard work but frequent efforts to find additional sources of diligent labor. The use of indentured servants, brought over from Europe with strict work requirements for a period of years before the contract was satisfied, was one indication of this. So were the frequent conflicts between rural families and children sent to them for periods of work. This practice was common enough in agricultural settings, as we have seen, but the American context may have generated an unusual number of runaways and disputes, with children objecting to the demanding work burdens placed upon them.

Many American farmers in the colonial period, and on into the nineteenth century, also owned their own land. Slaves were a huge exception, of course, and there were many agricultural laborers, some of whom had no chance of ownership. Compared to many agricultural societies, however, in which landlords controlled big swaths of land and labor, or in which family ownership was complicated by manorial dues or rents, ownership was unusually great in the colonial American context. This could in itself be a spur to hard work, along with the other conditions of American rural life: the result of effort would visibly pay off for oneself and one's family, not for some resented aristocrat or (as in Latin America) estate owner.

*   *   *

There was one labor system in colonial America that was unquestionably unusual, though not unique: the growing system of slave labor, particularly though not exclusively in the southern colonies. Here is the second colonial precedent that must be evaluated in terms of comparative work patterns.

American slavery—in what became the United States, but also in Latin America—constituted one of the most exploitative slave systems ever widely developed. While owners varied in their demands, the system encouraged the extraction of the maximum possible amount of labor, particularly among field hands working in commercial agriculture on large or reasonably large estates. Not only formal ownership was involved: the threat of force to exact labor was always present. The human impact was substantial. As a woman, a former slave, put it, reflecting on the earlier nineteenth century: "The things that my sister May and I suffered were so terrible.... Work, work, work. I been so exhausted working. I was like an inch-worm crawling along a roof. I worked till I thought another lick would kill me." Only Sundays provided a bit of relief, but even then most slaves had to work on family chores, possibly on a small plot of land; any real leisure was rare. Children began to pitch in early: the woman in question began taking care of her master's children and helping older women in their spinning when she was eight.[3]

The most common work routines, at least by the late eighteenth and early nineteenth centuries, as cotton cultivation began to spread (though tobacco cultivation had similar basic patterns), involved gang labor, working under overseers equipped with whips, which they were willing to use quite freely. As one slave put it, "If you had something to do, you did it, or you got whipped."[4] Plantation owners and commentators frequently complained about the cruelty and crudeness of overseers, but few did anything about their use. Women were pushed toward productivity standards—for example, in pounds of cotton picked, with 150-200 pounds a day a normal expectation—essentially the same as those for men. Larger cultural conventions about women's delicacy were ignored where slave labor was concerned, except perhaps for the opportunity for a few women to be identified for more purely domestic chores (where the work, however, might be as demanding as in the fields). Fourteen-hour days were common in the summer, often in intense heat. According to one calculation, slaves worked eleven to thirteen hours a day at least 261 days a year.

Slave labor, in sum, had some of the features of American agricultural work more generally, in that it was hard and physical. But these features were exacerbated by the slaves' lack of any voice on work routines, save on the rare occasions when there were chores for the slave family itself, and by the constant hard driving and violence.

A former slave in 1840 described what his mother had done in North Carolina: she took care of fourteen cows, milking them daily; she watched all the children of the women working in the fields; she cooked for the whole slave crew; she was responsible for the washing and ironing for the master's family; and at night she tended to her own family, alternately sewing and napping until she could do no more. With understatement he noted, "My mother's labor was very hard."[5]

Not surprisingly, many slaves tried to resist some of the harshest exactions, and particularly the violence. Their resistance—individual acts of defiance or evasion more than periodic collective protest, which roused white reactions of a different sort—plus the need of slave owners and their sympathizers to justify the slave system to themselves, tended to produce stereotypes about African American laziness or dislike for work. Discipline was essential, in this view, because slaves on their own would naturally idle about. In broad outline, this was a common upper-class stereotype about lower-class workers under their control—factory owners would often say the same about their workers, as we will see—but it had particular impact when put in a racial context. And it had lingering echoes even after the slave system ended.

Slavery in the English colonies in North America ultimately embraced several million people, though only about a tenth of all Africans brought to the Americas, so it is hardly surprising that its significance survived the institution itself. The bigger long-term questions about American slavery involve its comparative characteristics and its larger legacies to American work.

Significant debates have raged over American versus Latin American treatment of slaves in the eighteenth and nineteenth centuries. Both slave systems, exploiting labor for commercial profit to an unprecedented degree, pressed work conditions far more harshly than most traditional slavery had done. Brazilian slaves were more likely to be freed by their masters in a society where formal racism was less developed. But Brazilian slaves also died earlier than their U.S. counterparts, because American owners more quickly realized that they would save money by encouraging slave reproduction whereas Brazilians depended far longer simply on importing new slaves. As one observer noted in the nineteenth century, "it was considered cheaper, on the country plantations to use up a slave in five or seven years, and purchase another, than to take care of him."[6] So the driving of slaves at work, though obviously fierce, and undoubtedly increasing with the spread of cotton production, may not have reached its potential peak in the United States overall.

At the same time, it is vital to recognize that in many parts of the Americas by the eighteenth century, slaves provided the only available labor to take advantage of the new, global sales potential of goods like tobacco, sugar, and cotton. These export sectors simply could not have developed so rapidly, in an increasingly capitalist economy, without this labor until larger streams of migration provided cheap wage-labor alternatives. In this sense, slavery was fundamental to the emergence of American economies. It was, of course, finally abolished—around 1863 in the United States, a bit later in Brazil and Cuba. But its imprint did not end with the institutions. Attitudes toward African Americans and their work persisted; so did the tendency to employ this group in difficult but low-paying tasks; so did the widespread assumption that in this group even married women would hold jobs. Here were components of the work experience that survived into modern conditions, indeed to some extent to the present day. Did the knowledge of slave treatment also affect attitudes toward other workers? We will see that the United States pioneered innovative systems of acceleration and control of technically free workers. We will also see that there were several reasons for this, including the cultural zeal for hard work itself. But while the modern innovators had no direct experience with slave labor, knowledge that this labor had existed, that workers could be coerced toward demanding productivity goals, might well have exercised some subliminal impact.

\*   \*   \*

A final feature of the preindustrial American approach to work involves the possibility that some special cultural values applied to labor as a result of Protestantism, particularly New England Puritanism. The topic begins, however, in Europe, in the aftermath of the Protestant Reformation. Many historians have argued that Protestants, arguing that God has predestined salvation, which cannot be won through prayer or rituals in the Catholic fashion, somewhat ironically came to believe that the capacity for hard work was a sign of God's grace as well as a protection from sin. In other words, though strictly speaking one could do nothing to advance salvation, which God had predetermined, if one worked hard, one was demonstrating God's favor. The idea of a "calling" emerged, in which people might find a special area to which they could devote their labor and thus demonstrate divine blessing. The distinction was subtle between earning heavenly reward and using work to demonstrate God's choice, but it could be drawn. And certainly, in more straightforward fashion, Puritan hostility to too much luxury could easily translate into a praise of simple habits, including hard work. There is no question that many Protestants, and perhaps particularly Puritans, spent a great deal of time condemning idleness. In related fashion many English Puritan leaders condemned "parasitic" people, sometimes including aristocratic landlords, who seemed to live off the labor of others. Here, too, there are hints of a special work ethic.

Certainly, as many Puritans attained some commercial success, a belief in work as a God-given capacity could help ease tensions between religious conscience and actual material profits: if the latter were merely a side effect of righteous labor, surely appropriate spiritual priorities could be retained.

How much Protestantism, and particularly English Puritanism, emphasized special work qualities has been debated. Uneasiness with business life could easily transcend the praise for work, so the relationships are at the least quite complex. It is also true that some minority Protestant groups—the Quakers would become an even clearer example—might have devoted themselves to hard work and business achievement less because of special religious qualities than because they were seeking opportunities in commercial life that their minority status denied them in landowning or politics.

As English Puritans made their way to colonial America early in the seventeenth century, it is possible that they could combine their general sense that work expressed divine favor and inhibited idleness and vice with the special work demands of a frontier environment. It is important to note that some of the early organizers of colonial settlement in New England specifically looked for people with strong work values. The failure of the earlier effort at Jamestown, Virginia, was widely blamed on poor discipline, so even aside from religious underpinnings, a work commitment received special emphasis in many subsequent ventures. John Smith, one of the backers of New England's colonization, openly discussed how much he had suffered from the idleness and "loitering" of many earlier Virginia settlers. John Winthrop, governor of the Massachusetts colony, specifically insisted in 1629 on the need to find people with the internal drive to "worke."

Certainly, New England's religious as well as political leaders wrote frequently on the subject of work. They made it clear that work is a demonstration of God's selection for salvation—"work is the godly in prayer"[7]—but expected the unsaved to work hard as well, though more for personal gain than for community benefit and the demonstration of sainthood. A great deal of discussion focused on differences in motivation among equally hardworking people: the saved should work hard but without concern for worldly results, because this was not life's purpose. But while the theological niceties were vital here, many ordinary Puritans might take away a simpler message about work's central importance to a good life. Puritan sentiments also prompted New England governments to seek to regulate bad habits, like excessive drinking, that might limit the devotion to work. And, again as a practical matter, the harsh soil of New England made devotion to work a practical necessity in the early years, as farmers struggled for sheer survival as they labored to clear the land.

Another factor contributing to the unusual attention to work in the colonies, and particularly New England—again, within the larger cultural framework established by Protestantism—was the relative absence of settled class distinctions. Ultimately, clear gradations of wealth would emerge, but in the early decades most people were joined by the common necessity of working fairly hard; and the need for practical skills, like carpentry, gave considerable prestige to groups and individuals who would have been lower on the social scale in Europe. The more general Protestant emphasis on the dignity of labor found particular resonance in British America, with praise for hard work of any sort, even at the hands of a day laborer.

Writings on the importance of work and discipline dotted the New England landscape in the seventeenth century. John Cotton's collection of sermons, *The Way of Life* (1641), was a particularly elaborate attempt to show the need for "diligence in worldly business and yet deadness to the world."[8] Again, all people should work hard; idleness and sloth must be generally condemned; but only the holy would work without being ensnared by profits or other worldly gains. The practical injunctions were less complex, and they anticipated elements of the middle-class work ethic later on: "Rise early, and go to bed late ... and avoid idleness"; take "all opportunities to be doing something, early and late." The idea of using time carefully began to spread among Protestants on both sides of the Atlantic, but again the American emphasis may have been stronger, if only because of the greater insistence on the sense of religious duty and the louder protests against any form of idleness.

Not all, or even most, colonial Americans were Puritans. But New England values did gain a somewhat wider audience, particularly by the early nineteenth century, because the region harbored an unusual number of authors and publicists. Heirs of New England values also fanned out widely, from the later eighteenth century onward, into upper New York and widely in the Middle West. We will soon turn to signs of a special American work ethic in the nineteenth century, when industrial opportunities came into play; but it certainly owed something to earlier traditions, and to the extent that New England Puritanism had already provided hints of a national or at least special regional approach toward work, later American emphases become even easier to explain.

*   *   *

We turn, in the following chapter, to the major changes in work brought about by the Industrial Revolution and its wider implications beyond the factory system per se; and then, after that, we will return to American variants on these changes. Premodern work conditions did not, however, yield easily, either in the United States or elsewhere. Many kinds of work long directly retained premodern features. This was particularly true of agricultural labor, even when some new equipment was added. Housewives and other domestic workers retained some premodern qualities in their work, and some traditional crafts hung on as well. And observers have pointed out that college students still today in some ways retain premodern work characteristics—working at various times during the day, mixing work and leisure, determining something of their own pace despite promptings from professors. Change definitely occurred in work patterns overall, and premodern standards provide a baseline by which the nature and impact of these changes can be evaluated, either explicitly or implicitly, both by experts and intellectuals and by ordinary people who lived the changes on a daily basis. But continuity must be recognized as well, both in actual work patterns and in values and judgments. Premodern work systems had survived, in broad outline, for many hundreds of years, so it is hardly surprising that many people found ways to retain connections with them.

The special American premodern legacy concerning work must be regarded as somewhat tentative, and certainly complicated. Cultural factors and actual agricultural conditions may have produced some degree of special commitment to work, but this must not be overdrawn, as against patterns common in preindustrial settings. The existence of demanding slavery (and some related concerns about slaves' resistance to work and possible laziness) reflected key divisions in American society that would have prolonged consequences. Divisions could extend beyond slavery itself: southern estate owners, though often personally hardworking, would fashion an ethic of gentility and leisure very different from the values being preached in New England. Again, there was no single colonial American work culture. Whether slavery encouraged nonslave Americans to think about distinctive kinds of work pressures and discipline that could be imposed on other working populations—for example, immigrant workers in later factory settings—is also open to debate. American work systems and beliefs had some distinctive components before nineteenth-century industrialization, but it is not clear how much they predetermined later responses, when work began to change more systematically.

# Notes

1. *The Autobiography of Benjamin Franklin,* ed. Leonard Labaree et al. (New Haven: Yale University Press, 1964), 52–53.

2. Eric Sloane, *Diary of an Early American Boy: Noah Blake* (New York: W. Funk, 1965); Mary Beth Norton et al., *A People and a Nation: A History of the United States, Vol. 1: To 1877* (Boston: Houghton Mifflin, 1982), 72.

3. Jacqueline Jones, *Labor of Love, Labor of Sorrow: Black Women, Work and Family from Slavery to the Present* (New York: Vintage, 1985), 13.

4. Jones, *Labor of Love, Labor of Sorrow,* 18.

5. Jones, *Labor of Love, Labor of Sorrow,* 42.

6. Carl Degler, "Slavery in Brazil and the United States," *American Historical Review* 75 (1970): 1004–28.

7. Jones, *Labor of Love, Labor of Sorrow,* 86.

8. Jones, *Labor of Love, Labor of Sorrow,* 120.

# Further Reading

## On Slavery

Laura Foner and Eugene D. Genovese, eds., *Slavery in the New World: A Reader in Comparative History* (Englewood Cliffs, NJ: Prentice-Hall, 1969). *See also* Eugene D. Genovese, *Roll Jordan Roll: The World the Slaves Made* (New York: Vintage, 1976). See also Jacqueline Jones, *Labor of Love, Labor of Sorrow: Black Women, Work and Family from Slavery to the Present* (New York: Vintage, 1985). Slave labor in rice-growing areas is treated in Peter Wood, *The Black Majority: Negroes in South Carolina from 1670 through the Stono Rebellion* (New York: Knopf, 1974).

## On Colonial Work (and Particularly the Puritan Work Ethic)

Stephen Innes, *Creating the Commonwealth: The Economic Culture of Puritan New England* (New York: W. W. Norton, 1995). *See also* Jonathan Prude, *The Coming of Industrial Order: Town and Factory Life in Rural Massachusetts, 1810–1860* (Amherst: University of Massachusetts Press, 1999). The classic statement on the Protestant work ethic generally is Max Weber, *The Protestant Ethic and the Spirit of Capitalism* (New York: Dover, 1958); an almost classic study of Puritanism is Perry Miller, *New England Mind in the Seventeenth Century* (Boston: Beacon Press, 2000).

# CHAPTER 4

# The Impact of Industrialization

We have seen that changes in work began to develop in many parts of the world in the seventeenth and eighteenth centuries, providing a backdrop to the more dramatic developments of the Industrial Revolution itself. Some of the changes had been further extended by the particular conditions and values of British colonial America. It was, however, the Industrial Revolution that began to create the conditions associated with modern work, first in the factories, but then (though with certain modifications) in other settings. Older work long coexisted with modern work; preindustrial expectations and habits persisted. But modern work began to be born in the later eighteenth century, which is why from a historical standpoint "industrial" and "modern" are essentially equivalent, even beyond the factory floor.

The Industrial Revolution, centered initially in parts of Britain from the late eighteenth century onward, spread to sections of Western Europe and to the United States by the early nineteenth century, and then reached other parts of Europe, Russia, and Japan by the late nineteenth century. The spread of industrialization continues to the present day.

The basic definition of industrialization is easy; the consequences, momentous. Early industrialization was marked by the application of steam power (and also wider uses of waterpower) to manufacturing, particularly in spinning and much weaving and in metallurgy, and by the rise of new factories. Inevitably, dramatic new technology (steam power and novel transmission devices) and the massing of labor in factories—that is, novel work organization—had a major impact on the experience of work. To claim that it revolutionized the nature of work within a few decades would hardly be an exaggeration.

It is important not to press too far. Outright industrialization initially affected only a small portion of the labor force. Many people continued agricultural and craft work with relatively little change, at least for a time. Growing work sectors, like domestic service in the middle-class homes of expanding cities, actually seemed to extend traditional types of labor. Early factories, in pioneering societies like Britain, were small; many employed fewer than fifty workers.

They could seem novel to people accustomed to more traditional settings even so, but it was not as if former peasants transitioned directly into a contemporary automobile plant.

On the other hand, some spillover from industrial impact on work might quickly affect larger categories; craft labor, for example, fairly early shifted in response to what was going on in factories. Rural workers, producing for growing urban markets, might experience change as well, not only in industrial societies themselves, but also in societies of distant suppliers such as Latin America. Furthermore, the shock effect of industrialization tended to expand with each new experience. Russian workers around 1900, many of them former peasants, did walk into giant factories, among the largest in the world, often with over a thousand workers.

Another complexity: some of the features of industrial work that most bothered tenderhearted historians a century after the fact were probably not the most troubling results of the factory system. Workers in the factories labored long hours; days of fourteen hours were not uncommon. The use of gas lighting (and later, electricity) might expand the length of the working day; and commuting time, walking to factories, could add strain as well. But hours of work were probably not, in themselves, completely shocking to workers accustomed to daylong efforts; it was only in combination with the more dramatic innovations that hours seemed to count for more. Women often worked in the textile factories, another point that would shock later, reform-minded observers. But the innovation would have been for them not to work, for as we have seen, female labor was part of the natural course of things in agricultural societies. The settings were new, which raised some novel issues; but women's work itself was not necessarily seen as a burden. Indeed, as women have more recently reengaged with the formal labor force in advanced industrial societies, the whole issue of early factory work has taken on a new cast, and reform efforts to regulate women's hours now seem more questionable, a greater departure from traditional norms.

Children worked as well, and there were undoubtedly instances of huge abuse, particularly in British industrialization, including horrible examples of maiming by the new machines. But British exploitation of child labor was unusual; later industrializations, as in France, Germany, and the United States, went easier on children, partly because their leaders had the British example before them. The British exception, in terms not only of extensive and dangerous use of children but also of dragooning of groups of orphans into factories with essentially no choice, seems to have resulted from a great sense of risk within early industrial investments and a felt need to exploit children because of their low cost. Reform pressure and greater industrial excess eased the worst treatment after three to four decades. Fairly quickly, it was not child labor but the decline of child labor that generated the most dramatic innovation in this category. New concerns did surface among workers themselves, as well as reformers, but they were more subtle than child labor itself.

New technology, and particularly the use of fossil fuel rather than human or animal power, and new work organization redefined many cherished features of work even more central to the experience than the use of women or children. Workers realized the changes quickly, but they were not necessarily in a position to do much about them. While factory work formed the center of change, spillover to other categories began to be identifiable within a few decades as well, wherever the Industrial Revolution took hold. The passage of time further enhanced changes for factory workers. While the first generation of factory workers in one sense took the biggest hit in terms of changes, because of the stark contrast between their traditional expectations and their new encounters, amplification was significant as well: machines got bigger and faster, factories grew to larger size and required even more impersonal forms of administration. The process of change seemed to feed itself.

*    *    *

It was in the 1830s that the French textile manufacturer Motte Bossut introduced the practice of placing a garland of flowers each week on the machine that had been most productive. Machines, not people, easily became the center of attention in the factory work process. Their output capacities were amazing by any traditional standard: a mechanical spinning machine, tended by a single worker with perhaps an assistant or two, could generate a hundred times the amount of thread an individual using manual spindles could. Mechanical looms were less awesome, but even they upped productivity three to four times by the early nineteenth century. Small wonder that manufacturers shifted their attention: machines were a golden goose.

Machines were also expensive and risky in the early days of factory industry. While initial equipment was modest by later standards, the investment was considerable given the limited resources of many early manufacturers. In point of fact, a number of early factories failed outright, so the risks were not imaginary. Lots of entrepreneurs were legitimately anxious about the security of their investment, particularly because they often did not have a very good understanding of how the machines functioned. Many of the constraints of the work environment in early industrialization flowed from these very real pressures—sustained as well, of course, by the desire to make a quick profit.

For example, it was widely believed during the first decades of industrialization that only by pressing the work day to thirteen or fourteen hours would there be any margin of earnings; the first twelve hours were thought to be sufficient only to generate the pay for the workers and the upkeep and amortization on machines and plant. These beliefs were often wrong; they were surely self-serving on the part of the factory owners; but they were widespread and help explain why the workday became so extended in many early factories.

The new pressure to work, partly to make sure the machines kept rolling, also led early factory owners to combat traditional festival habits. Many traditional workers, peasants and artisans alike, had, as we have seen, been accustomed to a number of days per year that could largely be devoted to feasting and community entertainments. These customs were more difficult to maintain in the context of an urban environment, where workers were surrounded by strangers rather than people familiar with local rituals. But above all the festivals ran afoul of the regularity work now seemed to require. Fines and other mechanisms were used to repress traditional festivals, which did dramatically shrink in number. Specific work sites—like the coal mines, where earlier tradition dictated some days off, for example, to celebrate St. Barbara, the patron saint of miners—saw very explicit conflicts that gradually eroded the customary celebrations. Early industrialization, wrapped around the demands of machines, unquestionably cut back customary leisure time, with festivals the most obvious victims.

The presence and primacy of machines impinged on work in other ways. Many workers, particularly of course those from the countryside, commented on the deafening noise of the equipment. (Today, visitors to industrial museums with operating machinery are always given earplugs, because of the dangers to hearing; but no such amenities were available for the workers themselves.) Many textile factories operated with windows closed, because it was believed that outside air might damage fiber; this increased the noise levels and also the dust that pervaded the factories.

Physical dangers were an obvious problem amid rapidly moving machine parts. Because of cost concerns, and scorn for the workers, in the first decades of industrialization, manufacturers often failed to put up even rudimentary safety devices, such as screens to keep arms and legs away from the equipment. The same industrialists often developed a convenient belief in worker imprudence, explaining many accidents as the result of worker carelessness. Even child workers were often described as foolishly getting their hands caught in a machine, losing some fingers in the process. Factory owners might voluntarily pay an injured worker a small amount in compensation, but this was unsystematic, without any sense of obligation. Metallurgical plants and mines were riskier still, with recurrent major accidents throughout the nineteenth century. Only gradually, mainly toward the end of the century, did improved equipment, but above all new state regulations and effective inspection, begin to reduce accident rates, though these would remain a problem in some settings even to the present day.

The most systematic impact of machinery, however, involved massive intensification of the pace of work. Here is where machines, not people, really dictated practice. The new facts of the matter were stark: to run efficiently, machines had to be kept going once activated, because of the energy and time required to get them up to speed. Workers, as a result, had to be predictably available and deprived of opportunities for personal moments of downtime. Beyond the constancy of the machinery was the additional fact that, steam driven, it could operate at high speeds, with production on the whole increasing with speed. Here, too, workers had to accommodate.

The results showed in many specific practices virtually everywhere that factory systems were launched. Workers' arrivals and departures, and any breaks, were strictly regulated by clock time; clocks became the devices that merged worker habits with the needs of machines for regularity and predictability. Shop rules and strict foremen required workers to arrive at the factory within a fifteen-minute margin; if they were late, they would not be allowed to enter for at least half a day and would sacrifice that amount of wages and usually be assessed an equivalent fine. Dismissal time was similarly clock based. During the day, breaks, including meal periods, were typically extremely limited, in order not to lose attendance on the machine, and stringent rules were directed toward unauthorized absences.

A standard factory regulation thus read: "The bell denotes the hours of entry and departure in the factory when it first rings. At the second ring every worker should be at his work.... It is forbidden under penalty of fines to abandon the workplace before the bell indicates that the work site is closed." And further: "The porter is also forbidden to let any workers in or out [of the factory] without the foreman's permission during the hours of work." Lock-in factories have been understandably compared with another modern institution, the prison.[1]

Timing rules convey only part of the story. What was happening in the early factories was a quiet war against traditional worker habits. Whereas most traditional workers could often indulge personal irregularities on the job—pausing to chat, wandering around to relieve monotony, even sneaking an occasional nap—the machine regimen, as interpreted by employers, imposed stringent regularity. Accordingly, factory rules, backed by fines, deliberately legislated against precisely these habits. Even singing on the job was banned (machine noise might have inhibited it in any event) because it harked back to the customary mixture of work and relaxation that was now in principle to be outlawed. Every attention must be given to the job.

What was sought and what was actually attained could be two different matters. In the employer view, workers continued to ignore good work habits, despite rules and supervision. A common calculation—again from France in the 1830s—was that workers only gave 72 percent of their full capacity to the job, simply slowing up or taking breaks despite employers' best efforts. This kind of calculation, supported by no particular data, encouraged employers to think that their obligations to workers were limited: since performance was below par, work conditions and pay could be below par as well. And the calculation also encouraged further efforts to increase the stringency of work regulation—and as we will see, American initiatives ultimately would play an unusually important role in this process.

There was some sense, at the same time, that workers successfully internalized some of the new work requirements after an initial generation or two. The experience of child labor, some argued, helped workers better understand the relevance of clock time and greater punctuality. One of the purposes of modern schooling was to inculcate a time sense in children, so that by the point they started work, the idea would seem completely natural—still an implicit goal of educational systems in industrial societies.

Other aspects of the machine-based work pace were less easy to assimilate, and as noted, they tended to intensify over time. Many British workers around 1900 claimed that because of stricter rules and more rigid supervision, opportunities to sneak naps in odd corners of the factory, which had still been possible in the 1870s, had virtually disappeared, meaning that work regularity was more daunting than ever before.

Certainly, the pace of machinery tended to increase, if not steadily, at least periodically over time. In the 1890s, to take another case, new mechanical looms were introduced from the United States. These Northrop looms were so highly automated that one worker could tend sixteen or sometimes even thirty-two of them, in contrast to earlier decades, when a single individual would mind one or at most two mechanical looms. To be sure, the physical exertion involved often decreased. Early machines frequently required workers still to activate part of the operation manually, and considerable strength might be required (particularly in weaving; some forms of spinning were less demanding). By the later nineteenth century, particularly with the spread of electric motors, the elimination of human power was far more nearly complete. But the accelerating speed of the equipment, so many workers claimed, exacted a new toll in nervous energy, simply to keep up with the whole operation.

The claim of nervous exhaustion came to be something of a watchword for many workers in industrial societies after several decades. A German worker noted that after a day of work, "my eyes burn so that I can hardly sleep." He specifically claimed that his limbs "shook" after a day on the job, and contrasted this with an agricultural childhood when work lasted all day but still left enough energy for some singing and conviviality in the evenings. Employers and others in the middle class remained skeptical for the most part, more concerned with what they saw as workers' tendency to slack off than with the burdens of pace. Here was one of several points of recurrent dispute about the basic nature of modern work.[2]

*   *   *

Skill levels and broader issues of the meaning of work constituted a second crucial area, related to machines and pace but requiring separate comment. Early factories required a number of highly skilled workers, often brought in from relevant craft sectors. The workers who installed and maintained machines, for example, had a mixture of older metalwork skills and newer knowledge. Most factories also needed a few construction workers. Brand-new skills emerged. Early industrial steelmaking, for example, demanded a group of workers called puddlers, who manually reintroduced carbon and other chemicals into molten iron after impurities had been removed. These workers commanded substantial salaries and took great pride in their special talents, moderated only by the knowledge that work in extreme heat, amid considerable physical danger, often produced short working careers. Locomotive engineers, another new category, often boasted loudly about the power they felt as they drove their iron monsters through the countryside. Even machine-based textiles and coal mining had clear skill gradations, up to levels that involved considerable expertise.

High skill, however, was not the characteristic component of the factory system, and indeed machines made sense only by replacing many skills and allowing the use of lower-paid categories of labor. Explicit efforts were devoted to figuring out ways to make skilled workers less essential. Puddlers, for example, after a period of vital service, were really eliminated as a skill category when new methods for steelmaking, like the Bessemer process of 1856, allowed automatic reintroduction of necessary chemicals. The whole sector of machine building, which for several decades was essentially a small-shop, craftlike industry, though with many new specific skills, saw a substantial deskilling at the end of the nineteenth century. More-automatic processes—for example, in boring holes through metal parts—allowed machine production to be conducted by workers with far less experience or training. The pattern was pervasive.

And this meant, with obvious though often temporary exceptions, that the typical factory worker was semiskilled. Most men and women in the factories needed a few months of training to reach acceptable proficiency, and several years of experience before they attained full capacity. But they did not need much formal apprenticeship, and apprenticeship programs decreased steadily in factory settings, if they were ever formally installed at all.

Semiskilled status obviously reduced workers' bargaining power. It was relatively easy, except in conditions of really meager labor supply, to replace factory workers, which often happened during strikes or when individuals were singled out for disruptive behavior. At extremes, many workers felt the indignity of being replaced by women or foreigners or people regarded as racially inferior—ugly feelings, by modern standards of political correctness, but understandable to a degree when one realizes the dismay that loss of skill could cause.

There was more than bargaining power involved. Emphasis on low skill levels, combined with the results of mechanization, found growing numbers of factory workers confined to fairly limited phases of the production process. Instead of building whole machines by the later nineteenth century, for example, semiskilled machine builders (who might sometimes be women) did a few operations over and over again—for example, guiding machines that drilled holes in one kind of metal part that would then be bolted to another part by the next worker. The sheer number of occupational categories increased, but this meant that many workers were doing smaller and more circumscribed tasks. Not surprisingly—though it is impossible to claim that this reaction was brand-new—many workers noted directly or indirectly that they were frequently bored. Some claimed that only by daydreaming could they get through their days, particularly since they had so little opportunity to move away from their work for a moment's respite or brief socializing.

The whole process of reducing skill levels, along with the obvious fact that in capitalist industry workers had no direct ownership stake in the firms that employed them, prompted the great social theorist Karl Marx in the 1860s to write extensively about the meaninglessness suffered by modern workers. Marx contended that industrial conditions separated workers from any real sense of participation in the products they created, so that they felt no real stake in the manufacturing process. His term for this condition of meaninglessness in work was alienation. The concept makes good sense in theory. Certainly, it is possible to argue that, compared to traditional craft or agricultural workers, who oversaw many stages in the production process and could feel some real connection between their labor and a finished item—possibly, in some of the crafts, even an artistic item—factory workers confined to a limited phase of manufacturing would have a hard time seeing anything of themselves in the resultant output. And some unusually articulate workers did talk in terms of alienation, claiming directly that their work had no meaning, that they were given no more credit than animals might gain for the results of their labor. At the same time, however, alienation was hard to translate into active protest goals, and many workers probably managed to make some adjustments that would keep them short of existential despair. Some degree of alienation, however, may have been widespread, if not commonly expressed, and certainly workers were quite aware that their share in the overall production process was shrinking, their confinement to increasingly monotonous tasks becoming steadily more pervasive.

*   *   *

Closely related to lower skill status and mechanization was the whole issue of the direction of work—of taking orders from someone else, often someone not directly perceived as a worker himself. Bosses were not a brand-new work issue, but the nature of the issue was truly transformed in factory conditions.

We have seen that, in traditional work, most workers could hope to rise to a position where they would make their own daily decisions, constrained certainly by environment and economic circumstance and sometimes by community pressures. In principle—though this did not always work out in practice—most artisans could hope to rise from apprentice to skilled journeyman to master. Even journeymen who could not complete this process, and who might certainly harbor resentment that the final stage eluded them, nevertheless had the satisfaction of having master artisans work alongside them, in conditions of partial equality, and of being treated as semiequals socially as well—for example, taking meals with their employer. A minority of rural workers never had a chance to gain landownership and similarly would face a lifetime of wage-labor employment. Slaves, in some societies, constituted a huge exception to the ideal of ultimate self-direction, save when they were manumitted. But most peasants expected to gain access to land, which would give them control over their own daily routines, just as many artisans could aspire to day-to-day autonomy after a period of youthful dependence.

Similar hierarchies affected women. Girls might work under the direction of their mother or some other mistress, but most could hope, through marriage and maturing, ultimately to have a household of their own, where again they could determine their precise work routines and set their own specific standards.

With factory industry, most people, for the first time in human history outside of some forms of slavery, could never aspire to work without direct supervision.

Intriguingly, when factories first started, there were some limited experiments in giving considerable leeway to individual workers. Many early factory owners thought that the most efficient way to organize, say, mechanized spinning or weaving was to identify a skilled operator who would oversee an individual machine and be responsible for employing and directing a small team of workers—often including children—to assist him (or sometimes her). The idea was to replicate artisanal or decentralized direction in the factory. The option was facilitated by the fact that many factories were quite small, allowing the owner to have some sense of what was going on in the whole operation.

But this system, when launched, was always quickly abandoned. Employers lost confidence in workers' capacity to direct. If they failed to discipline their crew such, for example, that absenteeism increased, a machine might be down for a half day or more. Even a spat between a skilled worker and his assistant-nephew could throw the production routine off balance. Many workers also seemed to lack the technical knowledge to determine when a machine was malfunctioning, an obvious danger when a small problem turned into full-scale collapse. Indeed workers had every short-term incentive to drive their machines hard when their pay was related to output, and neglect to report troubling noises or other signs of breakdown.

As a result, decentralization was replaced by more-systematic supervision of labor from outside the ranks of workers. Shop rules, of course, provided some centralized guidance, setting standards for work behavior. But these were goal statements, not monitoring devices. To bridge the gap, and to take supervisory initiative away from workers themselves, factory owners installed a new category of employee, the foreman, responsible for overseeing crews of workers, usually with power to hire and fire, and reporting directly to the factory manager.

Foremen were an interesting breed. Mostly they were former workers, but their decision to join the lowest rungs of supervision separated most of them firmly from the working ranks. A few might still try to socialize with workers, at the corner tavern, for example, but most took on more middle-class airs. Even their dress distinguished them, for they would rarely work the machine directly, and their clothing aligned them with the rest of management.

These were the people who told workers what to do on a daily basis, to the extent that sheer routine and the pace of the machine did not do the trick. The demands on foremen, as true middlemen between management and worker, were huge. They were under constant pressure to meet high production quotas while keeping problems such as machine malfunctions and worker grievances under wraps to the greatest extent possible. Small wonder that many foremen, despite their own backgrounds, turned out to be hard drivers, unsympathetic to workers' job issues.

It was also true that foremen had the potential for considerable abuses of power. They could privilege relatives. They could press for sexual favors from women workers. They could assign workers who gave them trouble to the most difficult or least rewarding work. They could and did fire or fine without having to offer explanations to any higher authority, constrained only by the need to keep production going.

In this situation, many foremen came to personify for many workers both specific injustices and labor's general lack of power to determine daily conditions and work assignments. Disputes were frequent and sometimes violent. Foremen frequently berated workers, cursing them publicly and, particularly in the case of younger workers, administering beatings. Individual workers or groups might easily reply in kind. A group of women French textile workers noted around 1900 that their work and pay were not all that bad, but the foremen were deplorable: "They treat us like animals." Favoritism, unnecessary criticism, yelling—these were some of the common foreman behaviors that could push workers to the edge. Small groups frequently walked off the job to protest personal mistreatment, and once in a while a specific incident helped spark a truly considerable labor protest. More-typical incidents were small and often brief. Frequently a group of disgruntled workers would storm off the job after a foreman insulted one of them but then gather in a bar, down a few drinks, and decide that going back to work was the best course of action after all. It was petty and recurrent tension, not systematic grievance, that most commonly marked this aspect of modern factory work.

Of course, not all foremen were clumsy or abusive. Some managed to maintain a certain camaraderie with their former mates. Generally, however, the relationship was a tense one. Workers did not control their conditions or routines. They were bossed by people clearly separate from themselves, with different goals and interests. A sense of considerable powerlessness was not only understandable, it was accurate.

*   *   *

A final basic innovation in modern factory work is harder to assess, because the workers affected addressed it less clearly. This involves the relationship between work and family. For many workers accustomed to traditional standards, the removal of jobs from home settings and family collaboration was a huge change, and it must have seemed quite uncomfortable, even unsettling. But comment was either missing or fairly oblique.

Many early factory workers did note the stress of working alongside strangers, in contrast to familial and community surroundings. This difficulty eased a bit with time, as worker neighborhoods developed and a sense of group and class solidarity developed, though there was usually a good bit of turnover as well, so the stranger aspect did not disappear. A few workers, including women, even noted their enjoyment of meeting new people, in contrast to more customary constraints.

Early factories often allowed workers to keep their children close by, using them as assistants or at most farming them out to another relative. Here, clearly, was a way to maintain some association of family with work and also to expand family earnings and keep children under safe supervision. As factories expanded and became more impersonal, with more interventions by foremen, this familial quality became harder to assure. Many workers saw their children assigned to others, possibly to complete strangers, and this was clearly unacceptable. This disruption of family-work connections, not child labor itself—which after all was widely expected—was what prompted many British workers by the 1830s to urge laws that would limit child labor—an indirect sign that the separation of work and family was causing real pain.

Most working-class families adjusted further to the separation by instituting a new gender division of labor. Women could work until marriage and childbirth, because their earnings were vital to their family of origin and might allow some savings on which marriage itself could be based. But once mothers, most women were expected to stop working outside the home in favor of child care and household maintenance. Some productive work might continue, such as taking in boarders or laundry, but not factory work itself. Only a minority of married women seemed to prefer continuing factory labor, entrusting their offspring to some other relative. And of course there were married women whose husbands were inept, injured, or dead and for whom factory work remained essential. But the big response to the home-work separation was the much sharper differentiation of male and female roles.

This meant, however, that men had to adjust to a radical rift between their work lives and their family lives. Of course a few adult male relatives might work in the same plant—family assistance in finding jobs preserved some links. But the severance was considerable for most men. There is no question that working men's daily ties to family were greatly reduced.

Many workers directly lamented the sheer time away from family, the fact that their hours of work and after-work exhaustion made it difficult to share much with their children. This could be deeply felt. On the other hand, many workers also developed a kind of masculine culture that might exacerbate the tension, spending time with their buddies rather than heading home at the first opportunity. There was relatively little comment on the impact of isolation from the family on the work experience itself. We know there was great change, but its ramifications are harder to trace.

\* \* \*

For the group most radically affected—factory workers—the changes in work that resulted from industrialization obviously overlapped. The driving pace of work and lack of control over the daily routine could be felt as part of a single tension, made vaguely worse by the separation from family context.

Individual reactions to change undoubtedly varied. Some workers might be so grateful for their jobs, particularly if they came from a rural background where lack of land had made earnings irregular, that they played down any deterioration in their lives. Some workers with special skills like machine building that commanded higher wages might actually enjoy the challenge and innovation of the industrial environment. But, as might be expected, the overwhelming evidence suggests considerable maladjustment and concern, perhaps particularly acute in the first generations of factory work but never entirely overcome.

When historians first began to pay extensive attention to the industrial working class, particularly in Britain, they focused heavily on what became known as the standard of living debate. This was an argument, often pitting socialist/Marxist against capitalist historians, about what happened to wages in the first decades of the factory system, and whether workers' nutritional levels and housing improved or deteriorated (and along with this, what happened to their health). The debate was never entirely resolved. It is clear that low wages burdened many workers, that while clothing improved a bit (because factory production reduced prices), slum housing could be appalling in rapidly growing cities, and quality and quantity of food could be a problem as well. Frequent periods of unemployment, when factories dismissed workers because demand for their output faltered, contributed to a sense of insecurity as well; many workers had to pawn their meager possessions during slumps, only to buy them back, if possible, at inflated costs later on. The fact that food prices usually went up in early industrial slumps, while wages and employment dropped, added to very real problems, pushing some urban workers well below the poverty line and directly contributing to rising death rates.

Overall, however, it has become clear that in the medium and certainly long runs, for societies that managed to industrialize extensively, standard of living issues are not the main point. Within a few decades in Britain it is incontestable that workers' living standards improved, though large pockets of grinding poverty remained. And of course the uncertainty of early wages and the periods of unemployment undoubtedly fed back into the work experience itself. In many British working families, for example, fathers were often given the only meat available at dinner, simply because it made family economic sense for adult men to keep their strength up. On the whole, nevertheless, it was the changes in work, not living standards off the job, that really altered most decisively and over the long haul.

Workers showed their sense of the changes at work in many ways. Early in the Industrial Revolution in most countries, groups of workers (some from factories, some from the craft sector) demonstrated basic concern by attacking machines directly, arguing that they were ruining work life and that only their elimination could bring jobs back to appropriate standards. This action was called Luddism, after a series of protests in Britain between 1810 and 1820, where workers grouped under the leadership of a probably mythical figure called Ned Ludd. Luddism would crop up in France about a decade later. Attacking machines was a literal and symbolic statement that something was going fundamentally wrong with the world of work when evaluated by traditional criteria. Even after formal Luddism declined, individual acts of sabotage against machines might continue—putting sand in gearboxes, for example. But Luddism proper was always put down by the authorities, usually with vigorous police repression; Luddism could not be tolerated if a society was going to industrialize. Interestingly, many magistrates—themselves unconvinced that modern work was heading in the right direction—expressed sympathy with the Luddites. But attacks on private property, which Luddism involved, could not be countenanced, and workers learned that this recourse, however heartfelt, was not really available.

Individual actions for many decades into industrialization reflected the new pressures of work and allowed personal adjustments as well, without, however, attacking the industrial system directly. Several patterns were involved. Early on, many workers, fresh from the countryside, would leave the factories during the summer, particularly at harvest time, when work back home was plentiful and operated according to more traditional standards. This option declined with time, as workers urbanized and lost their rural connections, but it was an understandable first impulse—much to the dismay of employers, who bemoaned the inconsistency of their labor force. Simply taking time off was another frequently used option. Workers whose wages allowed a bit of margin would use the surplus to buy time away from work, not showing up for a day or so, in order to have more time at their own disposal. There was risk here, of course, for factory owners might fire them outright; but if their labor was needed, they might get by for a while with this kind of personal alleviation of work pressures.

Most widespread of all, and impressively durable, was frequent job changing. Many workers changed factories three or four times a year when economic conditions permitted. There were several goals. A new job might offer marginally better pay, and since there was little reason for loyalty to an existing firm, there was no reason not to explore this option. Sometimes merely the hope that a new job would be better was enough to prompt a move, particularly if the existing assignment involved a disagreeable foreman or some other specific grievance. Job changing might allow a few days of downtime between positions, another way to gain some respite from the grind of industrial work. The habit persisted. Even at the end of the nineteenth century, factories in established industrial centers like Germany were reporting 1,000 percent turnover or more each year, a clear suggestion that workers were voting with their feet, not against modern work itself, which seemed immovable, but against too strict a regimen. There were limits to the option, of course. It depended on other jobs being available, and this was not always the case. Older workers found they could no longer take the risks of changing jobs, because of employers' preference for younger workers, who were presumed to be quicker learners and stronger. But the frequency of job changing—a clear inefficiency, from the manufacturers' standpoint—shows some of the ongoing tensions that modern work generated.

Finally, of course, there was direct protest against work conditions, though short of outright Luddism. Factory workers faced a variety of barriers to protest in virtually all instances of industrialization. The fact that they weren't well acquainted with one another made organization difficult, at least until urban conditions stabilized a bit. It was not easy to formulate goals: work might seem unpleasant in some ways, but short of attacking the industrial system outright, it was difficult to know what to ask for. Many workers might have more immediate concerns, about food prices, for example (the standard of living issue), and become involved in protests not directly related to work. Labor organizations were illegal in any event in all early industrial settings, and police were actively used to attack labor demonstrations. Employers identified, disciplined, and even fired individuals suspected of being agitators. Further, in all early industrial revolutions, except in the United States, workers lacked a vote, which long complicated efforts to use the political process to deal with labor issues.

But protest movements did develop, and, revealingly, they increasingly took the form of strikes—refusal to work—rather than more traditional riots. Wages were a key issue; strikes often broke out against reductions of wages or a failure to return pay to previous levels even after an economic recession ended. But workers also frequently walked out to protest an abusive foreman or a work accident that, in their view, should have been prevented. Strike movements, and the related formation of labor union organizations, oscillated in frequency in the factory sector, but by the end of the nineteenth century they became a force to be reckoned with throughout the industrial world. While they did not redefine the essentials of industrial work—the pace continued to mount, deskilling continued to occur—they did encourage some important adjustments, setting up a second chapter in the story of modern factory work.

Clashes between workers' and employers' conceptions of work were often quite stark. Workers could feel that their jobs had spun out of their control and violated cherished beliefs about what work should be all about. British workers, for example, tried to cling to what some called a "lump o'labour" concept, whereby only a certain amount of effort need be expended for a certain amount of pay—an idea that ran directly against employer insistence on constantly mounting productivity. Not surprisingly, amid pressures to increase the pace and the harsh direction of many foremen, many British workers talked about being treated no better than slaves or no better than sheep in a New Zealand stockyard. For their part, employers recurrently worried about challenges to their essential control over the workplace; efforts to bargain directly about working conditions were among the least likely to succeed either through negotiation or through strike activity. Even more, they were constantly tempted to see their workers as lazy and ungrateful, because so few willingly lived up to the new expectations attached to factory work. Thus, as we have seen, by the 1840s many French industrialists argued that workers were only putting out about two-thirds of the effort of which they were capable, and which employers thought they should be able to rely upon, because of individual attempts to adjust pace and effort to more endurable levels. Modern work could easily become a battleground.

*   *   *

Before turning to longer-run adjustments, whether as a result of protest or not, one other ingredient must be established among the basic changes that accompanied the advent of modern work: the clearer emergence of a new middle-class work ethic.

Middle-class people in Europe doubtless harbored elements of a special work ethic before industrialization. Merchants often preached, and sometimes exemplified, the virtue of diligence. Many Protestants saw work as a vital discipline against sin and might believe that hard work and attendant economic success were a sign of God's favor. By the eighteenth century, as we have seen, Enlightenment thinkers often praised work in this world and used a work standard to criticize the idleness and profligacy of the aristocracy. As the French Revolution neared, several theorists argued that respectable, propertied, middle-class people clearly deserved a vote, because they so obviously contributed to the social good, in contrast to the parasitic aristocrats. In all of this, there were clear components of a new celebration of the values of work.

But it was the early industrial setting itself, after the French Revolution and related reforms had cleared the way for a more vigorous assertion of middle-class values, that praise of work reached something of an apogee. Most early industrial revolutions in Western Europe were accompanied by a new breed of publicists trumpeting the values of hard work and urging that work was a foundation of personal success.

In Britain, the leading cheerleader was a writer called Samuel Smiles, whose works sold widely among middle-class readers and among others, including many artisans, who hoped to figure out how to get into the middle class. Smiles's books were filled with examples of people who had started out humbly but whose hard work had propelled them steadily upward; rags-to-riches stories were a staple of this new genre. Along with the stories came more specific advice: get up early; do not be distracted by gambling or other wasteful leisure pursuits; in recreation, seek opportunities that will contribute to work itself, like uplifting reading or (a bit later) healthy exercise; teach children the virtues of work from an early age. The overall message was clear: hard, well-organized work was a moral act, its own reward—but it would also lead to greater success and upward mobility in a middle-class world.

The same literature, of course, commented unfavorably on the work habits of many ordinary people. Too many people were lazy. Too many people drank heavily or otherwise indulged in habits that not only wasted money but also prevented appropriate diligence on the job. Obviously the result was poverty, but the point was that this poverty resulted from individual fault. No one had to fail if he worked hard and appropriately disciplined his spending.

This kind of work ethic was endlessly repeated in children's reading, in casual newspaper columns, and in formal self-help pamphlets. The approach was optimistic in many ways, compared to more traditional upper-class thinking. After all, the work-ethic folks were arguing that poverty was not an inevitable human condition, that people were not tied to the economic and social station in which they were born but could use their own efforts to rise higher. When, around 1800, the Prussian government changed school materials to emphasize the possibility of improving one's condition by one's own hard work, rather than insisting that the poor will always be with us, it was offering a fundamental restatement of how to think about the individual's relationship to society.

But the same work ethic could bear very harshly on middle-class reactions to the poor and to the new issues in factory work. It was easy to dismiss complaints or signs of strain as a demonstration of laziness. Why shouldn't the pace of work increase, since work itself was a virtue? And what about all these informal devices workers were using to introduce a bit more personal control into their daily lives, like changing jobs—wasn't this a sign of inadequate devotion to work, a quest for easy escape routes?

Clearly, the new middle-class work ethic was itself an important contribution to changes in work lives. Many people came to believe in the ethic. Many middle-class people, including early factory owners, did work very hard, sometimes arriving in the factory earlier, and leaving later, than workers did. At least some other people might internalize the new work ethic and use it as the basis of attempting, at least, to rise in society; there were genuine rags-to-riches stories in early industrialization, though far fewer than the middle class liked to assume. Though the term was never used in the nineteenth century, there was in the new ethic the potential for a real addiction to work, a disorientation when not on the job. Factory owners who never took a day off, who sent their families off on vacations in which they did not participate, or joined only on weekends, were poster people for the new work ethic, but they may have had trouble focusing on much else.

Certainly, the ethic also added to the complexity of work in the factories. Middle-class observers, who knew little about actual factory life, easily talked and thought at cross-purposes with what workers were experiencing. Their notion that work was ennobling contrasted vividly with workers' experience. The result was another constraint on workers: bosses who had no way of understanding their experiences or values.

Revealingly, at the end of the nineteenth century in both Europe and the United States, new interest developed in identifying high degrees of nervous strain, which for a time came under the heading of neurasthenia. But whereas experts argued that many middle-class men suffered from neurasthenia becase of hard work, the condition among working-class men was blamed on bad habits and dissolute lifestyle. The notion that workers, too, might be working too hard was very difficult to accept in respectable society.

*     *     *

Disputes were not simply matters of principle: they also were rooted in some very specific antagonisms. Temperance activities were a case in point. In all the industrializing European societies, temperance advocates and organizations sprang up to urge greater control of drinking. In some cases the inspiration was religious; British Methodism, for example, was a vital source of temperance activities. But regardless of precise stimulus, temperance debates focused concerns on proper work habits. As factory rules themselves consistently indicated, drinking should be limited in the interests of careful, diligent work.

For many workers, in contrast, drink was a vital solace precisely because of work. For some, drink and work had long combined, as in the artisanal habit of taking a glass or two to ease into the work day. Everywhere, taverns proliferated in the working-class sections of town. Belgium counted the highest number in the mid-nineteenth century, with one bar per twenty-seven inhabitants in the industrial cities. The bars provided not only drink but also conviviality in a situation where living quarters were too cramped to provide social space.

Not surprisingly, many workers fiercely resisted temperance demands, and indeed temperance advocates never succeeded in regulating this aspect of work-related life. But the conflict simply deepened middle-class impressions that some workers, at least, were simply incapable of developing proper work habits.

In truth, this was not a simple class struggle. Many individual workers abstained and actually joined temperance groups. Many middle-class families—doubtless including some who officially espoused temperance for others—drank heavily. Many labor leaders, including key socialist advocates, themselves urged temperance on their charges, for sober workers would be more effective participants in protest. But the battle over drink did translate broader divisions over work into some concrete disputes.

*   *   *

With actual factory work imposing key new practices, with middle-class interest conditioned by commitment to an ethic that was itself partly new, how could any accommodation be reached amid the tensions that clearly dominated the work spheres of industrializing societies?

Three major approaches developed. Specific reforms were designed to help certain individual classes of workers for whom modern work seemed one way or another inappropriate. More gradually, a combination of negotiation and reform began to limit work time. And, along with this, workers themselves developed an approach to work focused more on rewards, less on intrinsic satisfactions—an approach called instrumentalism, in which work, rather than defining life, becomes an instrument to achieve a better life in other respects.

Middle-class reformers began early to worry about the impact of modern work on children, because of its dangers, its pace, its exposure to strangers (and possibly through this to bad moral example). As more and more people began to believe that children even in the lower classes should have access to schooling, in part to improve their longer-term work capacity through skills like literacy and numeracy, another kind of comment on child labor developed.

British laws limiting the employment of young children, and their hours of work, in particularly risky industries like mining, began early in the nineteenth century. France passed its first child-labor law in 1841, after long debate; Prussia had passed such a law in 1839. These early laws were quite limited: they bore primarily on children under twelve; they limited hours rather than banning factory work entirely except for the very young; and they applied only to factories of a certain size, not to other kinds of child labor. They were also badly enforced for many decades, as both employers and many parents sought to evade their impact. Gradually, however, they did win some effect. By the 1870s, compulsory school requirements and the employment of paid factory inspectors, charged with identifying factory violations, really began to affect behavior. Furthermore, as we have seen, many parents had second thoughts about sending younger children into factories. Finally, larger, more-automated equipment eliminated some of the children's tasks. For example, early spinning machines had external bobbins, around which thread was wound; the thread often broke, so young "bobbin boys" would retie it even as the machines continued to operate. By the 1860s, thread broke less often and retying was automatic, and the children were not needed in the most up-to-date factories. Child labor would continue to spread in early factories in newer industrial regions, like the American South in the late nineteenth century, where lower wages were at a premium and equipment sometimes a bit outmoded, but it faded in the original centers.

Gradually as well, laws extended their impact, limiting hours even for children aged twelve to sixteen and extending coverage to other work sites. The process was completed only in the twentieth century in Western society, but within half a century of industrialization it was already clear that the classic relationship between children and work was beginning to break. Childhood became redefined as a time for schooling, not for work—a truly historic change.

By the 1840s, similar thinking began to be applied to women in the factories, though exclusions never went as far as in the case of children. Legislation in 1847 limited hours of work for women in factories in Britain. The idea was that factory work was too stressful for women unless it was artificially limited and that women needed some time to take care of domestic duties. Many male workers, including those in early unions, supported laws that would emphasize their special work role and also improve their bargaining position for wages by reducing women's availability. Women continued to have important functions in some factories, in textiles, for example, and later in chemicals, but in most Western countries their formal involvement in the urban labor force declined for many decades.

Adjustment number one, then, though it was forced on certain groups without full consultation, involved basically a statement that modern work was too tough for all the types of workers who had participated in traditional work and that new limits were vital. These changes emerged gradually in the industrial pioneers, like Great Britain; they tended to be adopted earlier in the industrialization process in later cases, such as Japan (at least for children) and Russia.

Adjustment number two, which came into the picture particularly in the final third of the nineteenth century in the industrial countries, involved limiting the hours of work even for adult males. If work was in some ways more unpleasant and, particularly, more intense, and if there was no agreement on how to change these trajectories on the job, then at least the time devoted to work could be reduced. Groups of workers began to use strikes and union agitation to win shorter workdays—down to twelve hours, later to ten (a movement around 1900), in some cases (like coal mining) down even to eight. Political action supplemented the process. Parallel campaigns began to work for a full weekend off (what the French by 1900 were referring to as the "English week," with at most a half day of work on Saturdays) and occasional vacation days during the year. The change was gradual and uneven and was sometimes undermined by pressure to work overtime, a problem that persists today. By 1900, however, most workers, and even elements in the middle class, were enjoying workdays that left some time, not just for sleep, but for recreation and family life. The modern pattern of a daily routine divided between work and nonwork—not the traditional pattern that intermixed the two—was significantly modifying initial industrial trends. Of course, within the shorter workday intensifications continued, so complaints about nervous exhaustion hardly ended, but there was measurable change in the structure of work life.

The third, instrumentalist adjustment began to surface in the 1850s and spread gradually but ultimately quite widely. The instrumentalist deal was this, in oversimplified form: workers implicitly agreed to basic conditions of modern work, including their substantial lack of control, in return for improved wages (and, later, benefits). Employers found demands in this vein more understandable than pressures on work itself, over which they sought to keep tight controls; the goals fit aspects of the work ethic, in which work was seen as the basis for social gains. In appropriate economic circumstances—when demand was high and the need to keep valued workers great—workers could indeed win real improvements, either through individual bargaining or through strikes or union actions. Instrumentalist goals by 1900 were the most common targets of labor action, because workers could agree on their desirability and because, of all the major demands, they stood the greatest chances of success.

Instrumentalism was often accompanied by a growing ability to think about other things on the job: a hoped-for consumer purchase, a socialist victory in the future, anything but the task at hand. An imaginative German worker, who in fact hated his job, said that he got through the day by pretending to be an artist: "Forms and pictures pour from my mind's eye, O that I could paint them all. O that I were free." More ordinary workers simply focused on random daydreams.[3]

Instrumentalism related closely to another adjustment, the importance given to the male worker's role as family breadwinner. Here was where work and family could be closely attached, or reattached, even though in a somewhat indirect or impersonal way. Many workers poured their devotion to children and family into their pride in holding a job and bringing home at least a survival wage. And if, through instrumental action, the wage allowed a bit more, all the better. Here was a vital, if fairly modern, badge of mature manhood, agreed on by all members of the working-class community and approved as well by middle-class observers. How much it compensated for the daily separation between work and family can be debated, but it surely provided emotional as well as material rewards.

Instrumentalism, the breadwinner role, and reduced hours did not mean that workers ceased to expect any satisfaction from work itself or to find disappointment when their expectations were not met, or that they did not continue to gain some pleasure from aspects of the work setting. Combinations were complicated, and as always personal calculations varied. By the twentieth century, some other adjustments modified early industrial conditions as well, particularly where union representatives won the right to represent workers who had grievances or to bargain over certain aspects of work and pay conditions. Here, the previous loss of control might be partially modified. These concessions were hard to gain in factories, however, where employer resistance was powerful.

Overall, however, the degree of change remained the most striking result. Workers faced a variety of significant innovations in factory work, most of which continued and even intensified. The encounter was further complicated by the real gulf between the values most workers retained, based loosely on a sense of earlier work traditions, and the new middle-class ethic. Adjustments occurred, but they brought further change—for example, in the differential involvements of different family members in modern work, or the new if desirable problem of what to do with nonwork or, as it was increasingly called, leisure time. Many workers successfully negotiated the changes, for human adaptability to various work settings has long been considerable; but most felt some loss, and many, even amid some of the reforms, felt profoundly alienated.

*   *   *

Industrialization's impact on work spread beyond the urban middle class and factory labor, though on the whole the level of innovation was somewhat less stark or at least somewhat more gradual in other areas.

As cities and the middle classes grew, the number of domestic servants expanded rapidly. This became the most common occupation for urban women through Western Europe, partly of course because factory jobs became less available or were viewed as inappropriate. Servant work was in many respects quite traditional. It appealed to earlier women's specialties in household and child care. It occurred in a domestic environment, though not the servant's own. It was not fast paced but stretched throughout long days. It involved much personal contact. And indeed, many people had been domestic servants before; it was the rapid expansion of the category that was particularly striking. Such positions allowed women to work but maintain contact with many earlier standards. Of course there were drawbacks: pay was low, and the rooms offered for live-in servants were often unpleasant. Having middle-class women as bosses presented many opportunities for conflict, and complaints about the "servant problem" multiplied endlessly. Opportunities for sexual exploitation by male employers were considerable as well. As many servants noted, factory work, for all its modern pressures, might seem preferable to the highly confined life of a servant and the highly individualized work supervision. And there were innovations: many servants were expected to live up to newer standards of household hygiene and newer ideas about child discipline. They might be required to be, or urged to become, literate, for participation in a modern household was difficult if one could not read. Servants in some ways were caught between largely traditional work standards, which had real drawbacks of their own, and modern demands that might make many servants, often of rural origin, seem really wanting. Small wonder that servants often quit or changed jobs (and almost never intended to keep on after marriage). Other adjustments included quiet protest actions like spitting or even urinating in the family soup. Servanthood persisted well into the twentieth century and expanded in societies outside the West, but it began to decline in industrial cities by 1900 partly because middle-class families, using new household technologies, had less need for assistance and partly because the women involved preferred other work options.

The impact of factory work on urban craft workers was intriguing, and in some ways unexpected. Many types of craft work expanded in the early decades of industrialization. Growing cities needed more construction workers, furniture makers, and the like, and the operations were not susceptible to factory production. Many craft workers, in turn, maintained traditional styles of work without significant modification.

But there were new pressures, and they provoked sometimes anguished response. Alert craft workers realized that their manufacturing styles were losing ground to the vastly more productive factory units, even when there was no direct competition. It was easy to resent the new wealth and power of the factory owners and the types of work they represented. Adaptations of factory styles made their way into the crafts directly. There was new effort to increase hours of work, though craft workers almost always avoided the extremes of some of the factories. Apprenticeships were cut back so that workers could begin production earlier and costs could be contained. Many furniture makers, for example, complained that they were increasingly required to make furniture as rapidly as possible, to standard designs, without the individual creativity and artistry that they believed were customary in their field. And with shorter apprenticeships, this trajectory was enhanced, for the younger workers lacked the degree of skill and independence of their older colleagues. In this situation, many master artisans began to act like small employers rather than colleagues and coworkers. It became increasingly difficult to rise from journeyman to master. Some masters stopped housing their journeymen or eating with them—again a suggestion that factory-style relationships were creeping into the crafts.

Ultimately, of course, many crafts were either converted to factory operations or at least affected by new technologies. By the later nineteenth century, furniture factories had been set up. Shoemaking shifted from traditional cobblers to factories (often staffed by women workers), except for the finest-quality brands. In construction, while skills remained important, the use of structural steel and preformed concrete by around 1900 cut back the number of skilled positions required; it took little training to assemble some of these components. Printing was dramatically affected, again around 1900, by larger and more-automated equipment, and some presses filled with women and other semiskilled workers in what had been one of urban Europe's most prestigious crafts.

Except in cases where factories replaced craft work outright, craft work never fully merged with factory modes, for both technical and human reasons. Technically, certain industries, like construction, could simply not be fully automated. It remained essential to have carpenters and masons, and new craft categories, like electricians, were added. This was a question not just of skill but also of a degree of autonomy on the job. Many construction workers continued to make specific decisions about what to do during the workday, about how to resolve certain problems, even when there was some general oversight from a site supervisor. Other skill areas were only partially altered by new equipment: diamond cutting was an obvious example where craft centers continued to predominate. Beyond the technical, many craft workers proved adept at forming organizations—not guilds any longer, for these were outlawed in most places, but new kinds of craft unions—that protected elements of work tradition more successfully than factory workers could achieve. Craft unions, spreading widely in the industrial countries after about 1850, not only helped keep hours of work down but also maintained apprenticeships, if at reduced length, which helped preserve a sense of skill and also limited competition for craft jobs. Printers' unions, thanks to good organization and periodic strikes, were able to retain skill categories even amid advancing mechanization, with work rules that limited how much type a given worker could be required to set during the working day.

Predictably, craft workers remained more likely than their factory colleagues to claim identity and meaning in their jobs, a distinction that would continue into the later twentieth century. But craft workers, too, effected some compromises, admitting that they no longer had the control or artistic autonomy that their predecessors had maintained. A degree of instrumentalism entered in here as well; groups such as printers were among the first to begin to bargain for higher wages in return for surrendering certain customs in the workplace itself.

Rural work was less affected by industrial principles in most of Europe, particularly where peasant holdings predominated. Changes occurred with the gradual introduction of new equipment such as tractors or cream separators. Many peasants, converting more fully to market production, found themselves involved in new kinds of commercial relationships, which among other things convinced them that some formal education was desirable. But there was no wholesale conversion to mechanization or impersonal supervision during the industrialization period in most of Europe.

Modern work principles spread strongly, however, to a final category, rapidly expanding after about 1870: the white-collar section. Here ultimately, after factory work, was the most important scene of change.

Small numbers of people had served as secretaries and clerks in traditional society. While not necessarily of high status, the work carried some real prestige. The fact that it was not manual, given the customary pecking order of social thought, gave it some glamour. In a few societies, such as the Balkans, clerks deliberately grew a fingernail extra long to demonstrate that they did not sully themselves by working with their hands. More substantively, clerkship meant literacy and some education. In the earliest days of industry, members of the manufacturer's family—a wife, a son—might assist with office work. This provided prestige directly and, where sons were involved, suggested the possibility of rising from clerkship to the solid middle or even upper-middle class, as part of lifetime mobility.

From about the middle of the nineteenth century onward, the number of people needed for clerical positions, broadly defined, began to increase dramatically. By the 1870s, this was the most rapidly growing set of occupational categories in Western Europe, outstripping even blue-collar expansion. Corporate offices needed secretaries, file clerks, and what we would now call receptionists. Department stores, another innovation that first emerged in the 1830s in Paris, needed large numbers of sales personnel. Banks and other operations needed tellers and cashiers. Whole new occupations sprang up around novel technologies—telephone operators were a case in point.

At the same time, with the steady growth of primary and secondary education, the pool of qualified white-collar workers also grew rapidly. Growing numbers of women also entered the field. While some white-collar occupations long retained unusual prestige—being chief secretary to a leading corporate manager or political figure is a powerful clerical job even today—the expansion both of jobs and of suitable occupants created a dramatically new framework.

And into this framework most of the principles of modern work were quickly poured. White-collar work never became exactly like factory work. White-collar workers, as the name suggests (women can be referred to as white-blouse workers), dressed like the middle class and often had middle-class aspirations. Employers kept most of these workers on salaries rather than daily wages, partly to reflect a slightly higher status and partly with the deliberate aim of keeping them separate from the working class and from working-class organizations like trade unions. Benefit programs, including retirement arrangements, were also usually both separate and superior. The tactic worked, in that white-collar workers (to this day) are less likely to strike and unionize than factory workers. Many white-collar workers exhibited what Marxists called a false consciousness, believing that their conditions were far more distinctive than they actually were. Among other things, pay levels were often not much different from those on the factory floor.

But the most important point was work itself. Technology soon intruded, if not to the extent that prevailed in factory life. New devices like cash registers and typewriters changed the face of much clerical work, reducing skill levels; many conventional male clerks, proud of their calligraphy, simply refused to engage with the new equipment. The pace of work also went up; secretaries were typically hired after being tested for how many words they could type per minute. In larger offices and in department stores, foreman-like supervision was installed to maintain proper discipline. Jobs were increasingly subdivided—file clerks, for example, were different from typists in the big offices—another application of industrial principles. Even noise levels went up, in the larger, cubicle-filled offices with scores of typewriters going a mile a minute.

There were some amusing extensions of efforts to supervise and speed up. Early in the twentieth century a German store owner installed a steam jet in the company toilet designed to go off after a person had sat for over a minute. No time to waste.

Office work continued to have some features that differed from work in the factories. There was more opportunity for informal socialization; no amount of monitoring could prevent people from chatting occasionally from desk to desk. The machines involved for white-collar workers did not impose the same degree of overwhelming discipline. And of course a sense of superior status—many secretaries dreamed of marrying the boss, to seize on a common image; many white-collar workers of both sexes planned for their children to rise higher in the world, more solidly into middle-class ranks—could help ease the work pressure as well.

On the other hand, as it developed by 1900, white-collar work also began to impose some additional constraints on workers beyond what the factory floor demanded. Many white-collar workers had to be trained in emotional control, so that they could be properly deferential and pleasant with the boss, in the case of secretaries; or smiling and solicitous in the face of even the most demanding customers, in the case of store clerks. Training in emotions management developed only gradually, but by the early twentieth century, manuals were frequently available to list the personal characteristics a good office or sales worker should have. Many workers found these additional job requirements extremely burdensome, sometimes even distorting their private emotional lives.

Not surprisingly, some of the same worker reactions developed in this setting as in the factories. There was a good bit of job changing; turnovers were high when economic conditions permitted. Many women intended to stay in white-collar work only for a time, prior to marriage; this reduced their concern about job conditions, because they were seen as transitory, but contributed to a complicated labor force. Outright protest, of course, was less common than with blue-collar labor, but there were many signs of strain. Instrumentalism was a particularly common reaction: white-collar workers, within a broadly middle-class environment, often became avid consumers, seeing their jobs as sources of pay for clothing and recreation. By the same token, their intrinsic job attachments were not much different from those of the working classes.

*   *   *

The development of modern work had one final, striking feature: its universality among industrializing societies. Patterns set in European industrialization were widely repeated elsewhere. Partly this resulted from direct imitation, but partly it flowed from the common demands of factors like powered technology.

Of course there were some individual variants. Industrialization in Japan imposed much the same work discipline as it had earlier in Western Europe. Artisans, who formerly had enjoyed the status of the highly skilled and insisted on considerable leisure time, found their work increasingly regulated and accelerated. There was a special twist on women's roles for several decades, into the twentieth century. Because Japan desperately needed to earn foreign currency to import fuel, raw materials, and up-to-date equipment, it relied heavily on exports from its silk industry. This, in turn, required extremely cheap labor, in sweatshop conditions. Many Japanese peasant families, themselves pressed for survival, in essence sold daughters to the sweatshop operators, who could closely regulate not only their work but also their housing and personal lives, working them extremely hard for very low pay. Only gradually, after 1900, did the Japanese develop a more balanced industrial approach, with greater emphasis on factory technology and growing recruitment of male workers. Ultimately Japan would also introduce some distinctive initiatives in factory industry that some observers argued built on older traditions of group solidarity deriving from Japanese Confucianism and feudal loyalties. But the initiatives dated mainly from after World War II, and they contrasted with the more conventionally modern work experiences and tensions characteristic of Japanese industrial life in the initial decades of the factory system.

Patterns in Russia were particularly interesting, for in the middle of the industrial process the Russians shifted from capitalist to communist organization. Again, the results generated some new departures in work life. Under Stalin, for example, peasants were increasingly forced into collective farms, where the Soviets attempted to install more factory-like work conditions than were common in agriculture. Large work crews were assembled, using powered machinery (though the Soviets had difficulty keeping this in adequate supply), and pledged to demanding production standards. The system did not function as well as hoped, in part because of peasant dissatisfaction at the lack of individual ownership and incentive, but it was an interesting indication of how far modern work systems might be applied. Soviet white-collar work also showed some distinctive features. The Soviet regime touted the importance of consumer standards but in fact tended to indulge white-collar workers as members of the working class. As a result, white-collar personnel, such as those at state-run department stores, tended to be surly and unresponsive. Consumer experience was thwarted as a result, and there were chronic inadequacies in the production of consumer goods; but workers were spared some of the pressures that had developed in the West.

In Soviet factories, however, modern work discipline was vigorously advanced. Factories tended to be large, which increased impersonality. The most striking feature, fully consistent with the larger modern work pattern, was a constant effort to increase productivity. Factories were assigned output goals, and managers had to work hard to meet them, pressing the labor force in consequence. As the pace of work intensified, many workers were also compelled to put in overtime, another effort to compensate for the lack of skill and experience in a rapidly growing factory labor force. Indeed, a semimilitary quality permeated the organization of work, partly to compensate for the absence of highly trained operatives amid massive recruitment from the countryside. Workers were encouraged to compete with each other for higher volume. In 1935 a coal miner in the Donets basin, Alexis Stakhanov, was said to have exceeded his personal quota by 1,400 percent, and a new prize category, the Stakhanovite worker, was established in his name. Soon workers in a variety of industries were seeking this award, mainly by speeding up their pace—indeed, a few aspirants actually died from the exertions involved. Here was a dramatic intensification of the standard industrial trend with regard to pace and personal effort. More broadly, "shock groups" of particularly zealous workers were used to model work for new recruits from the countryside, seeking to motivate and to intimidate by their productivity. A demanding work ethic was alive and well in communist society.

The public context for modern Soviet work was different, to be sure: workers were widely praised as heroes of the people, glorified in art and public pronouncements. Their symbolic standing was much higher than it had been in the industrialization period in the West. Other benefits, such as state-sponsored vacations, also eased industrial life. Whether this helped compensate for the daily routine is hard to ascertain. On the other hand, amid inadequacies of consumer goods, instrumentalism was harder to adopt; and the regime made sure that overt protest was rigidly repressed. Foreign observers in the 1930s, for example, were appalled at the number of armed police stationed at factory gates.

Modern work systems, as initially established in industrializing societies, had a final impact on work patterns even in otherwise underdeveloped economies. While it was impossible to replicate full industrial patterns on the agricultural estates and in the mines of nineteenth-century Latin America, owners could borrow from some of the Western innovations. Tentative efforts to limit leisure time and drinking, for example, in the interests of more diligent work showed the spillover from the new standards.

*    *    *

Overall, in the industrial societies themselves, work innovations were among the most striking features of the Industrial Revolution. Fundamental transformations occurred, and the most successful adjustments—from reforms to instrumentalism—simply added to the novelty. The patterns involved were easily applied to the United States, again by direct imitation and by parallelism. Within the common framework, however, the United States introduced some additional innovations of its own, creating something of an American version of modern work that could in turn influence other societies.

# Notes

1. Archives du Haut Rhin 1M123C1, Rules of Benck and Company.
2. Adolf Levenstein, *Aus Der Tiefe, Arbeiterbriefe* (Berlin, 1908).
3. Levenstein, *Aus Der Tiefe, Arbeiterbriefe.*

# Further Reading

## On Reactions to Modern Work

E. P. Thompson, *The Making of the English Working Class* (Harmondsworth, UK: Penguin, 1968) is a classic study of reactions to new work systems. *See also* Joan Scott, *The Glass-workers of Carmaux* (Cambridge, MA: Harvard University Press, 1974); Malcolm Thomis, *The Luddites* (London: Ashgate Publishing, 1993); Peter N. Stearns, *Lives of Labor: Work in a Maturing Industrial Society* (New York: Holmes & Meier, 1975); Lenard Berlanstein, *The Working People of Paris, 1871–1914* (Baltimore: Johns Hopkins University Press, 1984); Patrick Joyce, *Work, Society and Politics: The Culture of the Factory in Later Victorian England* (New Brunswick, NJ: Rutgers University Press, 1980).

## On Women

Louise Tilly and Joan Scott, *Women, Work and Family* (New York: Methuen, 1987); Mary Jo Maynes, Birgitte Soland, and Christina Benninghaus, *Secret Gardens, Satanic Mills: Placing Girls in European History, 1750–1960* (Bloomington: University of Indiana Press, 2004); Irene Padvaic and Barbara Reskin, *Women and Men at Work* (Thousand Oaks, CA: Pine Forge Press, 2002); Theresa McBride, *The Domestic Revolution: The Modernization of Household Service in England and France* (New York: Holmes & Meier, 1976).

## On Children

Carolyn Tuttle, *Hard at Work in Factories and Mines: The Economics of Child Labor during the British Industrial Revolution* (Boulder, CO: Westview, 1999); Sandy Hobbs, Jim McKechnie, and Michael Lavalette, *Child Labor: A World History Companion* (Boulder, CO: Westview, 1999); Robert McIntosh, *Boys in the Pits: Child Labour in Coal Mining* (Montreal: McGill-Queen's University Press, 2000); Colin Heywood, *Childhood in Nineteenth-Century France: Work, Health and Education among the "Classes Populaires"* (Cambridge: Cambridge University Press, 1988); and Neil Smelser, *Social Change in the Industrial Revolution: An Application of Theory to the British Cotton Industry* (Chicago: University of Chicago Press, 1959).

## On Work Management in Industrialization

Rinehard Bendix, *Work and Authority in Industry: Ideologies of Management in the Course of Industrialization* (Berkeley: University of California Press, 1974); Sidney Pollard, *The Genesis of Modern Management: A Study of the Industrial Revolution in Great Britain* (Cambridge, MA:

Harvard University Press, 1965); Peter N. Stearns, *Paths to Authority: The Middle Class and the Industrial Labor Force in France* (Urbana: University of Illinois Press, 1978).

## On White-Collar Work

Juergen Kocka, *White-Collar Workers in America, 1890–1940: Social-Political History in International Perspective* (Beverly Hills, CA: Sage, 1960); David Lockwood, *The Black-Coated Worker: A Study in Class Consciousness*, 2nd ed. (New York: Oxford University Press, USA, 1989); Michael Miller, *The Bon Marché: Bourgeois Culture and the Department Store* (Princeton: Princeton University Press, 1981).

## On Industrial Work in Russia

Kenneth Strauss, *Factory and Community in Stalin's Russia* (Pittsburgh: University of Pittsburgh Press, 1997); Sil Ruda, *Managing Modernity: Work, Community and Authority in Late-Industrializing Japan and Russia* (Ann Arbor: University of Michigan Press, 2005); Reginald Zelnik, *Labor and Society in Tsarist Russia* (Stanford: Stanford University Press, 1971).

## On Japan

Janet Hunter, *Institutional and Technological Change in Japan's Economy: Past and Present* (Oxford, UK: Routledge, 2006); Andrew Gordon, *The Evolution of Labor Relations in Japan* (Cambridge, MA: Harvard University Press, 1985); Janet Hunter, *Women and the Labour Market in Japan's Industrializing Economy* (London: Routledge Curzon, 2003); Tamotsu Sengoku, *Willing Workers: The Work Ethics in Japan, England and the United States* (London: Quorum Books, 1985).

# CHAPTER 5

# Modern Work
# the American Way

Industrialization began to take hold in the United States by the second and third decades of the nineteenth century, initially relying on equipment and factory schemes imported directly from Great Britain. This was the start of a genuine and ultimately highly successful industrial revolution, but like processes elsewhere it did not convert work systems overnight. Many Americans remained in agriculture; the nation did not become half urban until 1920, seventy years later than Great Britain. Other traditional work sectors long survived as well, and of course slavery persisted in the South until the Civil War ended the system. Traditional sectors were not changeless: urbanization and westward expansion created new opportunities for commercial agriculture, and Americans applied machinery, such as harvesting machines, to agriculture quite early, compared to Western Europe. Slavery intensified in the Deep South with the growing importance of cotton. Hard work was not just an industrial issue.

In American factories, work systems developed in ways very similar to the patterns of other industrial societies. It is important not to look for too many really distinctive experiences. New issues of pace, supervision, and deskilling emerged in the United States just as they did elsewhere. Ultimately, American factory owners would add to industrial innovations, and their contributions were important both nationally and internationally; but a clearly American tone did not emerge in the initial industrial decades.

Even in the longer term, it is vital to keep the fundamental comparative point in mind: the big development in modern American work history has been the conversion to basic modern forms, not some kind of national exceptionalism. Differences would have some significance on the margins, and even, as we will see, contribute to broader international patterns, but the installation of industrial labor and its spillover into other work areas was the core pattern.

American industrialization was conditioned by the fact that, given opportunities in expanding agriculture and the still-small population base, labor was in somewhat short supply, compared to much of Western Europe or, later, Russia or Japan. This fact, supplemented perhaps by the absence of a guild tradition with its heritage of suspicion of new technologies, encouraged an unusual reliance on machines and machine-based productivity gains, extending one of the trends basic to industrialization everywhere. Americans did not contribute many fundamental inventions to early industrialization. American inventors shared with the British key innovations in the development of the standardization of parts, which ultimately reduced skill levels in machine making, but otherwise the nation long imported most of the crucial technologies from Britain, France, and even Sweden. But American manufacturers were eager users of machines, because expanding the labor force was more challenging in the American context, and they often adapted equipment to make it more productive. It was thus no accident that, toward the end of the nineteenth century, the larger Northrop looms, with their much greater output per worker, emanated from the United States, as Americans sought more advantage from mechanical weaving equipment initially pioneered elsewhere.

To the extent that Americans emphasized technological solutions, they imposed more adjustments on the labor force: a more rapid pace, a greater specialization in work functions, and so on. By the 1850s and 1860s, additional pressures may have resulted from the fact that, thanks in part to a rapidly expanding national market and permissive legislation, unusually large corporations began to enter key sectors of American industry. This development encouraged the growth of factories larger than those in older industrial economies like Britain and added more-impersonal management and greater commitments to the kind of high output that would generate substantial profits. Still, however, the basic parameters of factory work remained within the recognizable framework of modern work, clearly overlapping with patterns in Western Europe. Key trends were familiar, from the first factories on to the mid-twentieth century.

A shortage of labor encouraged an unusual appetite for immigrant workers, a factor that began to come into play by the 1850s with the influx of French Canadian and considerable Irish labor into New England textile factories. Immigration and the commitment to technology would ultimately produce a more clearly definable American contribution to modern work.

In the early industrial decades, however, it was less the factory floor than American middle-class culture that generated the most distinctive American element. An exaggerated work ethic—not different from the middle-class values of Western Europe so much as more extensively accepted—affected middle-class work performance and ultimately the evaluation of the working class as well. Whereas the work ethic advocates in Western Europe claimed to see work as a key ingredient of personal and social progress, their American counterparts elevated work to a moral imperative. Early industrial developments set a basis here, doubtless building on the Puritan heritage, but we will later see how striking continuities and adjustments carried the theme into the twentieth century and beyond.

# The American Ethic

We have seen that American tradition differed from that of Western Europe in lacking at least two components capable of sustaining a premodern set of work values into the modern era. There was no aristocracy to suggest an alternative style of life to that of hard work. Americans aplenty worried about the brashness and greed of the new-style industrialist—intellectuals in Boston commented on it, as did Southern planters. But it was difficult to convey a fully developed alternative to work-based existence. Nor was the guild tradition available. American craftsmen could and did take pride in their skills, and some craft values partially survived the industrial onslaught in the United States as in Europe. But without a guild background it was harder to project a commitment to a more leisurely, artistically creative style of work (and indeed, for many purposes like decorative stonework, the top artisans continued to be imported directly from places like Italy).

It was also easy for Americans, particularly farming and craft families, to pick up a version of the Enlightenment idea that social value correlated directly to work. Historians have noted the emergence in the early nineteenth century of a small-producer ideology that stressed the special virtue of work, often attacking remote, big-city capitalists, who presumably did not toil so directly. This approach mixed older and newer elements of culture, but it could help support a more distinctive work ethic as well.[1]

American commentary was also less hesitant about suggesting the validity of ambition as a spur to hard work. Europeans, as we have seen, emphasized that people could use hard work and efficiency to get ahead, but they often conditioned this with a lingering sense that poverty was inevitable and that encouraging too many people to think they could rise in society might cause frustration and social discontent. Americans were often scornful of racial minorities and immigrants, despairing about their presumed idleness and bad habits; but they did not ultimately argue that messages about upward mobility needed to be qualified by concomitant pleas for people to remain in their social place. Racial prejudice constrained mobility in fact, which was crucial, but had less explicit impact on formal rhetoric.

In a sense, then, the American decks were cleared for an unusually vigorous assertion of the values of hard work. It was revealing that, even before the American Revolution and well before the emergence of Samuel Smiles types in Britain, Benjamin Franklin and his popular *Poor Richard's Almanac* had already laid out some of the sinews of the new work ethic, with his admonitions to go to bed early, rise early, and in general organize life around the kind of work devotion that would make one "healthy, wealthy and wise." To be sure, Enlightenment thinkers were praising constructive work in the same period, but without so much moralism or such specific time injunctions. The American lead here suggests a special openness to what became the newer middle-class values, again perhaps reflecting the absence of an alternative aristocratic ethic in addition to the role of the Puritan tradition.

By the 1830s, hymns to the beauties of hard work became commonplace. These virtues were trumpeted in readers for children, which drove home the point that hard work would allow a person to be the author of his destiny. Daily newspapers reflected the same belief. A crucial component—again, not uniquely American but given unusual attention in the United States—was the association of work with social mobility and the attendant belief that rising in the world was what any upstanding person should strive for.

A key theme, as various officials and publicists worked to establish a new sense of American nationhood, was that the United States was a land of opportunity, so long as people were willing to work hard to take advantage of it. A newspaper story from the 1830s cited a British laborer frustrated at his lack of a job and endemic poverty. To his complaints his wife responded, "There is another land where, if what we hear be true, ability finds employment and talent a sure reward." And indeed the couple packed up to cross the Atlantic to the Land of Promise. Or as another writer put it, in America "men succeed or fail ... not from accident or external surroundings" but from "possessing or wanting the elements of success in themselves"—beginning with hard work.[2] The vision was progressive, in the sense of freeing people from the idea of inherited, inevitable status, but it was also demanding: life was seen as an endless race to move ahead.

Work was central. Again, from a Massachusetts newspaper: "Idle men and women are the bane of any community. They are not simply clogs upon society, but become, sooner or later, the causes of its crime and poverty.... Every family motto should read: 'Be somebody. Do something. Bear your own load.'" Stories told of rich people who had risen by work from humble origins: "My father taught me never to play till all my work for the day was finished.... If I had but half an hour's work to do in a day, I must do that the first thing, and in half an hour.... It is to this habit that I now owe my prosperity."[3] Note, obviously, the modern twist: not just hard work, but efficient work, timed by the clock.

A corollary of the work-and-mobility package, also beginning to win wide acceptance by the 1830s, was the notion that children should do better than their parents, building on the latter's accomplishments through their own education and hard work. This was a message sent to Irish immigrants, who might not see much progress in their own lives but could count on their children, for whom "the rudest implements of labour may be the means of advancement to wealth, honour, and distinction." Here was another widely shared national belief that would easily survive at least into the later twentieth century.

The middle of the nineteenth century saw a large number of books about the wealthy in American society that pointedly used the occasion to emphasize how hard work was consistently at the root of great success. Thus *The Rich Men of Massachusetts*, issued in 1851, told of Seth Adams, whose father died and who supported his family by labor on the farm from the age of ten. Later going to

Boston, he put his habits to good use in setting up his own business. Robert Douglass, also fatherless, supported his mother and eight siblings and then turned his diligence to a business of his own, in candy making; he was widely known for his "efficiency." Phineas Allen, a printer's apprentice, was another "man of extremely regular business habits. Always about his business; a correct, go-ahead man" who started his own newspaper. And so the list went, with example after example. Newspaper obituaries provided another opportunity to tell the public about how successful lives were shaped by hard work. The theme was ubiquitous during the industrializing decades.

Other self-help pamphlets, pushed by prominent people like the newspaper editor Horace Greeley (who also urged young Americans to "go West" for success), urged that work capacity and related good habits formed the key distinction between those who made it and the more general run of men. Greeley thus noted that the young people who would succeed would largely shun leisure activities; they would count each hour and use it "to work efficiently"; they would do any kind of work, even if it seemed "ungenteel," in order to earn money to get ahead, and would never stand idle. Ultimately moneymaking would come easily to such a person, as the wealth piled up. "But the germ of all this spreading oak was in the tough acorn whence it sprang."[4]

The most famous prophet of this American work ethic, after Benjamin Franklin, was Horatio Alger, the American counterpart to the British Samuel Smiles. Alger wrote prolifically in the mid-nineteenth century, almost entirely on rags-to-riches themes. He published a whole series for young readers, addressing them both in books and in serialized stories in magazines. An 1867 effort, first published in *Student and Schoolmate* and then emerging as a book, featured Ragged Dick. Dick was a bad boy; he swore, gambled, and smoked. But he never stole, and he was open to good advice. A Mr. Whitney took him in charge, reminding him that "in this free country poverty in early life is no bar to a man's advancement." The key was diligent study and, of course, hard work over a long period of time. Dick resolved to persevere, realizing that he had only his own efforts to depend on.[5]

Clearly, as the prolific Alger's career itself suggests, Americans were being subjected to a real cultural bombardment. Not everyone, even in the fabled middle class, bought into the values, but it was hard to escape their influence.

To be sure, it is not clear that middle-class people actually worked harder in the United States at this point than their European counterparts did. Many American businessmen put in long hours, and many sent their wives and children on summer vacations while they stayed back to mind the store. But, as we have seen, similar patterns developed in the European middle class.

In addition to the cultural onslaught, the American middle class subjected itself to real pressures for success, along with vivid cautionary tales about failure. By the later nineteenth century, a variety of institutions had developed to provide credit ratings for business and professional people; Dun and Bradstreet was the most influential example. These ratings could be ruthless in their assessment of moral failings and poor work habits, including, of course, excessive drinking and gambling. And rates of business failure were in fact quite high in the early industrial decades (in Europe as well as the United States). This meant that many middle-class people had direct knowledge of friends and relatives who had not been able to maintain their social rank and were aware as well that their deficiencies would be noted in formal credit evaluations. It was hard, given the larger work ethic, to explain away failure, not only to outsiders but also to one's family and oneself. If work inevitably paid off, as the culture insisted, anything short of success must indicate deficient diligence. Poor health might provide a bit of an excuse, but bad luck or social barriers could not easily be invoked, since work should be able to overcome such obstacles.

It is also clear that different sets of social beliefs developed on the two sides of the Atlantic, based in part on divergent views of the role of work. By the late nineteenth century, and still today, Americans were far more likely than Europeans to exaggerate opportunities for upward mobility based on diligence and efficiency. Europeans, in contrast, downplayed the amount of mobility that occurred in their society (actual rates in the two cases were about the same, based on similar involvement in the processes of industrialization). Europeans, in other words, tended to think that durable social barriers could not necessarily be overcome by individual effort; Americans belittled social obstacles in their belief that everyone had a roughly even start in life and that hard work would win the day.

This divergence—and of course it involved not just ideas about work but a whole approach to the social order—arguably generated additional consequences over time, more clearly in the twentieth century than in the nineteenth. Even by 1900, it was clear that socialist political movements could not gain the same audience in the United States that they did in Europe. American insistence that socialism was a dangerous and foreign import played a role here; so did ethnic and linguistic divisions in the American working class. But a crucial factor was the extent to which Americans, even many immigrant workers, absorbed at least some belief that individuals should be able to control their fortunes through hard work, that poverty and social inequality were in large part results of individual failure. With this approach, socialism, arguing for a different social order and more collective assistance for those in distress, simply made less sense than in Europe.[6]

Partly because of this political rift, but also as a further result of different degrees of faith in the certainty of work-based success, Europeans would develop much more extensive welfare systems than Americans did, even when New Deal and Great Society programs are included. Differences were limited before 1945, though European schemes tended to emerge earlier than U.S. counterparts, but the gap widened with the postwar flowering of the European welfare state. Similarly, when in the 1980s and 1990s welfare programs came under attack because of economic constraints, Americans cut their programs back far more readily than most European countries did, in favor of insisting that the poor take their chances in the job market. A key reason for these significant disparities was the

American belief that too much welfare would undermine appropriate work habits, that individuals should be able to make their own way if they would only devote themselves properly to their jobs. Europeans, in contrast, proved readier to use the state to compensate for barriers to adequate living standards. Americans did believe that society owed access to education for a proper start in life; their commitments here developed earlier and more extensively than was true in Europe until the later twentieth century; but after that, good work habits should take over.

Finally, differences in the degrees of commitment to the new work ethic—again, it's vital to remember that many values were shared by a transatlantic middle class; the distinctions were in the degree and intensity of acceptance—showed in the different fates of temperance activity on the two sides of the water. Efforts to reduce or eliminate the consumption of alcohol reflected, of course, a number of factors. Religion played a role. Certain Protestant groups were typically at the forefront of temperance movements, and the United States, as an unusually religious industrial society, reflected this factor strongly. In the American context, temperance activities could also suggest anxiety about the habits of immigrants and an attempt to discipline them. But, in the United States as elsewhere, concern about the effects of drinking on work were fundamental to the inception of temperance activities; it was no accident that temperance and early industrialization went hand in hand on both sides of the Atlantic.

In this context, it was revealing that American temperance movements tended to surpass European efforts in many ways, with some admitted overlap with developments in Great Britain. American temperance efforts began earlier than those in most European countries. They moved more quickly toward attempts to ban drinking altogether, as opposed to an initial impulse simply to moderate the consumption of alcohol. By the late nineteenth century organizations like the Women's Christian Temperance Union and the Anti-Saloon League pushed vigorously for laws that would abolish the production and sale of alcohol, moving away from earlier emphasis on the reform of personal habits. And of course, uniquely among major industrial societies, the United States did in fact prohibit the manufacture, distribution, and transportation of alcohol through the Eighteenth Amendment to the Constitution, passed in 1919 and repealed in 1933. Furthermore, though Prohibition in one sense clearly failed, in that the public changed its mind about using the law for these purposes, it did permanently alter working-class drinking habits, greatly reducing reliance on neighborhood taverns even when they once again became legal. Here again, American commitment to an ethic of hard work, at least as a public ideal, and to removal of barriers to hard work moved well beyond European levels.

The most important questions about the special features of the American version of the work ethic obviously relate to work itself. The American version surely helps explain some of the work addiction, visible still in contemporary society, that differentiates the American approach from that of other industrial countries. We will have to trace the maintenance and enhancement of the ethic over time—after all, the fact that special features developed in the nineteenth century does not guarantee their impact today—but the potential connections are obvious. Elements of the American middle class have long been conditioned to define their lives in terms of work, and the impulse continues well after the throes of early industrialization have passed.

The second application of the American ethic involves dominant attitudes toward the work of others. Obviously, the extensive commitment to work has affected attitudes toward poverty and other social issues. It also, potentially, affected the organization of work itself. With work given such value, manufacturers and office directors had even more motivation than their European counterparts to seek maximum effort from their labor force. Here, too, a general pattern—the intensification of modern work thanks to industrialization—was given an additional boost, along with the commitment to exceptionally productive technology. Gradually—for this connection was forged a bit more slowly than the work ethic itself—Americans added innovations to the factory floor and the office complex.

## Industrial Work, American Style

The initial experience of factory work in the United States, in the early decades of the nineteenth century, was surprisingly favorable, particularly if measured by British standards. The key factor—in contrast above all to Britain, but also to other parts of Europe and Japan—was the labor shortage. With a small population and an expanding frontier, there were limits to the conditions early factory owners could impose on workers. Standard changes still applied; this was a new work experience in the United States as elsewhere. Pace, accidents, deskilling, impersonal direction all shifted. And some workers hated the result, leaving the factories at the earliest opportunity or suffering damage to their health and psyche.

Many workers, however, reported some compensations along with new stress. Many workers in the early New England textile factories were farm girls eager to make a bit of extra money to help their families (New England farms were becoming less productive) or prepare for marriage. They did not think of the factory commitment as lifelong, which may have cushioned their reactions. And there were some gains. One woman, writing to her father, noted that she was able to find a job easily, that it paid pretty well and that the rate would rise as she gained experience, and that she had a "first rate overseer." Many companies provided housing for workers that was regarded as adequate. Another young woman, commenting on the intense pace, noted with pride that she was as productive as any other member of her unit and that she was learning how to operate more machines more quickly than most. "I think that the factory is the best place for me and if any girl wants employment I advise them to come to Lowell [Massachusetts, a key textile center]." A third young woman, admitting there were many problems at work, noted her admiration for the human ingenuity embodied in the machines and her appreciation of the plants and artwork that employers put in the workrooms. She also welcomed the moral guidance of her overseers, the medical care and religious facilities provided, and the opportunity to earn wages that would enable her to assist aged parents.[7]

This was, obviously, not the same package that early factories had offered in Britain, and it was notably better than conditions in other American textile centers. Employers in places like Lowell, Massachusetts, had to offer greater amenities to attract workers initially, and they did not see workers from the farms of New England as totally different from themselves. Reports on housing, on Sunday schools, on décor, all suggested unusual levels of attentiveness. Even more important were pay scales that permitted workers some sense that they had a margin above subsistence, often to fulfill family obligations (there was less sense of an early devotion to new consumer pleasures of the sort that would later accompany instrumentalism). All this, in combination with an intention of leaving the factory after a year or two, produced an attitude that could then appreciate some of the interesting aspects of modern machinery or the opportunity to meet new people among the throngs of strangers in the labor force. Work changes, in other words, could be encountered as a mixed bag, not simply a set of deteriorations cushioned by compensatory pay.

This was not, however, a durable reaction. As American industry prospered, it also began to recruit new types of immigrant workers—French Canadians in the New England mills, for example, by the 1840s. In combination with more efficient equipment, this influx began to loosen the labor shortage and so lighten the constraints on management, including the need to offer attractive wages. Quickly, work experience in the factories began more closely to resemble conditions in Europe and thus the more standard features of modern work. Quickly, indeed, American manufacturers were able to intensify the characteristics of modern work in ways that added a permanent national mark to the industrialization process.

By the 1880s, the combined interests of American managers and corporate directors, on the one hand, and growing expertise in both engineering and psychology, on the other, began to produce the movement that would become known as scientific management. The United States was not the only source of this movement. Germany, another rising industrial power, also generated important research, particularly in industrial psychology, though some leading figures ended up holding academic positions in the United States. But the larger thrust of scientific management was distinctively American. One management expert, Peter Drucker, has even termed it "the most powerful as well as the most lasting contribution America has made to Western thought since the Federalist Papers"—and indeed the impact went well beyond Western confines as well.[8]

While several figures launched studies in scientific management, the movement became particularly associated with Frederick Taylor, who began his research in the 1880s. Indeed, French industrialists and labor leaders would later refer to the whole efficiency thrust as Taylorization. Taylor's emphasis rested on the possibility of carefully measuring worker motions and timing them, setting production standards that workers would have to live up to if they were to receive a full wage. The goals, obviously, were to make workers' behaviors more uniform and to speed up the whole work process toward greater productivity at potentially lower cost. Engineers, with their technical training and their capacity to study human factors as they would the workings of machines, began to become far more important than foremen in regulating the workplace. This potentially eliminated some of the favoritism and personal bullying with which foremen were often associated, but it also limited the flexibility and variety of work, and it greatly extended what was already a key feature of industrial work, the heightened pace (and related loss of workers' control over their own daily routines).

Two factors—beyond the sheer drive for greater profits in an increasingly competitive global industrial environment—helped anchor this movement in the United States. The rise of engineering as a discipline was obviously crucial, but this was not distinctive to American shores. Rather, the commitment (at least in principle) to a particularly stringent work ethic on the part of owners and managers made it seem both logical and justifiable to push factory workers even harder than before. If work was valuable in its own right, more, and more-efficient, work could be seen as even more rewarding. Along with this, however, came management reactions to an increasingly immigrant workforce around the turn of the century, a workforce filled particularly with eastern and southern European entrants (and a few African Americans and other minorities as well). It was easy for largely native-born, or at least Anglo-Saxon, managers to see immigrants as inferior and therefore to accept levels of work regulation and intensification that might not otherwise have been tolerated. It was easy for them, as well, to see these workers as intrinsically lazy and evasive (a widespread managerial view even of a native-born labor force) and therefore requiring an unusual amount of prodding.

Time was the crucial factor in this whole movement. It could be measured; workers could be assessed, stopwatches at the ready, according to the speed and efficiency of their movements. "Time-and-motion" studies, and work standards based on their results, sat at the core of the scientific management approach. Of course these procedures might eliminate jobs; of course they could increase workplace fatigue. But leaders like Taylor rejected these criticisms—Taylor himself reputedly became incensed when asked about fatigue—because the goals of greater productivity outweighed other concerns. (Taylor also claimed he could provide scientifically determined optimal rest periods.) In Taylor's view of the work ethic, workers would truly want to earn their wage, and so measures that brought them, literally, up to speed were fully justifiable.

Taylor recruited a variety of additional experts to the principles of scientific management, as many companies established personnel research units and as a growing array of consulting opportunities became available. Time-and-motion studies were applied to a steadily expanding array of work settings, particularly in factories but occasionally in office settings as well. A 1912 inquiry already identified at least fifty-two industries in which one or more companies had introduced "labor-saving" management.

Scientific management was widely attacked, particularly by workers and labor organizations. The overriding objection was the increasing treatment of men (and women) as if they were machines, but loss of autonomy and the sheer pace of work were specific issues also. Not infrequently strikes arose over the introduction of time-and-motion standards, though because employers insisted on their right to determine conditions of work, the protests rarely gained durable victories. Indeed, several industrial engineers in Taylor's wake began to work not only on efficiency goals but also on inculcating greater worker obedience. On the other hand, many workers continued to be able, informally, to resist some of the new standards and modify their work routines in practice—sometimes with assistance from foremen, who also objected to their loss of autonomy under the new systems. The one definite bright spot, however, from the labor standpoint, fully approved by Taylor himself, was that manufacturers might be able to offer higher pay as efficiency improved; they would still save money, but workers would benefit as well. Obviously, this approach built on, and confirmed, the instrumentalism of many American workers, who were compelled to work in systems they found unpleasant but compensated in ways that might improve their lives off the job.

Efficiency engineering led directly to a second American innovation early in the twentieth century, the introduction of the assembly line, initially in Henry Ford's automobile plant. Assembly lines moved products steadily past specialized groups of mostly semiskilled workers, where they repetitiously performed particular motions (tightening screws, for example) as quickly, and with as little thought, as could be managed. Ford's goal—extending the time-and-motion principles—was to make workers as machinelike as possible, with effectively no independent initiative or decision making. The assembly line, distinctively American in origin like scientific management more generally, served really as the apotheosis of industrial-style work. It too spread rapidly in industries where its applicability was possible at all. Ford and his colleagues claimed to offer top dollar to the workers involved—Ford's famous $5 day was symbolic here. Ultimately, assembly-line principles allowed certain processes to be automated altogether, reducing the sheer number of machinelike workers. But the innovation had lasting effects on work itself.

Inevitably, time-and-motion principles and assembly lines spread well beyond the United States, beginning in the first decade of the twentieth century. Various European countries imitated these practices extensively, as did Japan. Canadian Pacific introduced new systems. Russian leaders—and particularly Lenin, after the 1917 revolution—were deeply interested in the new principles, as part of their zeal to accelerate industrial production. The wartime production needs in many countries between 1914 and 1918 boosted attention to efficiency programs. "Made in America" remained an important aspect of scientific management: it is vital to remember how and why this development sprang from United States conditions. But ultimately the developments contributed to the intensification of key features of industrial work around the world.

# White-Collar Work

Many features of white-collar work in the United States—including the rapid growth of the category—replicated developments in other industrial societies. American offices and stores were quick to adopt typewriters and other new technologies that reduced traditional skill levels and helped speed up the work process. New forms of supervision were introduced, in some imitation of factory patterns.

Two characteristics stand out as candidates for some national distinctiveness. In the first place, the development of new kinds of labor expertise among the ranks of industrial psychologists and the like easily spilled over into the white-collar category. Efficiency experts performed time-and-motion studies on clerks and typists, trying to avoid wasted motions and discourage distracting socialization. The idea of piping in music to promote greater work zeal applied particularly to office settings, where noise levels otherwise were not overwhelming. Playing music forty-five minutes each hour, then pausing for fifteen minutes, proved most effective in getting maximum effort out of office staff without their awareness that they were being manipulated. Obviously, offices could not exactly be converted to factory environments, because more personal interactions were required and the levels of technology were lower. But scenes from typist pools, with workers sitting in rows, repeating similar tasks under supervision, deliberately evoked the factory floor. American managers led the way in office standardization.

The spread of personnel departments—and 31 percent of American corporations had such units by the 1930s—fostered other efforts directly to adjust white-collar workers to the demands of their jobs. Counseling services aimed at helping workers overcome emotional or mental difficulties, but with an eye to making them more work-serviceable and limiting the impact of off-the-job problems on work performance.

American conditions, and the ready availability of industrial psychologists, contributed to other changes in white-collar work. For example, screening of many white-collar workers, particularly those who would interact directly either with management or with the general public, became increasingly deliberate, and personnel tests were often applied. The idea was to use tests to fit personalities to job functions. The Humm-Wadsworth personality test, first used at Lockheed Aircraft in the early 1940s, was designed to weed out troublemakers and identify workers likely to be manipulable and docile; one of the test's authors claimed that 80 percent of all problem workers had testable deficiencies in temperament. In principle, and doubtless often in fact, the goal was to improve the work experience as well as productivity: when people were suited to their jobs, workers and manager alike could gain. But testing also suggested an additional set of norms for work, standards that white-collar workers as well as managerial employees needed to measure up to, as part of acceptable work performance.

Testing related directly to the growing importance of job interviews in the white-collar sector, in which applicants would be rigorously screened by personnel experts to make sure that their attitudes, dress, and background were suitable for the job at hand. Increasingly, this brought aspects of what might have been regarded as private life into direct contact with the demands of work. One's family values, personal habits, even leisure interests now were framed in terms of their relevance to work.

In the workplace, and particularly for the white-collar categories, a new goal involved driving all emotionality from the work site, replacing it with entirely rational behavior. Secretaries, for example, were told to keep emotions in check. Whereas traditional secretarial manuals had emphasized trustworthiness and responsibility—now less salient characteristics, as secretaries had fewer responsibilities and more supervision—work advice now turned to temper control. A good clerk would greet even the most unpleasant boss with a wide smile, and anyone with a quick temper was "faced with the problem of remedying these defects." "The secretary should never forget that in order to please people, he needs to exert himself."[9]

Foremen, similarly, were urged to keep their anger under control, for their task now was not to browbeat workers—machines and industrial engineering norms now assured the appropriate pace and productivity—but to make sure disputes did not disrupt the work process. As one set of guidelines for foremen urged: "Control your emotions—control your remarks—control your behavior." "It is of the utmost importance that the foreman remain cool," as a 1943 personnel relations article put it. Salesmen faced similar injunctions, and a whole series of training workshops opened up to teach people appropriate sales behavior. Dale Carnegie was a key guru in the 1920s and 1930s, urging that salesmen always keep a handle on their emotions even when customers were at their most disagreeable. As Carnegie put it, talking about restraining himself when faced with a particularly nasty client: "I had the satisfaction of controlling my temper, the satisfaction of returning kindness for an insult. I got infinitely more real fun out of making her like me than I ever could have gotten out of telling her to go and take a jump."[10]

Programs to test, supervise, and educate white-collar personnel obviously extended to department store personnel. Many stores by the 1920s instituted elaborate programs to teach salesclerks how to dress and behave like model middle-class citizens, including managing their emotions—even when their middle-class customers did not do the same.[11]

For some white-collar workers, these new behavioral demands could be assimilated without too much difficulty. For others, however, the strain of measuring up to the need for emotional control might be quite telling. A telephone operator: "You can't be angry.... You have to be pleasant, no matter how bad you feel." Similarly, a foreman in the 1950s told a sociologist-interviewer that he always went home from work "frazzled" from the effort to keep peace with people "at all levels."[12]

The movement continued through the twentieth century, with additional kinds of training sessions and faddish socialization schemes essentially pointed in the same direction, to incorporate new levels of control into the workplace. Here, obviously, was a new or at least enhanced constraint in work that differentiated white-collar work from the more physical constraints long present in factory labor.

The impulses were of course common to much white-collar work everywhere, but because of the particularly strong standing of American personnel experts, and the larger cultural belief that anything, even emotional autonomy, could and should be sacrificed to effective work, the rules, testing, and training went furthest in the United States. Revealingly when, much later in the twentieth century, McDonald's restaurant chain spread to Russia, a key management requirement was to redo the traditional, rather surly Russian sales approach in favor of emotionally controlled, smiling hamburger jockeys. Expectations of cheerfulness in American white-collar workers were particularly high.

The overall approach could take a toll on workers, just as new factory rhythms had done. A major sociological study in the later twentieth century found many American white-collar personnel—flight attendants were a key example, carefully schooled in emotion management—increasingly incapable of figuring out what their real emotions were, even off the job. The strain of constantly pretending, living up to the new standards of emotional restraint, affected the whole of life—another case of modern work spilling beyond its official boundaries.[13]

Beyond special work systems and emotional requirements, some American white-collar workers, by the second quarter of the twentieth century, were also experiencing a special kind of alienation that, while again not unique, called attention to particular aspects of the national work culture. The findings, developed in a number of sociological studies between the 1930s and the 1950s, ran as follows. White-collar workers were not subject to classic work alienation in the style of some workers in factories, where work seemed to have no meaning and undermined the human dignity of those involved. Rather, some white-collar workers, reaching middle age, began to realize the absolute disparity between their American-dream-like expectations and the reality of their prospects. They had seen a job as a clerk or a salesman as a first step toward upward mobility into the solid ranks of the middle class, into managerial or entrepreneurial jobs. These hopes kept them going amid tasks that were often repetitious or, when dealing with surly customers, positively unpleasant. But while American culture emphasized mobility and the link between diligent work and later success, most white-collar jobs ensnared their occupants for a lifetime; the hoped-for mobility did not arrive. Workers might compensate, of course, by emphasizing consumer pleasures, or hoping for the greater success of their children (white-collar workers were quite likely, in the United States and elsewhere, to invest considerably in education for their offspring), or, in the case of women, pulling out of the labor force in favor of marriage. For some workers, however, the bleak realization of being trapped in a low-level job could not be avoided. This was a new form of alienation, based on hopes inspired by the work ethic, to which American workers were particularly vulnerable.

Playwright Arthur Miller in 1947 captured this alienation in his classic portrayal of salesman Willy Loman, caught in later middle age in the realization that, in a lifetime of hard work, he had accomplished almost nothing. His greatest work achievement, he poignantly states, was building a back porch for the family home; at least, here was an achievement he could point to as a result of his labor and his creativity.[14]

## The Work Ethic Revisited

A final category of American work values and behaviors began to emerge in the later nineteenth century, ironically associated with the undeniable growth of leisure and consumer patterns. In both Western Europe and the United States, a variety of new recreational activities expanded from the middle of the nineteenth century onward. As hours of work gradually dropped, and as workers increasingly adopted a partially instrumentalist posture toward their jobs, new kinds of leisure indulgence made sense (though many workers still could afford very little commercial leisure, particularly once they married and had children). Equally striking was growing middle-class interest in leisure activities. In the United States, historians have traced how changes in middle-class work life could lead to growing dependence on leisure satisfactions. More and more businessmen, for example, found themselves confined in management hierarchies rather than seeing any real opportunity to become entrepreneurs in their own right. The idea of success continued to be framed in terms of business ownership, but fewer and fewer people could really aspire to this. Similar developments occurred in many of the professions. Lawyers, for example, now often operated in large law firms rather than independent practice, again having to sacrifice values of independence for economic security in an increasingly corporate environment.

Many of the new forms of leisure, including the widely popular films and radio shows of the 1900s that sedulously avoided work settings, were simply escapist, serving as alternatives to labor and probably reflecting the need for contrasting outlets and experiences. Music hall performances, for instance (called vaudeville in the United States) offered humor and some suggestions of sexuality—nothing that could be construed as anything but a pleasant antidote for work life. Professional sports had an escapist element as well, as did the movies, which increased in popularity after 1900. As industrial societies matured, in other words, work no longer defined the whole of existence. Americans participated strongly in this change, often leading the way in developing new leisure forms such as mass-market films. The result was an important shift away from the work constraints of early industrial society.

Three complexities must be noted, however. Some of them applied to maturing industrial societies generally, but most of them took on a particular flavor in the United States, reflecting the ongoing power of the middle-class work ethic.

First, a surprising number of the new leisure forms and consumer outlets continued to be marketed to Americans—and particularly the middle class—in terms, not of escapist pleasure, but of their contribution to work capacity. Vacations, for example, were not presented as opportunities for adventure and contrast so much as necessary opportunities to recharge the batteries—particularly essential for harried managers or professional people—in order to return to the job with greater vigor than ever before. Sports, particularly participant sports, provided chances to learn discipline and competitiveness, and by 1900 possibly teamwork as well—vital qualities for successful performance on the job. Football particularly was widely promoted as a preparation for job discipline and teamwork. And sheer physical conditioning, by improving health and energy, would contribute to work as well. In the early twentieth century, a growing fascination with hobbies, like stamp collecting or making model cars, also reflected a belief that recreational activities should be self-improving, providing greater knowledge of technologies or world geography while not literally replicating the daily job. By the same token, leisure activities that were too purely hedonistic, that had no work-related value, continued to be widely criticized, even as they also continued to gain ground. Thus gambling or excessive drinking or frenzied dancing were widely criticized. It was not a contradiction, in this context, that an expanding leisure life coincided, in the United States, with the effort in Prohibition to eliminate drinking altogether—though of course the effort failed.

Point one, then: access to new leisure opportunities, an important development, was conditioned by some effort to promote them and evaluate them in work terms. This is not surprising; the hold of the previous work ethic surely made it logical to seek a transition in which leisure might be defined in more traditional language. Nor was the transition American alone. But many Americans had a particular stake in continuing to see themselves preparing for work, even when not actually working, rather than trying to escape.

Point two shades off from this transitional rhetoric: while some of the new leisure forms were indeed escapist—whether or not also intended to help people restore spirits and energies to return to their jobs—some modern leisure embodied direct work qualities and were valued in part on that basis. Many hobbies allowed people to indulge craft interests, pulling away from corporate management or professional settings but often working very hard to satisfy creative goals. Participant sports were often very serious business, requiring the same kind of discipline and effort that were supposed to go into work itself. Even for spectators, certain sports might drive home modern work values while providing release. Growing fascination with statistical records (like batting averages in baseball) and sheer speed mirrored qualities on the job, helping people internalize goals of greater productivity and careful measurement. Most modern sports also followed the clock, another direct link with the world of work. American historians once spent a considerable amount of time debating whether modern leisure converged with work or contrasted with it. The obvious answer is, both. But the extent to which much leisure reinforced work qualities and values reflects the continuing power of a vigorous work ethic. Indeed, the term later given to healthy exercise—"working out"—made the link quite directly.

Finally, and this was the most striking American point, the rise of new leisure interests was accompanied, by the 1920s, by a surprisingly dynamic and direct reassertion of the work ethic itself. To be sure, many observers in the 1920s and beyond discussed—and often lamented—the decline of this ethic. They pointed to the undeniable surge in leisure interests; to working-class instrumentalism, where jobs seemed to come second to other priorities; and to middle-class disillusionment in an increasingly corporate economy and with jobs that, even for their group, were increasingly specialized and potentially monotonous. In 1927 a New York writer, Langdon Mitchell, blasted the United States for too much indulgence and a resultant boredom; while his remedy was greater devotion to high culture, a renewed devotion to work might also provide a path. Many of the changes the critics cited were real, and undoubtedly for some people did challenge older work values. A leading historian has more recently argued that by the 1920s the work ethic was "gutted," despite some rhetorical gestures, because of changes in the workplace brought about by maturing industrialization and the new nervousness of advice givers.[15] Certainly, the workday changed shape for many, with the clear delimitation now of a period designated for nonwork activities (though it was often substantially consumed in fact by commuting and family chores). And there were health experts who were actively urging Americans—or, more particularly, middle-class males—to take things easier, in favor of their health. The idea that work and stress could damage health certainly gained ground as Americans turned from concerns about older types of contagious diseases to new worries about heart ailments and blood pressure, about unseen deteriorations that might be triggered by overloads on the job.

But what was striking, amid some shifts in cultural context, was the renewed and public commitment to work in the United States, as if the work ethic was so central to national identity—at least in principle—that it had to survive countervailing forces. Thus a famous study of an Indiana town in the 1920s (called Middletown by Robert and Helen Lynd; in fact it was Muncie) featured a chapter, "Why Do They Work So Hard?"[16] The observers claimed that workers obtained little satisfaction from their jobs but put in longer and longer hours. They saw consumerism as the only answer to the conundrum: Americans must be working harder, not because of real devotion to their jobs, but because they were so committed to buying more and more goods. But their actual evidence featured blue-collar workers talking explicitly about how interesting their jobs were, how they helped to relieve the monotony of life more generally. And for the middle class itself, and particularly the growing professional sectors such as law, medicine, and engineering, there is considerable reason to believe that work was still seen as a fundamental source of pleasure and identity.

A host of interwar novels explicitly celebrated the virtues of hard work. Ellen Glasgow's *Barren Ground*, (1925) featured a heroine who rallies from a nervous breakdown by devoting thirty years to what had been a run-down family farm, making it the most successful operation in the region by dint of working around the clock. Work, in this story, cures. Sinclair Lewis's *Arrowsmith* helped launch the work-based canonization of the American physician, whose devotion to his job and ability to cast aside the enticements of luxury give him real meaning. To be sure, the doctor found that he did periodically suffer from overwork, but the remedy was a very brief vacation and then a return to the daily routine—a routine that provided him "the happiness of high taut insanity."[17] Work, here, is the doctor's only real love.

Advice literature increasingly followed suit. A doctor wrote in 1920, in *American Magazine,* that the idea that work is an affliction is "the greatest delusion in the world.... [T]he fact is that the happiest people in the country are those that get up and go to work." The message went on: "Work is the only means toward the one thing every healthy human being wants more than anything else in the world. And that is Accomplishment.... This has been the happiest period of my life ... because I love my work better than anything else on earth.... Even Heaven is ... a world of souls happy and blest because they are at work."[18]

Other articles continued the theme that work was the greatest cure for mental distress. Ernest Hemingway added his own biographical note: "To work was the only thing, it was the one thing that always made you feel good."[19] Hugh Wiley wrote in the popular *Saturday Evening Post*: "Most of the trouble (in the United States) will end when the people ... realize that the cure is useful work.... Work will buy life and happiness.... There is no honest alternative. Sweat or die!" To be sure, the message here was more social than personal, directed against labor unrest, but the valuation of work was strong on both levels. Another *Saturday Evening Post* article frankly proclaimed the joys of work addiction: friends may tell you to relax, but they can be ignored in favor of becoming a "habitual worker.... A week without work, and I was a wreck."[20]

The question was, in this discussion, not about work itself: the participants agreed it was a prime good. Rather, it was whether the work ethic was appropriate for everyone, or only for those, as in the professional classes, who had truly intriguing jobs. Some believed, of course, that factory jobs were simply too limiting to nurture a work ethic. But some industrial psychologists were, by the 1920s, involved in an attempt to make even this work agreeable by manipulating conditions so that all blue-collar workers would see value in their jobs. Other 1920s discussions featured efforts to show housewives how to make their work interesting as well. Outlets like the *Ladies Home Journal* contended that by using modern appliances and applying new standards to the home and family, housewives in fact could commit to challenging and varied tasks. The work ethic, in other words, was not necessarily divided by class and gender, though there were some new issues. Another *Saturday Evening Post* editorial urged that employers help restore pride to their labor force, so that for this group, too, work would not just be a source of revenue but rather an end in itself.[21]

The point is clear. Work values were indeed somewhat less clear-cut by the early twentieth century than they had seemed to advocates in the nineteenth century. But, particularly in the American context, this challenge merely galvanized extensive reassertions of the intrinsic importance and value of work. Obviously, not everyone was aware of these new messages, for they were directed primarily to a middle-class audience. Without question, however, a culture persisted in which workers in various sectors could feel authorized to proclaim a deep commitment to their jobs. Without question as well, a culture persisted in which some workers would feel encouraged to proclaim and act on a real addiction to work. Here, in fact, the signals were more explicit than ever before, precisely because the relationship between work and mental health had been challenged. Some people were aware that there was a potential for American craziness about work but were willing to argue that they should plunge ahead anyway. Even foreign observers began to note that some Americans took such pleasure in work that it became, for them, a kind of play. This was an argument popularizers could pick up as well. A 1922 *Saturday Evening Post* offering made it explicit: "When you get yourself properly trained, and conditioned for success in your work, your work itself will become your favorite play." Unquestionably, individuals in other industrial societies drew the same conclusions, but only in the United States did this approach become part of a larger culture.

## Conclusion

Basic features of modern work in the United States emerged in several different ways and in several different settings during the nineteenth and early twentieth centuries. Distinctiveness was often subtle, involving American emphases and degrees of application that extended some of the common features of the industrial process as it was experienced in places like Europe and Japan.

Both actual experience and work values were involved. The most striking single American innovation, the new engineering systems established on the factory floor, was something many workers came to live with on a daily basis. But work culture, along with the insistent emphasis on a vibrant work ethic, was a reality as well. It affected the ways Americans evaluated themselves and others, and it helped support some of the experiential changes. After all, if the value assigned to work was combined with considerable scorn for immigrant labor, exceptional factory discipline might seem to follow as a matter of course: it merely enforced "proper" work behaviors on recalcitrant subjects. Efforts to use work values to help justify and constrain leisure, and the pressure on white-collar workers to add emotional control to their approaches to labor, involved daily experiences and the larger work culture alike.

There was a certain amount of irony or tension in the American work example. A society that touted its democratic values in politics presented a highly authoritarian work organization, with little attention to workers' voice or, some would argue, workers' dignity. The effort to make workers as machinelike as possible must be combined with democratic political values in assessing the nation's global legacy.

The results differentiated the United States from other societies at least to some degree, and the effects would continue well beyond the middle of the twentieth century. But some of the results moved beyond the United States to affect other parts of the world. Most obviously, Taylorization and the assembly line began to intensify factory labor in Europe, Japan, and, most strikingly, the Soviet Union. More broadly, the United States soon came to be regarded as the gold standard when it came to personnel research and human resources activities. Other societies did not necessarily import all the American beliefs about emotional control on the job or sorting out workers through tests, but imitation was widespread. The United States contributed to the evolution of modern work in many other places.

Within the United States, the partially distinctive approach to work raised two other issues. First, the work ethic itself complicated responses to problems at work. Of course American management tried to police worker reactions, just as all early industrial societies did. Attempts to beat back unions and strikes were fierce. But insistence on the work ethic could make it difficult for workers themselves to define exactly and justify discontent with working conditions. If work was such a great value, too much complaining might reflect some individual deficiency or incapacity, not a judgment on work itself. We have seen that in the work ethic discussions of the 1920s, experts divided over whether factory labor should be expected to find intrinsic value in work, at least without major adjustments in working conditions (or at least a fair amount of psychological manipulation). Many American employers were, obviously, content to drive their workers without much concern about satisfaction. But the prominence of work ethic values might make it difficult to sympathize with categories of workers who sought to explain why their work was not rewarding. It could certainly complicate efforts by members of the labor force to explain why work did not sustain their dignity or even to capture these thoughts in private, for themselves. American culture made it hard to complain about work, even as American industrial conditions almost certainly made certain kinds of jobs less fulfilling.

This constraint did not impede the formation of an active labor movement from the late nineteenth century into the 1950s. But it was revealing that the United States did not develop a widespread socialist impulse. Several factors retarded American socialism: a successful campaign to persuade people that socialism was a dangerous foreign import, including the Red Scare of 1919; the belief that ordinary people could rise by their own efforts, so that a restructuring of society was not necessary; the diversity of the immigrant population, which could impede coordinated political action. But, as we have seen, beliefs in work could be actively involved. If work was a great value, then perhaps it should be pursued regardless of political and economic system. Here, too, there was no need for a socialist alternative. And, on the white-collar side, we have seen that beliefs about work could easily lead to a sense of personal failure and disenchantment, not to some collective reaction that would admit and generalize the frustration. Failure to make work lead to success in the American cultural context constantly threatened to reflect on the individual, not the system.

But this could relate to a second point: if it were even harder to protest American work than modern work more generally, particularly given the harshness of many actual work experiences under the goad of the industrial engineers or the personnel managers with their new efforts to regulate emotional response, the question arises: what kinds of compensations might develop?

For some, of course, particularly among the successful, work could seem to be its own reward, just as the work ethic argued. Though impossible to prove statistically before the later twentieth century, it seems likely that work addictions were particularly likely in the modern American setting. But what about those who, though unable to offer an explicit alternative value system, found work unsatisfying, a burden to be endured? Here, it can be suggested, by the early twentieth century a particularly strong instrumentalist impulse was likely to emerge. If work was somewhat unpleasant, if workers increasingly were treated like machines or emotional automatons, then surely the only recourse was to seek consumer rewards in response. The United States did not invent modern consumerism, but by the early twentieth century American prosperity and the special vigor of American advertising moved consumerism to new levels. Opportunities to buy big-ticket items—even, thanks to Ford, an automobile, for many people—and opportunities to indulge in escapist fare at Hollywood-dominated movies made perfect sense in instrumental terms. Immigrant workers, among others, could see their decision to come to the United States, often despite demanding work situations, justified if they could claim a consumer standard of living superior to what they had left behind.

Again, the American choice of instrumentalism, where the work ethic itself did not fully satisfy, belonged to a larger modern current throughout the industrial world. It simply went a bit farther, in part because American work pressures went a bit farther as well. But in this response lies another potential dilemma: if consumer satisfaction justified so much of life, then how hard might one have to work to afford appropriate satisfaction? The dilemma was only suggested by 1950: it would emerge more strongly later in the American experience, along with the ongoing effects of national values and work systems themselves.

Basic reactions to work, finally, did not exhaust the impact of industrialization, either in the United States or more generally around the world. We turn in the following chapter to another vital set of topics. the differential experience of key groups in connection with modern work, where, again, the United States both joined and differed from the broader global patterns.

# Notes

1. Gary Nash, "Also There at the Creation: Going Beyond Gordon S. Wood," *William and Mary Quarterly* 44 (1987): 606–10; Tony Freyer, *Producers versus Capitalists: Constitutional Conflict in Antebellum America* (Charlottesville: University Press of Virginia, 1994); Stephanie McCurry, *Masters of Small Worlds* (New York: Oxford University Press, 1995).

2. Stephan Thernstrom, *Poverty and Progress: Social Mobility in a Nineteenth Century City* (Cambridge, MA: Harvard University Press, 1981), 57, 63.

3. Thernstrom, *Poverty and Progress*, 67.

4. Horace Greeley, "Hints toward Reforms," in *Lectures, Addresses, and Other Writings* (New York: Harper & Brothers, 1850), 16.

5. Horatio Alger, *Ragged Dick*, ed. Richard Fink (New York: Collier Books, 1962).

6. John H. M. Laslett, *Failure of a Dream: Essays in the History of American Socialism* (Berkeley: University of California Press, 1994).

7. Cited in Thomas Dublin, ed., *Farm to Factory: Women's Letters, 1830–1860* (New York: Columbia University Press, 1981), 101–4.

8. Peter F. Drucker, *The Practice of Management* (New York: Collins, 1954), 280.

9. Edward Kilduff, *The Private Secretary* (New York, 1951), 50, 57.

10. Harry W. Hepner, *Human Relations in Changing Industry* (New York: Prentice-Hall, 1938), 96; Annette Garrett, *Counseling Methods for Personnel Workers* (New York: Family Welfare Association of America, 1945), 71; Dale Carnegie, *How to Win Friends and Influence People* (New York, 1940), 2, 27, 68, 70, 156; R. C. Borden and Alvin Busse, *How to Win a Sales Argument* (New York, 1926), 7; Joseph Tiffin and E. J. McCormick, *Industrial Psychology* (Englewood Cliffs, NJ: Prentice-Hall, 1965), 188 ff.; Rexford Hershey, *Better Foremanship* (Philadelphia, 1961), 10; Glenn Gardiner, *Better Foremanship* (New York, 1941), 53–54; Charles C. Smith, *The Foreman's Place in Management* (New York, 1946), 119; W. E. Baer, "Do's and Don't's in Handling Grievances," *Personnel* 43 (1966): 40. R. A. Sutermeister, "Training Foremen in Human Relations," *Personnel* 20 (1943): 13; Burt Scanlan, "Sensitivity Training: Clarification, Issues, Insights," *Personnel Journal* 50 (1970): 549.

11. Susan Porter Benson, *Counter Cultures: Saleswomen, Managers, and Customers in American Department Stores, 1890–1940* (Urbana: University of Illinois Press, 1987).

12. C. Wright Mills, *White Collar: The American Middle Classes* (New York: Oxford University Press, 1951), 184; Arlie Hochschild, *The Managed Heart: Commercialization of Human Feeling* (Berkeley: University of California Press, 1983); Doncaster Humm and G. W. Wadsworth, "Temperament in Industry," *Personnel Journal* 21 (1942): 314–22; Leon Baritz, *The Servants of Power: A History of the Use of Social Science in American Industry* (Middletown, CT: Wesleyan University Press, 1960); Stanley Herman, *The People Specialists*

(New York: Knopf, 1968), 13. Arlie Hochschild, *The Second Shift* (New York: Penguin, 1989).

13. Hochschild, *The Managed Heart.*

14. Arthur Miller, *Death of a Salesman,* 1947.

15. Daniel Rodgers, *Work Ethic in Industrial America* (Chicago: University of Chicago Press, 1979); see also Martha Banta, *Taylored Lives: Narrative Productions in the Age of Taylor, Veblen, and Ford* (Chicago: University of Chicago Press, 1995).

16. Robert and Helen Lynd, *Middletown* (Fort Washington, PA: Harvest Books, 1959).

17. Sinclair Lewis, *Arrowsmith* (Whitefish, MT: Kessinger, 1925), 416.

18. Frank Crane, "The Greatest Delusion in the World," *American Magazine,* August 1920, 59.

19. Ernest Hemingway, "American Bohemians in Paris," *Toronto Star Weekly,* 25 March 1922. Reprinted in *Byline: Ernest Hemingway,* ed. William White (New York: Scribner's, 1967), 21–23.

20. Hugh Wiley, "Sweat or Die!" *Saturday Evening Post,* 10 April 1920, 31; Samuel G. Blythe. "Tapering Off on Work." *Saturday Evening Post,* 8 August 1925, 198.

21. Tom Lutz, "'Sweat or Die': The Hedonization of the Work Ethic in the 1920s," *American Literary History* 8 (1996): 259–83.

# For Further Reading

Steven Gelber, "A Job You Can't Lose: Work and Hobbies in the Great Depression," *Journal of Social History* 24 (1991): 741–66, and "Working at Playing: The Culture of the Work Place and the Rise of Baseball," *Journal of Social History* 16 (1983): 3–20; Melvin Adelman, "Baseball, Business and the Work Place," *Journal of Social History* 23 (1989): 285–301; Benjamin Rader, *American Sports: From the Age of Folk Games to the Age of Spectators* (Englewood Cliffs, NJ: Prentice-Hall, 1983); Allen Guttman, *Sports Spectators* (New York: Columbia University Press, 1986). Tom Lutz provides vital guidelines in this whole area in his article "'Sweat or Die': The Hedonization of the Work Ethic in the 1920s," *American Literary History* 8 (1996): 259–83. Daniel Nelson, *Managers and Workers: Origins of the New Factory System in the United States, 1880–1920* (Madison: University of Wisconsin Press, 1975). Steven Meyer, *The Five Dollar Day: Labor Management and Social Control in the Ford Motor Company, 1908–1921* (Albany: State University of New York Press, 1981). Harry Braverman, *Labor and Monopoly Capital: The Degradation of Work in the Twentieth Century* (New York: Monthly Review, 1974). Harvey Green. *Fit for America: Health, Fitness, Sport and American Society* (New York: Pantheon, 1986). T. J. Jackson Lears, *No Place of Grace: Antimodernism and the Transformation of American Culture, 1880–1920* (New York: Pantheon, 1981). Elton Mayo, *The Human Problems of an Industrial Civilization* (Cambridge, MA: Harvard Business School, 1946). C. Wright Mills, *White Collar: The American Middle Classes* (New York: Oxford University Press, 1951). Daniel T. Rodgers, *The Work Ethic in Industrial America, 1850–1920* (Chicago: University of Chicago Press, 1978). Roy Rosenzweig, *Eight Hours for What We Will: Workers and Leisure in an Industrial City, 1870–1920* (New York: Cambridge University Press, 1983). Stephan Thernstrom, *Poverty and Progress: Social Mobility in a Nineteenth-Century City* (Cambridge, MA: Harvard University Press, 1981). Scott

Sandage, *Born Losers: A History of Failure in America* (Cambridge, MA: Harvard University Press, 2006). W. J. Rohrabaugh, *The Alcoholic Republic: An American Tradition* (New York: Oxford University Press, 1979). Mark Edward Lender and James Kirby Martin, *Drinking in America: A History* (New York: Free Press, 1987). Susan Porter Benson, *Counter Cultures: Saleswomen, Managers, and Customers in American Department Stores, 1890–1940* (Urbana: University of Illinois Press, 1987). Ruth Schwartz Cowan, *More Work for Mother: The Ironies of Household Technology from the Open Hearth to the Microwave* (New York: Basic Books, 1985). Leon Baritz, *The Servants of Power: A History of the Use of Social Science in American Industry* (New York: John Wiley, 1965). Jackson Lears, *Fables of Abundance: A Cultural History of Advertising in America* (New York: Basic Books, 1995). Peter N. Stearns, *American Cool* (New York: New York University Press, 1994). Alice Kessler-Harris, *Gendering Labor History* (Urbana: University of Illinois Press, 2006).

# CHAPTER 6

# Rearranging Modern Work: The Young, the Old, and the Female

Wherever it occurred—in Europe, Japan, or the United States—the Industrial Revolution not only changed work patterns but also introduced new segmentations into the labor force. Some of these, like new divisions between male and female workers, built on differentiations that had been present to some degree in premodern work as well. Others, like the dramatic transformation of children's roles, were simply revolutionary.

This chapter explores the three key distinctions that began to be visible in the nineteenth century and, at least in two of the cases, that loomed even larger after 1900. New roles for women, and then new debates about what these roles should be, head the list, though in many ways they proved transitional rather than fundamental. More quietly, novel approaches to the relationship between older people and work ultimately formed a key component of the industrialization process, raising questions about the elderly, and about work, that are still being addressed today. Finally, the recasting of the use of children in work generated some intriguing conundrums that again still inform modern life. Overall, the new differentiations added to the basic impact of modern work on the broader patterns of life throughout much of the world.

The chapter deals both with general patterns and with particular American variants. On the whole, with respect to gender issues, the United States followed dynamics very similar to patterns in Western Europe, though there were some differences in rhetoric and politics. The relationship between old age and work also did not systematically differentiate the United States, though the strong emphasis on the work ethic had some complicating results on the American side. On the whole, however, it was the tension between childhood and work that ultimately produced the most strikingly American results within a context common to the industrial experience more generally.

The central theme in all industrial societies involved the growing productivity of industrial technology that forced choices about what groups should have first access to jobs. The problem was not evident in the first decades of industrialization, when machines were often still rather primitive and older work involvements—for example, of children—still seemed to apply. Soon, however, it became clear that not everyone needed to work for an industrial society to have ample, indeed sometimes excessive, output. This is where social values came into play in relation to new beliefs and new realities of work. Rightly or wrongly, briefly or over a longer haul, certain groups were judged less appropriate for modern work than others were. In the industrial societies, these judgments developed over a century or more, particularly from the 1850s to the mid-twentieth century, though there were some hints a bit earlier. Some judgments would have to be reconsidered later on.

The basic theme produced an obvious complication: as we have seen, industrial societies, in many ways headed by the United States, also generated an unprecedented degree of praise for the value of hard work and the social standing it should generate. Communist systems, with their support for proletarian valor, adopted much the same cultural system with different language. But if some groups could not be allowed to participate fully in work, what would the results be in terms of social value and a sense of personal worth? Not surprisingly, these were tough questions, which have not been fully answered even today.

In addition to the results of growing productivity, which forced some choices if certain categories of workers were to have reasonably good employment prospects, and some practical issues once work moved outside the home, the new distinctions in the labor force did entail a kind of beneath-the-surface consistency. While the middle-class work ethic unquestionably made isolation from work more problematic than ever before—a real issue for all the groups newly shunted aside—the modern belief (and fact) that work should be rigorous and demanding generated new notions concerning groups that might be harmed by work. When these notions combined with equally new or enhanced ideas about the frailty of women, the elderly, or children, the reduction of work opportunities might seem preordained. In fact, many of the assumptions involved were highly contestable, and this guaranteed some further changes in the future, up to and probably well beyond the present day.

# Women

Gender divisions have affected work since the onset of human society, and differentiation has always involved a combination of practical factors—like differences in certain kinds of physical strength or the obligations of child bearing—and beliefs and values that could artificially magnify separate work roles. In the long run, the greatest impact of industrialization and related changes, like falling birthrates, on work and gender will probably be to minimize divisions more than ever before in human history. But this was not the way the story began, and even today a considerable legacy from the early industrial period persists.

It was virtually inevitable that early industrialization would assign different kinds of work to men and to women, since the pattern had been so well established in premodern societies. For example, in the early spinning factories female labor predominated; men served only to activate the heaviest equipment and to provide skilled labor in machine installation and maintenance. After all, women had always done the spinning at home and in the domestic manufacturing system. They were the ones displaced by mechanization when the cost of factory-made thread plunged well below what manual labor could manage. They needed the alternative work; partly because of the displacement, women worked for lower wages than men. Weaving, on the other hand, presented a more complicated situation. In different places both men and women had woven before; the factory equipment involved was somewhat more complex than for spinning. As a result, both men and women worked in mechanized weaving, though with some specialization of function. Heavy industry—mining and metallurgy—had always been man's work. Even with new machines this type of work continued to require considerable strength and often posed special dangers; small wonder that it remained a proudly male province, even as the number of workers in heavy industry expanded unprecedentedly.

But industrial divisions between men and women did not just translate traditions into new settings. Several novel elements were involved, and they generated a rather complicated combination.

The fact that work was now located well away from the household raised some very practical issues for workers' families. Someone had to take care of children, do the shopping in the urban context, and provide some minimal level of household maintenance. Several arrangements proved possible. Women sometimes took young children to work with them in the factories, and employers might oblige in order to have the advantage of the women's labor and perhaps to orient toddlers to factory work. But this was an awkward arrangement and rarely persisted. A few institutions were established in the cities to take care of young children—a movement to provide nursery services developed in France, for example—but these might cost more than workers could afford and were rarely very extensive. More commonly, other relatives, including grandparents, might watch the children, allowing women to work. Overall, however, many families found that the only realistic option was for women to stop outside employment when the babies began to arrive. Only a minority of married women worked in the cities in the sense of holding defined jobs. In textile centers some women simply liked to work and paid for other child-care arrangements. More commonly, widowhood or an incapacitated husband explained a woman's continuing to work. Within a few decades, in working-class culture it was regarded as shameful for a married woman with an able-bodied husband to have to work outside the home.

Feeding into this was a growing sense among men that work should be their province, free from too much competition from women. Both material and status concerns were involved. Male workers increasingly realized that too much female labor drove down wages, because of overabundance of workers in general and the fact that women's pay was lower than men's by at least 50 percent for the same kind of work. Men also sensed that their own status was changing as skill requirements dropped and more and more work came under the supervision of others. The ability to claim that factory work was a man's job, and the related pride in pointing to men's breadwinning status, could serve as vital compensations. Small wonder that most labor movements quickly turned to defending the idea of a family wage—a level of pay high enough for a man to support the entire family, without depending on a wife's earnings—and pushed for the exclusion of women from many branches of work.

Compounding all this, finally, was a growing middle-class belief that respectable women should focus on domestic tasks and not sully themselves with the world of work. A common practice among early factory owners was extremely revealing: in the first generation, in many small factories the wife of the owner worked in the office, helping out as in the artisanal tradition. But with success, sometimes within a few years, the wives were pulled out and were typically replaced by male clerks. A key use of middle-class prosperity, in other words, was to separate male and female spheres much more fully than had been the case in older bourgeois traditions. The practice revealed again a curious ambiguity in the class's work ethic. On the one hand, work was a marvelous expression, the stuff of life; on the other, actual work in modern conditions could be seen as degrading, something that certain kinds of people—like women, like children—should be spared. On a more positive note, the middle class began building a special image for women, arguing for their greater moral purity and their natural capacity for domestic arrangements and child care. The ideal life should see men working furiously, proud of their achievements but aware that the new world of commerce involved a pursuit of profit and a level of stress that needed sanctification through the alternative sphere of home and family. Here, in what has aptly been termed a "haven in a heartless world," the special virtues of good women would predominate, and this meant that it was of paramount importance to keep these virtuous creatures away from the taint of formal commercial employment. By the middle decades of the nineteenth century, virtually the only middle-class women formally in the labor force in industrializing societies were widows or spinsters working in the few occupations that provided a veneer of respectability, such as serving as governess to a wealthy family or, occasionally, running a small shop.

Middle-class and working-class ideals did not exactly coincide, but they overlapped enough for most people to accept a reduction in the work roles for women generally, even at some cost in terms of wage levels. Legal measures to restrict women's work—which was never banned but often regulated in terms of maximum hours so that it became a less attractive alternative to men's employment—embodied this agreement.

All of this took shape in an environment in which the number of manufacturing jobs overall tended to fall in relation to the available population, most obviously in the textile industry. While work expanded rapidly in the growing cities, this expansion masked the displacement of hundreds of thousands of workers in the domestic manufacturing system, many of them women. On the whole, given tradition, the nature of industrial work itself, particularly in heavy industry, and the new familial and cultural factors of the industrial environment, women rather than men took the brunt of the job shrinkage.

This does not mean, of course, that women did not work. Running a middle-class household was a complicated task, even with the aid of a servant. Women were urged to work hard and efficiently, to keep modern types of household accounts, to live up to rising standards of hygiene and child care. The middle-class housewife had a work ethic of her own that overlapped to some extent with the ethic being urged more widely. Working-class women followed a slightly different pattern. They would normally hold jobs for several years before marriage, more often in domestic service than in the newer centers of employment. After marriage they would not only maintain a household but frequently would earn money doing laundry, taking in boarders, or manufacturing items, like artificial flowers, that could still be made at home. Most of the work of adult women in the cities would not count as formal employment: by 1900 women formed only 10 percent of the labor force in Britain in the terms the census takers used, only 30 percent in more traditional France. There was no question that, in terms of social perception and types of work alike, the gender divide had widened considerably, partially mirroring the new divide between work and home.

The early industrial picture had its gender complexities, quite apart from the interesting number of married women, particularly in the working class, who stayed in jobs partly by choice, sometimes noting that they preferred the excitement of the factory to the tedium of housewifery. Women with special needs, because of a disabled or drunken husband or simply durable single status, had to differ from their sisters, though they suffered in terms of social perceptions. Larger categories of women stayed in the labor force. Most adult African American women in the later nineteenth century sought jobs, often in domestic service, because of the tightness of the family economy amid low wages and frequent unemployment for men.

Regional variations entered in. We have seen that the French, with slower population growth than the British and more artisanal and rural production, did not move women out of the labor force to the same degree. By 1900, about one third of the formal labor force in France was female, over twice the census levels in Britain and the United States. More generally still, Russian industrialization, in a poor society with a strong continuing involvement in agriculture and a need to find cheap labor to help compensate for lower skill levels, depended heavily on women's work, both before and after communism. Women worked in many Russian factories and held a variety of jobs, both in services and in manual labor, in the cities—a fact that communist leaders would tout in arguing that their system provided greater gender equity than Western capitalism. Early Japanese industrialization depended on a massive amount of female labor, particularly in the silk sweatshops. Only gradually, as the Japanese developed more heavy-industrial sectors, did the percentage of male workers in manufacturing reach and then surpass the halfway mark. Over time, by the later twentieth century, the Japanese would pull many women out of formal employment, following patterns earlier suggested in the West.

The withdrawal of women from modern work, never complete in any region, had some obvious drawbacks, and it proved to be a transitional rather than a durable industrial statement. Most fundamentally, it was extremely costly to families and to societies as whole to limit such a large part of the population in terms of modern economic activity.

More concretely, the common early industrial patterns soon ran afoul of at least two other important trends. Throughout the early industrial decades, women acquired growing access to formal education—primary schooling at least for the working classes, often secondary education or, for a small but growing minority by the 1870s, college or university for the middle classes. The contrast between increasing education and a sense that women should not work was ultimately not sustainable. Even in the 1870s, throughout Western Europe, North America, and Russia, landmark cases in which individual women won entry into law or medicine provided evidence that earlier gender distinctions could not hold.

The second development, again in all industrializing societies, was the increasingly rapid drop in the birthrate, to three to four children per family in places like the United States by the early 1900s, and even fewer by the 1920s. Fewer children to care for could allow more volunteer activities or higher household standards, and a decline in available domestic servants created its own needs. Ultimately, however, women in various social groups might find new time on their hands.

By the later nineteenth century also, again throughout the industrial world, changes in the occupational structure itself began to contribute to a partial redefinition of gender and work. We have seen that the expansion of mechanization generated new opportunities for women, by lightening physical burdens at work and reducing skill levels. Though the move was resisted by male workers, women began to enter areas like printing and machine building. Newer light industries, like chemicals and appliance manufacture, also offered opportunities for women. Conversion of old crafts like shoemaking to factory production again produced a need for new sources of labor willing to work for relatively low wages.

Even more important, in the long run, was the massive need for new workers in the growing white-collar sector, where women could be ideal employees because of their education, their low pay, and their lack of commitment to older, now outdated methods of work—in the secretarial field, for example, women proved much more willing than men to adapt to the typewriter. Women were also vital in rapidly expanding professions, or near professions, like nursing, teaching school, civil service, and librarianship. The whole white-collar professional area needed numbers beyond what men could provide. White-collar jobs also involved a sense of respectability that helped cut through earlier objections to women's employment. In some cases, they even seemed to rely on qualities the culture of the times attributed to women: Who better than women to care for younger children in the schools, or provide comfort as nurses? Who but women could successfully sell to women in the burgeoning department stores, when it came time to display a fashion sense or simply a friendly warmth?

There was no immediate revolution here. Even by the 1920s, most married women did not formally hold jobs, particularly in the middle classes. Revealingly, while the number of women in professions like law and medicine did grow, though modestly, it proved difficult for many to combine this commitment with marriage; large numbers of professional women remained single. But women's involvement was inching up steadily. The routine commitment of unmarried women in the middle class as well as the working class was a huge change. All of this meant more direct exposure to the conditions of modern work, outside a domestic environment of any sort. It meant, for men—particularly in white-collar occupations—a new need to deal with female colleagues as part of the job structure.

And there were famous hints that more was to come. Both World War I and World War II, in drawing massive numbers of men away to the military fronts, opened vast needs for new workers in all urban sectors, particularly manufacturing. Women moved in rapidly, as a matter of patriotic duty and for personal excitement. In both cases the involvement proved temporary: returning veterans insisted on retaking their old slots, and women retreated to the pattern of quieter and more incremental gains. But the explosion revealed the artificiality of the gender arrangements imposed by early industry and, in the case of World War II, directly foreshadowed more fundamental change.

The United States displayed relatively few distinctive features in this early industrial history. We have seen that women enjoyed comparatively good factory conditions for a few decades, but this was a transitory advantage and soon yielded to the more general sense that factory work was not a respectable career choice. Even the early factory girls had assumed they would quit upon marriage. Through the later decades of the nineteenth century and into the twentieth, many immigrant women would work in factories, sweatshops like the New York garment industry, and domestic service, but as in Western Europe the tendency was to pull all but a minority out of the labor force after a family was formed. American enthusiasm for the work ethic was matched by a vigorous sense of the purity and fragility of good women, and the incompatibility of these virtues with durable employment outside the home.

The one national note that may be tentatively identified involves the unusual strength of American feminism as it formed from the 1840s onward, though

Britain and some other countries with Protestant cultures came close to matching American zeal. Work was not, it must be noted, the main focus of early feminism, a fact that was in itself revealing. Protecting women against male drunkenness and sexual exploitation and seeking legal equality and the all-important vote gained much greater attention. Feminists did not necessarily disagree that work and special female virtues did not easily blend, though they were as a matter of course opposed to any legal barriers to women's entry into any work field. But some sense of the advantages to women of the idea of special purity, and some real division between middle-class feminists and the working-class women who were actually in the labor force, limited the connection during the dramatic first phase of feminism as it crested after 1900.

The American feminist movement was among the strongest in the world by the late nineteenth century, and indeed was one of the earliest to emerge in part because of connections, dating back to the 1840s, with efforts directed against slavery. But despite this strength, and the undeniable vigor of work culture in the United States, it is difficult to point to a distinctive national feminist strand around work until later in the twentieth century. American feminists, like their European sisters, worked hard on equal legal rights for women and of course, by 1900, for the vote. They were adamant that women should have the right to attend universities and professional schools, supporting the growing though still small band of women doctors and lawyers. But while this effort was relevant to work in permitting respectable and even exciting career opportunities for women, it related more to legal issues than to sweeping redefinitions of gender and work in the eyes of most feminist leaders. No feminist leader opposed the idea of women working, but many were comfortable with primarily familial goals for most women, where a sense of special mission might define women's role with children and their commitment to motherhood. Feminism benefited considerably, in fact, from volunteer efforts of many middle-class women, who had not only abundant zeal but also considerable time on their hands precisely because they were not working in a formal sense. And, as in other countries, there was considerable utility for the feminist cause in seeing women as different from men, with different roles in life. Arguments for the vote could thus be based in part on a contention that women were more moral than men because they were less corrupted by workplace commercial values and motives, and that they therefore could bring new values into citizenship.

The biggest gulf between feminism around 1900 and an ardent embrace of women's work roles—and this was true in the feminist movement throughout the world at this point—involved social class. Most women who actually worked, certainly the minority who had formal jobs after marriage and child-bearing, were working class; most feminists were from a higher social level where work was still not expected, at least after marriage. Feminists tried to bridge the gap with workers, often sympathizing with unionization efforts (not only in the United States but also in Britain and elsewhere) and calling attention to unsafe or immoral job conditions.

An exemplary kind of debate broke out in Seattle between 1918 and 1920. Women workers, mainly from blue-collar families, had been increasing in number. In 1900 they had constituted 18 percent of the city's labor force; by 1920 they were up to 25 percent. Working women saw in feminism a means of appealing for the legitimacy of their jobs and the importance of being able to earn a living wage. Many men, including labor union members, opposed this competition and sought to defend men's exclusive right to pay levels that could support whole families. As the debate proceeded, working-class feminists became increasingly articulate about the need to see women's roles as going well beyond the family and housewifery. But middle-class feminists hesitated. Some opposed married women's working; others expressed doubts because of the centrality of family functions to their image of what women should be doing. Some of them even defended trade union views that women had no right to the kind of family wages that men should command. Ultimately, the combined opposition and ambivalence defeated the efforts of working-class women in Seattle, and membership in feminist labor organizations dropped off. The debate, however, had not ended, it had just been rescheduled for a later decade.[1]

Again, it is hard to find a distinctively American tone in all this, except to the extent that the strength of feminism brought out more clearly the divisions over work roles. It is important also, however, to remember the more silent trends taking shape beneath formal feminism. By 1920, in the United States as in Western Europe, the level of women's participation in work was creeping up, thanks to new needs and opportunities and also, through the expansion of white-collar work, new types of jobs. Here was another preparation for a future set of American initiatives that would in fact stand out more fully.

*   *   *

It's obvious from a contemporary vantage point that the first industrial construction of women and work, varied in any event, proved impermanent. We will later discuss the important reengagement of women and modern work as it developed from the 1950s onward. Here also, the United States, with its strong valuation of work, may have served as a bellwether, particularly in turning a new generation of feminism to a sharp focus on the importance of formal jobs over housewifery. Equally clearly, however, important legacies would remain from earlier decades in the United States and elsewhere. Women's pay continued to lag behind men's for equivalent jobs, though the gap narrowed a bit. There was still some dissent about the propriety of women's commitment to the same kind of work ethic that men were supposed to have and a host of practical problems—particularly in the United States, partly because middle-class work standards were so demanding—about how to juggle work and family life. A major new relationship was forged between women and work, in contrast with initial industrial reactions, but important issues and disagreements remained.

# Older Workers

Old age had always posed a potential problem for workers. Despite low life expectancy—which was mainly due to high rates of infant mortality; if one survived childhood, chances of living to at least early old age were not too bad—traditional societies saw a number of people survive into their sixties or even beyond, even in the lower classes. Seven percent of the French population was over sixty in the late eighteenth century. But with most work imposing strong physical demands, there was always a chance that injury or ill health would reduce a worker's capacity. While no systems of formal retirement existed—among other things, they would have seemed prohibitively expensive in agricultural economies—many workers simply had to cut back. In these cases, family support was vital; but there were always instances of old people without family assistance, forced to beg or seek public accommodations in places like hospitals (mainly, in traditional societies, institutions where the very poor went to die) or simply starve to death.

None of this created a comprehensive sense of old age as a work problem, however. Partly this was because the problems were so individually variable—some older people retained a strong work capacity. Partly it was because other groups, particularly the very young, were so much more numerous that the elderly as a category were hard to visualize. But partly also it was because most agricultural societies insisted in principle on a considerable amount of deference for the old. This was strongly featured in Confucianism and most African cultures—Western society was a bit more ambivalent about the qualities of the elderly—but it operated to some extent almost everywhere. Part of this deference, in turn, involved a belief that the elderly possessed a particular level of wisdom that was vital for family and social life. Older women or farmers might not have the physical qualities their younger relatives could contribute, but they remembered techniques and values that had their own importance in the workplace. Most obviously, older members of professions like the priesthood or the magistracy were particularly esteemed; not for nothing was the ruling group of some American Protestant churches referred to as the elders. True, even here an individual older person might retire from active life, often with the means to do so because of prior job success. But many people stayed in harness until death or returned to work in a crisis, as did the famous Roman statesman Cincinnatus, who was called back to political service after retiring to his farm. The elderly expected this kind of lifelong association with work, and society valued it. Not surprisingly, in colonial America when people lied about their age or sought to alter their appearance, it was usually to seem older than they actually were.

Industrialization gradually but vigorously altered this relationship. A number of factors contributed to major change. Family disruption was one. Many modern workers separated from their extended family, left back in the village. They might hope to return home when work got to be too much for them, but they might not be sure of their welcome; and they might not want to leave the familiar city at that point. Birthrates began to drop fairly soon after industrialization began. This meant that many people had fewer children to rely on if their work capacity diminished. A bit of bad luck, or a dispute with a couple of kids, and the customary support—never entirely reliable even in traditional societies—might not be available. To be sure, working-class families often offered protection. The number of older parents living with younger adult children actually went up in the nineteenth century in places like Britain; the elderly could help provide child care in an urban environment, and adult children, particularly daughters, did continue to feel a sense of responsibility when their parents' work capacity dropped. But there was a growing problem for many older people, which logically increased their reliance on being able to hold a job.

From the standpoint of the larger society, the same recourse might seem essential. For, with lower birthrates and gradually improving health levels, the percentage of elderly in the population gradually rose. In 1914, 15 percent of the French population was over sixty, more than double the percentage of a century and a half earlier. Here, too, societies might have had a clear interest in trying to make sure that as many members as possible of the growing group continued to contribute their work.

Individual and social logic, however, was countered by three other forces, which increasingly made the old age–work relationship problematic. In the first place, some modern jobs were difficult for older people to perform well. Many early machines required considerable physical strength to operate, at a time when many older people—even at sixty—suffered from failing health. The new category of service work often demanded literacy and numeracy, and old people, into the twentieth century, were less likely to have these skills than their younger, educated relatives. Not surprisingly, from the early industrial decades onward until well into the twentieth century, older workers generally saw their earnings drop after age forty and their periods of joblessness increase. They were simply less sought-after.

Second, many younger workers and their representatives actively feared the competition of older workers and eagerly pushed them aside for their own security. This is where the productive capacity of the new economy became increasingly evident. Often, there were simply not enough jobs to go around. In this situation, many labor unions began to urge that some alternative be provided for older workers so that opportunities could be available for others. The Great Depression of the 1930s solidified this thinking in many industrial societies.

But third, and ultimately most important, the cultures of many industrial societies turned against the elderly, at least concerning qualities relevant for modern work. Modern work connoted speed, even where special strength was not required, but it was hard to associate the elderly with speed. The pace of work, so central to the modern experience, and assumptions about old age simply did not harmonize. Modern work celebrated new learning, the ability to adopt new devices and master new techniques. Again, assumptions about the elderly hardly featured these qualities. It was easy to conclude that old age and modern work did not mix. By the late nineteenth century many employers adopted this view, preferring younger job applicants almost across the board. And many labor leaders agreed: they might hope for good treatment for elderly workers, but off the job, not on; work was for the younger and swifter.

Indeed, partly because of the apparent implications of modern work and its incompatibility with later age, old age came to be seen as an almost pathological condition, at least in the Western world, by the later nineteenth century. Physicians learned more and more about how old bodies and old minds almost inevitably deteriorated. Popular imagery increasingly picked up the theme of decline and incapacity. As a French labor leader put it, "An immutable principle is that at 50 years a man, and especially a worker, is exhausted." And, "at that age [65] the least infirmities with which they run the risk of being afflicted are paralysis or decay."[2] American doctors and publicists contributed strongly to this general view. A Dr. French, in 1892 wrote that "the old man's bank is already overdrawn. He is living from hand to mouth." He urged that laws ban labor "beyond the term which physiological science accepts as consistent with soundness and vigor." A Dr. Loomis added: "After sixty, failure [of the old] to recognize the changing condition of their vital powers and continuance in their business habits of earlier life, after this period, are no better than suicide." Despite or perhaps because of the middle-class commitment to an ethic of hard work, Americans seemed particularly willing to accept the idea that work and age should not mix.[3]

In the process, obviously, what was once valued from the elderly in work was now increasingly either rejected or contradicted. A deteriorating condition, physically and mentally, could hardly be associated with special wisdom and experience. And in a work world that emphasized innovation, in societies where most learning now came through formal literacy rather than the stories of older relatives, it was difficult to see special wisdom residing in the elderly, even in occupations with no intense physical demands.

The result of all this, for many decades, was simply a growing personal and social problem. Old people became more numerous. Their job prospects became less certain, and in some cases family support faltered as well. Yet they had no option but to keep working if they possibly could. Small wonder that, even early in industrialization, a sense of hopelessness often developed. A group of French textile workers in 1830 expressed a common sentiment: "When we grow old, we'll go to the hospital, or we'll die, and that will be that."[4]

Historians and sociologists have vigorously debated the clash between industrialization and the work of the elderly. There is no question that images of decrepitude were vastly overdrawn and overgeneralized. In fact, the same improvements in health conditions that allowed more people to live into old age did wonders for work capacity as well. Misery was very real; for decades, industrialization did complicate work performance of people whose health was deteriorating. But this was not a uniform condition. Furthermore, particularly after the first decades of the Industrial Revolution, new technology, by reducing strength requirements, in principle made it easier for older people to hold certain kinds of jobs. As schooling became more uniform, older people were almost as likely as the young to know how to read and calculate. And while speed might suffer a bit, many older workers had experience and reliability that might more than make up for this deficiency. There was, many argue, at least by the late nineteenth century, no inherent clash between work and old age.

Whatever the relationship in principle, however, there is no question about what happened in fact. Employers bought into the common modern culture, in hiring practices that often discriminated against the elderly and in dismissals in times of economic decline that pushed them off the job first. Labor leaders, as we have seen, doubtless sincerely believed that old people should not have to work, but they had massive self-interest as well in seeking to reduce competition within the labor force and clear the field for the young. who, as members, were the future of their movements. Many workers, accepting the culture or simply anxious about an uncertain future or seeing the real problems of some of their older relatives and colleagues, came to agree as well: in a proper industrial society, the elderly should not have to work.

The obvious solution, and ultimately the one widely adopted in all industrial societies once leadership realized that there was sufficient wealth to afford it, was increasingly widespread formal retirement. Some combination of personal savings, company pensions, and social insurance had to be developed to make the modern logic that old age and work did not mix with modern reality as well. Labor movements began pushing for pension systems vigorously by the later nineteenth century, and particularly in the craft unions, insurance programs even earlier had sought to provide a bit of protection. The German statesman Otto von Bismarck's social insurance program of the 1870s, designed (abortively) to win workers away from socialism, also included some old-age insurance, though not initially enough for anyone to rely upon. The welfare states of the twentieth century, including even the otherwise hesitant United States, uniformly provided retirement funds.

Rather unexpectedly, widespread retirement spread first among white-collar workers, not the factory workers most directly affected by strenuous physical demands. Employers found it desirable to offer pensions to white-collar personnel to help guide them away from the labor movement. Revealingly, the first large American corporation to develop a pension scheme was the American Express travel agency, in the 1870s. The U.S. government also took an early lead within the nation as a whole in allowing civil servants to retire or reduce their work commitments in later age. Flush with some funding, and with values that might also encourage personal saving, white-collar workers did begin to retire in large numbers. By the 1920s, only 5 percent of the white-collar labor force over age sixty-five in France were still at work. At the same point, about 40 percent of blue-collar workers were still on the job, for lack of alternative resources. But the trend was clear, and later expansion of social insurance would accelerate the trend.

Soon after World War II, retirement became a general phenomenon throughout the industrial world, an unprecedented development in human history. The innovation reflected the equally unprecedented wealth of industrial societies, all the more impressive in that the numbers of the elderly kept growing. But it also reflected the important new cultural dissonance between beliefs about work and beliefs about old age.

Interesting variations developed around the common theme. The French tended to settle on age sixty as the point at which retirement should be offered, perhaps persuaded by their particularly vigorous rhetoric about decrepitude, and also by the labor movement's strong commitment to reducing competition. Japan would also opt for age sixty. Here, the common pressures were supplemented by Confucian deference to the qualities of the elderly, now best expressed through social support for a peaceful, work-free existence. In the United States and Britain, perhaps a bit less deferential, sixty-five was long agreed upon as a logical retirement target. But in Scandinavia, where the welfare state otherwise reached an apogee, but where life expectancy and health in old age were also particularly strong, age seventy was seen as an appropriate goal. These differences make it clear how much the phenomenon depended on cultural and political, and therefore variable, factors, not some ineluctable dynamic in old age itself. They also raise vital questions for the future, as many societies, as we will discuss in a later chapter, face new issues about the first modern solution to the problem of old age and work.

Retirement options, when backed by acceptable funding levels, alleviated, if they did not entirely eliminate, a very real problem in industrial societies. Fairly quickly—by the 1940s in the United States, after the 1936 passage of the Social Security Act—families began reducing their sense of financial responsibility for older members in favor of government funding and insurance arrangements. More important from the standpoint of work, retirement options stimulated two additional developments that added their own complexities to the experience of modern work.

During the second quarter of the twentieth century, though based in part on earlier proposals, dominant discussions shifted from seeing retirement as optional to viewing it as mandatory, at least for large categories of workers. After all, if work was too much for older people, surely it was a kindness to make sure they did not have to face it; and once adequate pensions were in place, at least in principle, there was no clear barrier to this resolution.

Labor leaders typically favored the mandatory approach. For if retirement was useful in reducing labor competition, clearing the decks of older workers entirely would be even better. There was a further benefit: with retirement mandatory, unions could press for raising pay by seniority. This rectified the problem many workers had previously faced in later middle age, as in cases where pay began to fall after age forty. But employers might be persuaded if, through mandatory retirement, it was understood that the process of raising pay with levels of experience had a clear terminus at age sixty or sixty-five. Many labor leaders also believed that mandatory provisions protected individual workers from employer pressure to work longer than they wanted to. It perfected the separation between work and old age. Presumably, many workers agreed; certainly, there was no huge pushback from the rank and file when mandatory provisions were introduced.

Employers could also favor the approach. It rid them of the painful task of distinguishing between the few workers they might want to keep and the majority that, on the assumption that old age and modern work did not usually mix, they would prefer to get rid of. Required retirement fit a bureaucratic approach to the work process, eliminating more complex and individualized decisions. It was striking, by the later 1940s and 1950s, that American employers seized on the new availability of social security benefits to introduce mandatory retirement provisions, even though these had not at all been intended by the framers of the act, who saw social security as a cushion for the elderly in need not as a component of a compulsory system. Mandatory provisions survive widely in industrial societies to this day; in Canada and most of Western Europe, retirement is mandatory at age sixty or sixty-five, for example, regardless of individual wishes.

Quite widely, then, in industrial societies the idea and experience of retirement spread from the late nineteenth century onward. The Depression (with its massive unemployment, which wider retirements might alleviate) and then the spread of welfare states capped this trend. The concept of mandatory exit spread in the United States through corporate practice rather than by law, but it was standard practice nonetheless by the 1950s.

The mandatory approach always offered some interesting exceptions, of course. Owners of businesses or farms could not be forced to stop working, for after all they were laboring on their own property. Politicians and certain categories of judges were also not subject to retirement in the United States and elsewhere. Partly this reflected the self-interest of individuals who wanted to stay close to the seats of power, but partly it reflected a residual bow to the notion that the elderly might have some special wisdom to offer.

For most people in the employed classes, whether blue collar, white collar, or corporate, mandatory provisions came to predominate, adding another innovation to what was already an unprecedented approach to work.

The second development, which helps explain the lack of serious objection to the mandatory approach, was the extent to which many groups came to depend on retirement as a further adjustment to some of the downsides of modern work, at least when viewed over a lifetime. Even before mandatory provisions kicked in, so long as pensions were available, massive majorities of workers chose the retirement option. Ninety-nine percent of French factory laborers, for example, retired by age sixty by the late 1940s. Clearly, workers were voting with their feet: whether or not modern work was endurable—as opposed to unavoidable—for a few decades of life, there was no question that most workers came to expect a period of life in which it would disappear. Beyond the retirement years, many workers doubtless got through a decade or so by looking forward to them, even as work became increasingly meaningless. Like shorter hours and instrumental rewards earlier, retirement came to complete a trade-off package in which modern work, despite its drawbacks, could be made acceptable.

But this trade-off varied with the group of workers involved. Where pension conditions permitted, unskilled and blue-collar workers everywhere showed the greatest interest in retirement, getting out even earlier than required when they possibly could. Not surprisingly, this suggests a particular distaste for work at least as a lifelong experience, and specifically a sense that old age and work did not neatly mesh, and a high degree of reliance on retirement. Close on their heels were white-collar workers, in most countries only about 5 percent less likely to take early retirement options when available. The variance, though small, might suggest slightly less onerous work and less incompatibility with advancing age and, perhaps, a marginally greater commitment to a middle-class work ethic. Vastly different were the business and particularly professional classes, despite the fact that, with higher incomes, they could in principle afford the retirement option particularly readily. These groups were far less likely to retire early, at least completely, and far more likely to find ways to work at least part-time even after the mandatory age was reached and passed. Retirement, clearly, illustrates and refines an understanding of modern work, and modern work ethics, that is highly variable depending on background and job type. (Gender differences surfaced as well, with women typically retiring earlier than men; but this may largely have resulted from different ages at marriage, with wives retiring at the same time as, but younger than, their spouses.)

Developments in the United States generally fit within the larger patterns of the industrialized societies. Obviously, the nation resisted the most extreme approach to mandatory retirement, staying away from age sixty—a modest reflection, perhaps, of a greater belief in the personal value of work as well as a desire not to devote too many resources to social spending. But the choice of sixty-five as a norm was fairly typical.

Two distinctive points did emerge, one leading to a really striking departure after the 1960s. First, American workers often outdid their foreign counterparts in the actual ages of retirement, using relatively high levels of national and personal prosperity to abandon work well before they were required to do so. By the 1970s, the average blue-collar worker was retiring at age sixty, and certain categories with strong pension benefits, like automobile workers, pressed below fifty-eight. They were doing this despite the fact that the choice lowered their social security payments; it mattered more to get out of work. These patterns may reflect the unusually strong belief among many American doctors, noted above, that work and old age did not belong together. Certainly, the strenuous pace of American work, particularly on the factory floor, made many Americans particularly dependent on the retirement bargain to make the arrangement endurable. Of course the blue-collar situation was not universal: as elsewhere, other groups retired slightly less eagerly, and professionals in the main stayed on the job as long as they could.

Second—and this operated in complete tension with the widespread eager-ness to retire—the United States generated a particularly elaborate gerontologi-cal literature that worried about the effects of retirement. The literature began to emerge in the 1950s, just as mandatory retirement became a reality for most employed categories.

The argument was simple, and it reflected the survival of a vigorous work ethic in the nation's middle class. Work was, or could be, good. It gave value to life. It served as the basic source of power in a modern society. It followed that, by forc-ing or even encouraging people to retire, policymakers were condemning them to a later age that would become increasingly meaningless and marginal, with the elderly held apart from participating in the decisions that made modern society operate. Retirement, especially mandatory retirement, was the human equivalent of putting horses out to pasture, a statement of uselessness in a society in which utility counted for everything. Many of these same experts went on to speculate that retirement would be an unpleasant experience, precisely because it lacked the zest and significance of work, and pointed to the many cases where death closely followed the last day on the job.

Similar discussions occurred in other societies, for the issues were quite gen-eral; but they stirred particular passion in the United States because of the clash between ongoing work values and the practice of retirement. The debate involved issues of fact: most Americans in reality said they enjoyed retirement, though they often added how important it was to keep busy; the rising death rates soon after retirement might primarily reflect the fact that the people involved were fairly old—there was no clear retirement spike in the death rate overall. But above all, the debate involved issues of principle: about what life was all about, about what gave meaning to later age, about whether social significance depended on work alone.

Whatever the merits of the case, the debate began by the 1970s to stimulate another major American innovation. A variety of groups, spearheaded by the Gray Panthers, an old-age advocacy group mainly deriving from former professionals, arose to proclaim that mandatory retirement, and perhaps systematic retirement of any kind, was both unjust and unfair. This new approach contrasted with the more common kind of old-age interest-group argument, exemplified by the American Association for Retired Persons, that concentrated on defending retirement and seeking larger pension benefits. The Panthers specifically argued that older people should work whenever possible, because work was healthier than retirement and because a working older population would gain a greater voice in society at large. Their main focus was to attack mandatory retirement; using civil rights language, they protested the deprivation of individual choice. But their work-ethic message had even larger implications. Their specific arguments would ultimately generate the abandonment of mandatory provisions in the United States, almost uniquely among industrial nations. As we will see in assessing contemporary work, the result was a clear American exception to established policies as the twenty-first century took shape. Work values and the idea of choice triumphed over pervasive beliefs about incapacity in old age, even as most industrial societies still hewed to a more conventional modern package.

# Children

The Industrial Revolution forced massive revision of accepted relationships between children and work. Work obligations were central to childhood in agricultural societies, as part of family economies both in the countryside and in the cities. Only a handful of children, mainly from the upper classes, substituted formal education for work. For most peasants and artisans, training occurred as part of work, though in some cases a bit of religious instruction might be inserted around the edges. Forming a family labor force was one of the key reasons for having children in the first place.

As we have seen, the earliest phase of industrialization, particularly in England, maintained this pattern. Children, often from a fairly young age, could be useful in the new manufacturing, and of course most continued to work outside the factories, in agriculture or the crafts, and the use of children there was not disrupted at all. Employers found children vital. We have seen that many work-ethic advocates cited examples of people who started working when young and used this experience as the basis for later success (while also somehow sandwiching in a bit of education), extending the new ethic to childhood itself. More generally, most families continued to assume that children would contribute, if not always by working directly in the household economy, at least by bringing some wages home from the factories.

Gradually, this traditional or modified traditional arrangement was challenged by a number of factors. Parents began to worry when their children's work came under the control of others. New machines made child labor less useful in certain circumstances. Middle-class reformers began to preach a new definition of childhood in which innocence should not be sullied by excessive work and in which education should usurp the place of labor in defining childhood itself. Child labor laws in the major European countries and in many American states began to translate this new vision into legal reality.

However, the new assumptions took hold only gradually, quite apart from lax enforcement of labor and school-attendance laws during much of the nineteenth century. Greatest concern focused on children younger than twelve; young teenagers continued to play a major role in the labor force. Here too huge social class distinctions applied. Middle-class children were withdrawn from work not only in early childhood but also into their teen years, so that they could acquire at least a partial secondary education. American high schools and European secondary schools filled with new middle-class entrants by the mid-nineteenth century, whereas only the rare worker child made it this far. Labor restrictions also applied mainly to the factories; many early laws distinguished between employment sites with over fifty workers and those with fewer. And many parents, including those concerned about factory settings, continued to assume that children should work. So child labor continued to burn bright on the farms, in craft shops, and in a host of urban settings. New opportunities emerged in white-collar settings for messenger boys and newspaper sellers.

Schooling spread gradually. Many parents realized that some education might be a family advantage. Famously, many French peasants by the 1870s came to understand that, in modern market agriculture, having kids who could read and calculate could be an advantage. School-attendance requirements stiffened at this point as well. Even Japan, a newcomer to industrialization, introduced a mass-education provision in 1872, which was being widely enforced by the 1890s. At this transition point in the later nineteenth century, girls often lingered for more education than working-class boys were allowed. Teenage boys could get useful jobs, bringing money back for the family. Acceptable work opportunities for girls were less extensive, and there was more advantage in giving them further training as secretaries or potential teachers. But despite differentials, the trend was obvious: not only early but also middle childhood was aimed at schooling, not work directly. And by the twentieth century, the number of boys as well as girls staying into secondary levels began to grow steadily.

These transitions took more time in the United States than might have been expected, given a national culture that was enthusiastic about education and given relatively early school-attendance requirements in the northern states. There were several reasons for hesitation and delay. The nation was industrializing and urbanizing very rapidly amid a restricted labor supply: it was tempting, for employers and families alike, to continue to use child workers when adults were not readily available. Racial assumptions might factor in. While many African American parents, after the abolition of slavery, worked hard to provide education for their children, white officials were often less enthusiastic, and limited and unequal school opportunities, plus family need, could push for the use of minority children. Massive immigration in the decades around 1900 played a huge role. Immigrant families, coming mainly from parts of rural Europe where attitudes toward children had not begun to change, simply continued to assume that their children would work, and American employers were on the whole only too happy to oblige. Italian Americans disliked having their children work outside the family, but they gladly put them to work on family farms or small businesses. Polish Americans more readily placed children in the factories or in domestic service.

As a result of these factors, and despite child labor laws and an undeniable growth in education, the use of child labor in the United States reached a peak between 1910 and 1920, when over 2 million children (aged ten to fifteen) were in the labor force. They constituted 18 percent of the total labor force, up from 1 million children and 12 percent of the total just two decades earlier. Point one, then, for American distinctiveness: massive labor needs and continued beliefs in the validity of work for children delayed full national conversion to the new model of childhood, in which formal work dropped away in favor of schooling. For a brief but important period of time, American trends seemed to be defying the trends operating in other parts of the industrial world.

But this lag also encouraged a huge burst of reformist sentiment in the early decades of the twentieth century, and this would become the more important source of national emphasis in the long run. Immigrants drew particular attention from indignant middle-class observers: parents who put their children to work in traditional fashion were irresponsible and un-American, and they must be transformed by legal mandates.

A host of books and articles drove home the point that work and childhood should not mix. Ellen Key's book *The Century of the Child*, published in 1907, made the basic points clearly. Formal work that took children away from "play and school" was an abuse in and of itself. Work was bad for children's bodies. Key claimed that working children were smaller and less healthy than the norm—only 8 percent were really "sound and strong." Loss of sleep was a central problem. Work also exposed children to the moral dangers of "the street," including crime and sexual temptation amid a host of bad adult models. Work, here, whatever its value for adults, had no redeeming features for children. It was not the way to get started.[5]

In 1904, the National Child Labor Reform Committee took shape, backed by a number of prominent philanthropists. For the next three decades, debate over child labor assumed national dimensions, gaining massive newspaper coverage of tales of abuse. In the mid-1920s there was even an attempt at a constitutional amendment, which did pass the Congress but failed to gain sufficient support in the states. Early New Deal measures, as the Great Depression added yet another argument by suggesting that jobs should be protected for adults, finally ended the most intense debate by eliminating most formal employment before the age of sixteen.

Arguments against the employment of children had many facets. For some, including the trade unions, the depressive impact on adult employment and wages was an obvious issue: children had always been appealing workers because of their low cost, and it would help other workers immensely if their competition could simply be eliminated. But most of the reform zeal focused on children themselves and their unsuitability for modern work. As a speaker in the New York Assembly put it in 1913: "To rescue ... children under 14 years of age from nicotine poisoning [in cigar factories], from the miasmas of the stock yards, and from the horrible conditions of the sweat shops is to accomplish something worth doing." Children's health was a key component of the reform argument, and vivid rhetorical and visual images of deformed and sickly children rang true amid general concerns about children's frailty. The need for schooling was another powerful plank. Though as we will see there was also some concern about the burdens schoolwork placed on children, there was little doubt that some form of education was now vital for future careers, as the basis for successful adult work, and that child labor impeded it. Moral danger was another problem, again echoing earlier nineteenth-century reformist rhetoric. Child workers in the cities were removed from family supervision and exposed to all the dangers associated with urban life. Widely touted newspaper articles and debates in state legislatures cited the massive incidence (real or imagined) of venereal disease among children in the factories and in street occupations such as messengers and bootblacks. "They lose their respect for parental authority … and become arrogant, wayward and defiant." Early marriage and degenerate offspring were other consequences of child labor, according to the reformers. "The ranks of our criminal class are being constantly recruited from the army of child laborers," a reformer claimed in 1909.[6] These general points were driven home by repeated testimony, often from children themselves, about physical suffering, lack of schooling, and other poignant reminders of deprivation, such as the absence of the chance to celebrate birthdays and other aspects of idyllic childhood.

The arguments against child labor had some interesting components. This was true everywhere, but because the American campaign was so particularly fervent, the issues stand out in national context. First, there was tension as to whether modern work itself was under attack, or just work for children. After all, health and moral issues could apply to adults as well. None of the reformers intended to undermine the work ethic for adults, but they did suggest some nagging questions. When the argument turned, however, to schooling or the need for parental control, the campaign was more safely compatible with a continued belief in hard work—just not for the kids. A second tension involved the transition between childhood and work, if and when the reform model prevailed. After all, the old arguments that child labor helped children learn work habits were more readily consistent with the work-ethic vision. Now that childhood and work were to be separated, how was the ethic to be accessed? Parents, other adult authorities, and children themselves might wonder about the gap between childhood and the ongoing work expectations of adulthood, and we will see that this issue gained particular importance in what became the American approach to modern childhood.

One point was abundantly clear in the early twentieth-century campaign: almost all forms of child labor were now under attack, and not just work in the factories. Many attacks were levied against the use of children on farms, where hard physical work could be menacing: "It is the long continuance at these tasks hour after hour, day after day … that saps the vitality and warps the bodily frame." Reformers were at pains to refute traditional concerns about idleness: play and schooling were the alternatives, and they would better prepare for adult life than formal employment could.[7]

There are counterarguments, of course. Not only idleness but defiance of parental authority loomed for those who continued to think that children should work. Reform might deprive children of "initiative and self-reliance" while undermining the right of parents to train their offspring. A 1925 newspaper cartoon pictured a farm boy resisting his father's request to help with firewood, saying. "I can't, it's against the law."[8]

But the antiwork arguments now clearly prevailed, and child labor in the United States began to decline rapidly. Rosters dropped by a full million in the 1920s, and by 1940 only 1 percent of all children ages ten to fifteen were employed. A few exceptions persisted. Newspapers, though backing reform, managed to persuade legislators that children were vital in delivering their wares, arguing that this kind of work built business skills. Only at the end of the twentieth century did new transportation methods displace this hallowed child specialty. Even earlier, other technologies supplemented laws and school requirements in reducing children's work: telephones, for example, eliminated the need for office messengers. The cumulative thrust, however, was truly remarkable, and despite a few anomalies (including continued use of children by migrant farmworkers), the United States came to lead the world in the separation of children from work.

Ultimately this was the main feature of American exceptionalism in this important category. Partly, perhaps, because American culture placed such strong emphasis on hard work, and definitely because Americans came to believe that children were fragile and vulnerable, concern about even vestiges of work pressures on children reached exceptional levels in the United States. Reform sentiment, in other words, did more than end a classic linkage, it stretched into other facets of childhood as well. Urged on by many psychologists—and the United States led the world in giving weight to psychological expertise—many American leaders and ordinary parents expanded their protective approach to children and the view that childhood should be as far removed from work as possible.

Several developments drive home this comparative point. By the mid-twentieth century, school-attendance requirements in most states extended to age sixteen, in contrast to fourteen or fifteen in most other industrial countries. In part, this reflected greater national prosperity, which meant that more schooling could be afforded, but it also represented a revealing effort to delay the confrontation with work. Experiments in countries like France, where a group of students who did not seem academically inclined were allowed to combine work and school in what amounted to apprenticeship programs by age fourteen or so, were not picked up on the American side of the Atlantic. School-attendance levels through secondary school and beyond rose in all the industrial societies by the end of the twentieth century, but in most cases the United States led the way.

Equally revealing was the special approach many Americans adopted toward schoolwork. There was no major resistance to the basic modern trade-off in which children were expected to exchange work for schooling, and in principle American enthusiasm for the positive results of education ran quite high. But school might imply work as well, and here American experts and parents introduced some of the same cautions they had learned to direct toward paid employment. Too much schoolwork might harm a child's health: there were many warnings in the decades around 1900 about damage to internal organs and posture from the hours spent hunched over a desk. Eyestrain was another common target. The most interesting crusade, however, involved homework, a new feature of schooling in the twentieth century. A real antihomework protest movement arose in the early decades of the century, mimicking the campaign against work itself. The editor of *Ladies' Home Journal* voiced a common sentiment: "Is it any wonder that children have to be called over and over again in the morning, and that they at length rise unrefreshed and without appetites for their breakfasts? When are parents going to open their eyes to this fearful evil? ... Is all the book-learning in the world worth this inevitable weakening of the physical and mental powers?" In fact, scores of American cities passed antihomework ordinances into the 1950s (and the movement modestly revived in some places after 2000). More to the point, even when homework was allowed, the United States differed markedly from Western Europe and the Pacific Rim in the modest amount assigned in most schools. Most immediately, the European pattern of relatively short school days but extensive out-of-class assignments was simply not replicated in the United States, doubtless for several reasons but above all because of a fear that too much work pressure was bad for the innocence of childhood. Americans believed that children should be in school, but they seemed happiest when schools emphasized a playful approach to learning and tried to avoid an atmosphere that smacked of work. And when homework was imposed, American parents may have been particularly ready to jump in and do some of it for their fragile offspring: in 2000, 58 percent of all parents admitted to helping their children "considerably."

While this is the most striking indication of the distinctive American separation of work and childhood, one other category contributed as well: the rapid decline of work assignments, or chores, around the house. In the early twentieth century, many child-labor reformers argued that work around the house would continue and would provide children with the introduction to the work ethic that their opponents claimed to be worried about. But this linkage too diminished rapidly. Some chores simply became obsolete: dishwashing machines reduced a classic assignment, lower birthrates lessened the need to help out with younger siblings, newer fuels meant that children did not have to help with coal or wood for heating. Beyond the inevitable, however, parents and children alike began to assume that most chores represented an unfair encroachment on children's time, burdened enough with schooling. Most experts and popularizers like Dr. Spock continued to preach the socialization value of chores, in the best work-ethic fashion. Spock specifically wrote that "participation in the work of the home is good for the child's soul and provides a basis for the very soundest kind of companionship with parents." Even in the 1990s, the American Academy of Pediatrics praised chores as "an essential part of learning that life requires work, not just play"—another reminder of an older kind of thinking about childhood and preparation for adult life.[9] But this kind of advice went increasingly unheeded. Many parents argued that chores did nothing to train children to work, indeed just the reverse—it was better to let kids avoid work than find it unpleasant. Many noted that they themselves lacked the patience to guide children in work; it was easier to do it oneself. Whatever the reasons—and they increasingly included active disputes with children who resisted assignments of any sort—the number of hours children devoted to chores had diminished to almost nothing by the 1950s. Kids in their late grade-school years put in the most time, a few hours a week; outright adolescents did almost nothing, particularly in the middle classes, unless their parents were single. In 1976, 41 percent of all high school seniors said they did something at home every day; by the mid-1990s this claim was down to 24 percent, and most parents would have argued that reality was lower still. Once again, even in the most personal of settings, childhood and labor expectations no longer mixed.

The separation of childhood and work, particularly along extreme American lines, raised a number of issues. One, of course, was what children were for, now that they cost money and contributed nothing to the family economy. Plunging birthrates suggested that many people were deciding against having children, or many children, though interestingly American birthrates remained a bit higher than the norm in industrial countries. Presumably, emotional satisfaction, or at least expectations, replaced work contributions in many families. Another very real issue in many societies focused on children themselves: now that they were so separated from adult experience, would they be able to find purpose in their existence, would they be able to connect what they did as children—in school or amid the growing array of games and media activities—with what they would later do with their lives? For a minority of children, as suggested by rising rates of mental illness and even suicide, the answers here were troubling, not only in the United States, where child suicide rates shot up between the 1970s and the 1990s before leveling off, but also in places like Japan.

Most obviously, how would a childhood separated from work produce an adulthood with appropriate work capacity? How would the extremely protective approach taken in the United States mesh with the nation's equally extraordinary insistence on high levels of work commitments in adult life? The answer varied with the situation, of course. Many Americans learned to work hard enough in school that the transition to more formal work requirements was not too difficult. For some, college experience—a time of unusual work pressure for many success-ful students, in contrast with the more laid-back undergraduate years at many European universities—was precisely where the bridge was forged. As pressure for academic achievement mounted in the United States, many parents and children combined to produce an exceptionally busy childhood, with outside activities supplementing and sometimes overshadowing the often modest demands of school itself. Thus sports, music, dance, and activity camps provided the same full days that adults would have to devote to work itself. Of course, this same formula produced inevitable, and possibly telling, complaints about overorganiz-ing children, a contemporary version of the older American tendency to seek to dissociate childhood from work. But the pattern suggested that, for many American families, pushing a work ethic onto children, if less through chores and formal employment than through intense and diverse training, was the way to reconcile beliefs about childhood with the larger commitment to work itself.

A tension remained, however, and some American children, growing up, could never quite escape a sense that adult work obligations were unfair, that childhood, defined as work-free, had really constituted the finest time of life.

## Conclusion

The relationship between modern work and special groups in society offers a complicated picture. The values involved easily became double-edged. Modern work was seen as absolutely vital to the most productive lives, but perhaps too rigorous for some groups. New ideas about innocence or weakness or fatigue seemed to require separation for certain categories. But while the picture of a playful childhood or domestic womanhood or peaceful retirement might be painted in glowing colors, closer inspection might reveal the costs of the separation from what modern society seemed to value most, which was work, still. Small wonder that many women and, in a few instances, increasing numbers of advocates for the elderly protested the separation and even managed significant reversals. Women, indeed, would substantially redefine their early removal in the later twentieth century, though issues and hesitations remained. The question of the relationship between work and the elderly would probably reopen in the twenty-first century. Childhood seemed most durably redefined, but the redefinition raised issues of training and meaning that have not been fully resolved.

In several of the separations, American approaches added some distinctive elements. The high valuation of work showed a bit in early American feminism but even more in some of the newer movements among the elderly. The American twist on childhood was more unexpected but also more substantial. It highlighted the rigorous element of the national work ethic, making it seem particularly inappropriate for children, but it also exaggerated some of the common modern issues around the purposes of childhood itself. Because it seemed so vital to separate childhood decisively from work—in part because work gained such intense definitions—childhood came to be viewed in particularly strong terms of innocence and vulnerability. In a complex set of relationships for three key groups in relationship to work, American approaches might seem particularly intricate.

## Notes

1. Maurine Greenwald, "Working-Class Feminism and the Family Wage Ideal: The Seattle Debate on Married Women's Right to Work," *Journal of American History* 76 (1989): 118–49.

2. Confédération générale du travail, XVII Congrès confédéral (Paris, 1912), 279.

3. A. L. Loomis, "The Climate and Environment Best Suited to Old Age in Health and Disease," *Transactions of the Fifth Annual Health Meeting of the American Climatological Association* (1888): 8–9.

4. J. P. A. Villeneuve-Bargemont, *Economie politique chrétienne* (Paris, 1834), 2: 281.

5. Ellen Key, *The Century of the Child* (New York: G. P. Putnam's Sons, 1907).

6. Alexander McKelway, "The Needs of the Cotton Mill Operatives," *National Child Labor Committee Papers* (Washington, DC), March 29, 1909; for state legislative debates, see Viviana Zelizer, *Pricing the Priceless Child: The Changing Social Value of Children* (New York: Basic Books, 1985).

7. Raymond Fuller, *Child Labor and the Constitution* (New York: Thomas Y. Crowell, 1923), 37–41, 46–47.

8. Sherwood Anderson, *Dark Laughter* (New York: Boni & Liveright, 1925), 25; Woods Hutchinson, "Leisure and Work," *Saturday Evening Post*, 1922, 46. See Tom Lutz, "'Sweat or Die': The Hedonization of the Work Ethic in the 1920s," *American Literary History* 8 (1996), 260–81.

9. Benjamin Spock, *Baby and Child Care* (New York: Pocket Books, 1976), 322, 464–66.

# Further Reading

## On Retirement

William Graebner, *History of Retirement* (New Haven: Yale University Press, 1980); W. A. Achenbaum, *Old Age in the New Land: The American Experience since 1790* (Baltimore: Johns Hopkins University Press, 1979); Peter N. Stearns, *Old Age in European Society* (London: Croom, Helm, 1977).

## On Children

Viviana Zelizer, *Pricing the Priceless Child* (1985; repr., Princeton, NJ: Princeton University Press, 1994); Peter N. Stearns, *Anxious Parents: A History of Modern Childrearing in America* (New York: New York University Press, 2003); Colin Heywood, *A History of Childhood: Children and Childhood in the West from Medieval to Modern Times* (Cambridge, UK: Polity Press, 2001); Lee Shai Weissbach, *Child Labor Reform in Nineteenth-Century France: Assuring the Future Harvest* (Baton Rouge: Louisiana State University Press, 1989).

## CHAPTER 7

# Global Trends in the Past Half Century: The Industrialization of the World

The nature of work changed in many ways, in many places, between the middle of the twentieth century and the present day. The most important development was the addition of many new regions to the ranks of industrializing countries. In 1970, only about 20 percent of the world's population was directly involved in fully industrial economies; by 2020, the figure may well be closer to 60 percent. Additions to the ranks of labor also included huge shifts in women's participation in the formal workforce in many established industrial centers. More tentatively, new questions were raised about older workers as well.

Amid all the changes, one essential consistency must also be maintained: the fundamental nature of industrial work did not alter greatly. Industrial work—and this now extended well beyond the factory floor—still emphasized rapid pace, dependence on increasingly sophisticated machinery, the direction of others, considerable specialization, and a substantial reliance on instrumentalism. More people were now directly exposed to this type of work than ever before, thanks to the new geography of industrial economies and the collapse of older barriers to women's involvement in modern work settings.

There were a few countercurrents to the dominance of the industrial model, however, and these also must be factored in. More people in the most advanced industrial economies were able to escape the most severe industrial settings by some combination of several devices: new types of immigrants took over some of the least popular jobs in modern economies; new rounds of technological innovation, particularly associated with greater automation and then the use of computers and robots, eliminated some jobs both in blue-collar and in white-collar ranks; the rise of service jobs created new opportunities outside the immediate confines of factories; and, on a rather different front, increasing vacation time and more systematic retirement could significantly modify, though not erase, common work pressures. Ironically, some of this "relief" actually confirmed patterns of industrial work, because, to the extent that such work could be left to "others" (and people often regarded not only as other but as inferior) or temporarily escaped, its basic nature did not have to be reexamined. The process of adjustment to modern work, in other words, continued in various directions, though without redefining the fundamental processes involved.

Two other developments were noteworthy. First, technological change requires additional emphasis. In many work arenas including the growing service sectors, dramatic new equipment affected jobs as well. It was the increasing automation of some processes, along with new immigration, that could relieve certain workers of the worst kinds of factory stress. The growing use of computers was hailed by many for a potential transformative effect on modern work drudgery. Here, however, new equipment served more to confirm and enhance some of the central features of modern work than to rebalance these features. Machine dominance, among other things, measurably increased. Second, particularly in the social effervescence of the 1960s, but also thanks to some new management theories and the involvement of new regions in the industrial enterprise, some discussion emerged about deliberately reorganizing labor to address some of the most problematic features of modern work as they had taken shape a century and a half before. These experiments were quite interesting, but their impact proved more limited than some reform advocates had hoped. The continued emphasis on a recognizably industrial definition of work was not yet reversed, so some of the older questions about the meaning of modern work and the adequacy of compensations like instrumentalism continued to be extremely relevant well into the twenty-first century.

Key trends over the past fifty years were not always mutually consistent; this was true both globally and in the most mature industrial economies such as those of Western Europe and Japan. For example, the massive entry of women into the labor force in places like Western Europe coincided with a steady increase in technology-based worker productivity and some resulting unemployment. The first trend suggested the importance of access to work as part of changes in women's lives; the second trend raised the question of whether there was enough work to go around. Both developments were important, but they did not point in exactly the same direction. On a similar note, in many parts of the world new patterns of immigration focused on unskilled labor slots, even as attention shifted increasingly to high-tech categories and technology-based job displacement. Not surprisingly, amid conflicting patterns, policies toward labor varied and also fluctuated. Some societies, for instance, tried to lower the retirement age, in part to protect work opportunities for younger citizens, while others, concerned about the dignity of older people or simply worried about the costs of rapidly growing numbers of the elderly, moved to do the opposite. Both decisions responded to real issues, but according to different definitions of what priorities were involved. Important efforts aimed at involving workers more fully in the production process, but rising consumerism suggested that instrumentalism might be outstripping involvement; more workers than ever before essentially gave up on achieving much work quality in favor of focusing on life off the job.

Finally, and again not surprisingly, it was not always easy early in the twenty-first century to determine what trends would predominate in the future. Some experts wrote persuasively about a massive decline of work, thanks particularly to new levels of technological automation. But commitment to modern work was actually increasing for some groups and in some regions. If there was a dramatic revolution in the offing—and it could be readily sketched in theory—it certainly had not yet occurred. Questions and debates must be added to the delineation of major developments.

## The Expansion of Modern Work: Peasants into Factories

In 2006, half of the population of the whole world lived in cities, the first time this level had been reached in the span of human experience. This meant that during the twentieth century, but with accelerating speed in the century's final decade, millions of people moved from the countryside, and usually fairly traditional rural work habits, to urban centers. There, of course, they encountered all sorts of work situations, including frequent unemployment and entirely unskilled jobs—hauling people or materials in carts, for example—that were themselves fairly traditional. But many headed into work sectors that clearly emphasized modern conditions, with extensive technology, a rapid pace, and impersonal management and direction. Large minorities of workers now clustered in factories, even in countries that were not officially designated as industrial. By the second half of the twentieth century, nations as diverse as Iraq, Mexico, Turkey, and Brazil listed at least a quarter of their entire labor force as factory operatives. Extensive service sectors also emerged; as in the industrial nations previously, service work did not impose quite such stringent conditions as blue-collar labor did, but there was a similar emphasis on fast pace and formal management, often with added requirements about emotional control or personality traits.

The spread of modern work affected even established industrial centers. France, for instance, still boasted a substantial peasant minority in 1945, but more-efficient methods of agricultural production and the lure of the city steadily eroded this class, as it fell to under 10 percent of the total population. This development—one French sociologist summed it up with the term "vanishing peasant"[1]—meant two things in terms of work. First, more and more peasants, while retaining some vestiges of traditional work habits, began to rely on new machines, like tractors and harvesters, and a greater emphasis was placed on output and pace, thus partially merging with work trends earlier developed in urban occupations. Second, many former peasants moved into factories and service sectors, filling the growing ranks of automobile manufacturers or office secretaries or department store clerks—where they encountered modern work conditions directly. The pattern was familiar from earlier decades of industrialization; it now simply became more widespread, affecting ever larger numbers of people.

Far more dramatic changes unfolded in countries like China and India, particularly from the 1980s or 1990s onward. As China became one of the world's leading manufacturing centers, millions of peasants moved into factory labor, sometimes shifting their residence to a city, but even more often filling the ranks of a massive stream of about 200 million internal migratory workers. These were the workers who turned out growing volumes of clothing, Christmas ornaments, and electronic goods—a massive array of consumer items sent around the world. China had been a global manufacturing center before, of course, but around craft production and rural workshops; the factory base and its anchor in modern work patterns were quite new for all but a minority of the Chinese now involved.

Every Chinese New Year saw these millions of workers crowding the trains to go back to their villages for a few days, the one defined respite in a year otherwise filled with work. In some provinces, a full third of the population fell into the migrant worker category by the early twenty-first century. Observers understandably emphasized the family disruptions this huge wave of migration involved. Many workers left children and sometimes spouses at home, to be cared for by grandparents or other family members. One such migrant, Xiao Qingtong, was asked how his daughter was doing in school: "How can I possibly know that? I really can't take care of so many things. My priority now is to make money." Children, for their part, often had little sense of who their parents were or even whether they loved them. Not surprisingly, tensions often developed with other relatives as well. A worker in a leather-bag factory came home for a holiday but fought with his older parents so much he moved his family into a nearby hotel. A local farmer noted, "They lead a pretty good life. They even have a car. But they don't take care of the elderly; they don't respect the aged."[2]

While family problems and the sheer disruption caused by migration captured the greatest attention, work changes loomed large as well. These former peasants were laboring long hours in factories frequently amid dangerous equipment (accidents were common), and with a pace of work and method of direction vastly different from their traditional expectations. Reactions included occasional protests, and obviously the preservation of ties to the home village, even amid family tensions, suggested a certain tentativeness in the commitment to modern work. Equally clearly, a pattern of instrumental response emerged quickly. Difficult work could be accepted because it produced income that was vital to sustain the family back home and that could also be used to enhance the worker's own consumer standards.

None of this constituted a new story. What was happening in China replicated, in broad outline, the experience of many Europeans or Japanese a century or more before. But however familiar in terms of the introduction to modern work standards and the compensations workers tried to develop, the experience was new to these workers and vastly expanded the impact of modern work in the world at large. And the sheer scale of the exposure, with the many millions of Chinese now involved, had no precedent.

The surge of India's economy involved some variants of this pattern, again with effects on millions of urban workers. Factory industry expanded, but even more impressive was the rise of a service sector. Increasing numbers of Indian workers, benefiting from familiarity with English, received outsourced jobs from the United States, the United Kingdom, and elsewhere; they responded to mail order requests, handled billing services, made travel arrangements, and in general provided long-distance linkages for customers in the Western world. The role of technology was obvious: satellite-based phone connections and the Internet (publicly opened in 1990) were essential to this distinctive expansion of modern work. But standard conditions of modern service occupations also applied. These workers were held to a fairly fast pace, under the watchful eyes of designated supervisors. They had to undergo special training, not only to make sure they presented the right American or British accent in English, but also to convey a sense of friendly openness in their customer contacts.

While sometimes less dramatic in terms of numbers of workers involved, the expansion of factory operations in other countries produced similar outcomes. In many instances, foreign multinational corporations set up production facilities in industries such as clothing, electronics, computer chips, even automobile parts, in places like Indonesia, Mexico, Vietnam, and Lesotho. Or, even more commonly, local contractors for the big companies made the direct investment. In either case, hundreds of thousands of additional workers, usually from rural backgrounds, were drawn in, gaining their first exposure to modern work settings. Specific conditions varied. There was no doubt about what the foreign companies were after: cheap labor, capable of providing the semiskilled capacities required for machine operations. At worst, conditions could suggest a revival of servitude, with local contractors often particular offenders: Workers in Lesotho's Korean-owned textile factories were locked in the plant from arrival until exit ten or twelve hours later; they were not even allowed to leave on brief lunch breaks. Passports of workers from China and the Philippines in textile factories in American Pacific territories like Guam and Samoa were confiscated so that if the workers caused any disciplinary problems, they could simultaneously be fired and expelled. Many factories in Indonesia immediately dismissed workers who ventured any complaint, despite the fact that accidents were frequent because of unprotected machinery and hours were exhausting, with no extra pay for forced overtime. International human rights observers indeed used the term "slavery" explicitly in describing some contemporary work situations. In Burma (Myanmar), for example, some foreign corporations made deals with the repressive military regime preventing some factory workers from quitting their jobs—much less protesting—regardless of conditions.

On the other hand, some workers found that managers in foreign firms were more courteous than local foremen. Furthermore, international campaigns against sweated labor—several pressure groups were launched in the United States and Western Europe—gained some success in calling attention to the worst abuses, particularly where well-known Western firms, like Nike, were involved. In 1996–1997, for example, carefully orchestrated campaigns against Nike's labor practices in Vietnam and Indonesia affected sales and image to such an extent that the corporation vowed reform. The emergence of implicit international standards for minimally acceptable working conditions hardly reached all of the people newly exposed to modern work—they had little impact in authoritarian China, for example—but they did add some complexity to otherwise familiar stories of early-industrial exploitation.

## Immigrant Workers

Along with the expansion of modern work in key parts of Asia, Latin America, and Africa came an explosion of immigrant labor in the mature industrial centers, as well as a few other places. Beginning in the late 1950s, new immigrant streams from the Caribbean, Africa (both northern and sub-Saharan), Turkey, and South Asia began to pour into Western Europe. By 1900 there were over 12 million immigrant workers in the then twelve nations of the European Common Market. Caribbean, Asian, and Latin American immigrants created the largest influx of foreigners into the United States in its history. Japan was less immigrant friendly, but even here labor needs required reception of some foreign workers, mainly from Southeast Asia. The states on the Persian (or Arabian) Gulf, oil rich and booming with construction projects, formed another, even newer, magnet. Over 80 percent of the inhabitants of the United Arab Emirates were expatriates, or expats, from all over the world but particularly from southern India, Pakistan, and Palestine. Egyptians and Palestinians worked in fairly large numbers in a few other parts of the Middle East outside their home territories.

Immigration was not new, of course. The new wave in some ways mirrored patterns around 1900, when large numbers of migrants from southern and eastern Europe, plus parts of east and south Asia, had moved into parts of North and South America, some of them staying permanently but others returning home after a stint of work.

The new migration, however, brought people to work from even more distant places than before, creating, among other things, heightened issues of cultural adaptation and local reception. By 2000, Muslims, mainly from Turkey and North Africa, had become substantial minorities in places like France, Germany, and the Netherlands, a sure sign of change. Several receiving societies, furthermore, placed restrictions on the migrants greater than those imposed by immigrant-receiving societies around 1900. Many European countries dubbed migrants like the Turks "guest workers," a euphemism that justified not only exploitative labor practices but also a withholding of citizenship, such that workers might be forced to return home when their services were no longer required. The United Arab Emirates, dependent on a massive amount of foreign labor, held the passports of most foreign workers so that they would automatically be required to leave when they lost their jobs. Migrants themselves, benefiting from more rapid transportation systems, often displayed an even greater desire to return to their points of origin after a work stint than their counterparts of a century before. Many Latino immigrants to the United States, for example, even when granted citizenship, returned home frequently and held back from fuller integration into the host society, though patterns varied.

Migrant laborers performed all sorts of work, and only some of the jobs imposed the most stringent modern conditions. There were factory workers, whose rural origins meant they experienced the same kind of abrupt encounters with modern technologies and work pace that emerged in industrializing areas like China. In Los Angeles, for example, Mexican immigrants predominated in clothing factories, where modern work patterns combined with low pay; native-born workers, both white and black, concentrated in electronics and defense factories where technology was more sophisticated and wage scales notably higher. There were service workers: many Indian expats in the Gulf states did office and commercial work of various sorts. In some cases, migrants already had experience with modern work: an important layer of well-educated, sophisticated urban professionals migrated from India, China, and other places to North America or Western Europe, maintaining middle-class work patterns with which they were already familiar. At another extreme, some migrants, particularly women, entered the ranks of domestic workers, providing cleaning services and child care; this was the case for large numbers of Filipino migrants, though there were also trained nurses in this segment. Domestic workers needed familiarity with some modern home equipment, but many aspects of their jobs, including the long hours, harked back to more traditional situations.

The bulk of the migrants, at least initially, were slotted into relatively unskilled jobs that local workers no longer preferred. Massive numbers were used on construction sites, for example, in the United States and the Gulf states. Latino workers in many parts of the United States also worked in food service and lawn care. Asian immigrants in the United Kingdom were only about half as likely as the native born to be in factories but more than twice as likely to be in distribution activities—mainly small shops—and transportation work. In many of these categories, long hours and extensive physical exertion again recalled older work settings, though there was some exposure to new technologies as well and sometimes an involvement with relatively impersonal management. Lower-level service jobs also drew significant numbers—bus conductors in the United Kingdom, taxi drivers in many places were cases in point.

Something of a double blue-collar labor market opened up in Western Europe and the United States. Local workers, familiar with modern work standards but also reliant on relatively high wages, concentrated in the better factory jobs while sometimes moving into service categories as well. The unskilled immigrants clustered separately, competing for jobs no longer of wide interest to the native population because of long hours and physical strain, low prestige, and low pay. These jobs characteristically involved some mixture of modern and more traditional features, though they could also help immigrants become accustomed to new forms of work and new types of technologies. Racial prejudice helped confirm the separate job prospects of many immigrants. Immigrants' own ambivalence about whether they sought to stay in their new location or return home after a few earning years added complexity as well. Many immigrant workers thought mainly in terms of earning money to send back home, in situations where job opportunities in the places of origin were failing dismally to keep pace with needs. Mainly south Asian immigrants in the Gulf state of Bahrain, for example, sent over $60 billion out annually—as much as the nation earned from its oil revenues; Central Americans in the United States regularly transferred large sums. Here again was a kind of instrumentalism that could make seemingly unappealing jobs meaningful. The dual labor market also, however, imposed special risks on the immigrants, for it could generate long periods of unemployment or underemployment in cases of economic deterioration. Substantial unemployment among immigrants, particularly North African youth, helped trigger bitter urban rioting in France in 2006.

Lots of questions swirled around the new reliance on immigrant labor. Would the workers involved gradually integrate into more fully modern kinds of work and into a single labor force? Did the workers who returned home help reshape work values and expectations in the traditional countryside? Would technology or new job needs on the part of local workers ever displace the intense need for unskilled immigrant labor (or would rapidly declining birthrates in places like Mexico ultimately dry up the supply of this labor)? Whatever the answers, there was no question that new migration patterns added not only to the complexity of modern work forms but also to the exposure to new working conditions.

## Technology: A New Revolution?

Productivity per worker rose sharply in the mature industrial societies in the decades after 1950. Ford Motor Company set up its first "automation department" in 1947, and companies in other industrial areas were soon exploring similar options. Many new machines reduced the number of processes that required human intervention; this was particularly true in factories but also applied to service categories. Some machines, of course, merely accelerated the speed of work. Electric typewriters, for example, reduced physical effort but led to higher output standards, in a fairly familiar example of ongoing industrial technological development. But many assembly lines were able to cut back on their labor force, thanks to automatic processes that tightened screws, packaged foods, counted items, or assembled parts with only a few human overseers. Automation in some factories as early as the 1960s produced situations in which a few white-coated technicians watched machines do virtually all the work, almost entirely replacing blue-collar labor.

The pace of technological change seemed to accelerate once again in the 1980s and 1990s. This was the point in countries like the United Kingdom, which had lagged a bit previously, at which per worker productivity really spurted ahead. Computer programs now could regulate complex combinations of machinery while also processing records far more rapidly and efficiently than any set of white-collar clerks could manage. Robots assembled automobile components faster and more reliably than assembly-line workers could.

It is important not to exaggerate. Some industries continued to depend on considerable manual intervention. Meat-packing plants, for instance, still required human effort to cut up carcasses as these moved along assembly lines at speeds that often prompted industrial accidents. Some countries proceeded more rapidly in aspects of the automation program than others did. The United States, for example, used robotics more sparingly than France and particularly than Japan, where reliance on robots was seen as an alternative to massive labor immigration.

Despite variety and inconsistency, the new technology measurably changed work in several ways. Some observers, indeed, claimed there was a massive disjuncture, arguing that the new machines created a second revolution as profound as the Industrial Revolution had been. One actually talked about the disappearance of work, predicting that everything would be done by machines. A futurologist, a bit more modest, also assumed that levels of work would drop decisively, so that people should learn to do other things with the bulk of their time—he suggested computer games.[3]

In fact, changes to date have been both more modest and more complicated than these attention-grabbing scenarios suggested. Three major consequences followed from growing automation, including the recent computer-aided spurt.

First, automated procedures unquestionably reduced the need for some semi-skilled factory workers and in the process created new opportunities for trained technicians. Between 1980 and 1990, thanks to more automated procedures, the U.S. Steel Corporation was able to produce the same amount of steel with only one-sixth the labor force (20,000 as opposed to 120,000 workers). Computer controls in the chemical industry allowed major firms to reduce their workforce by half, as some plants virtually ran themselves. This kind of transformation significantly modified one of the key features of industrial labor for many people. Work still involved interactions with technology (indeed, machines set the standards for work even more than before), and it still required a fast pace and impersonal direction. But the degree of personal involvement with assembly lines, with resultant physical and sometimes nervous stress, could be diminished. In the chemical industry, for example, work became vastly cleaner and safer, mainly involving monitoring gauges and reading charts. On a larger scale, automation furthered the trend of rebalancing the labor force between blue-collar and white-collar workers in favor of the latter.

Second, new technologies unquestionably created new anxieties about jobs and may turn out to generate persistently high unemployment rates in mature industrial societies. The worry is undeniable: in 1996 a *New York Times* poll revealed that 40 percent of all American workers were unsure their jobs would survive in a changing economy. This degree of insecurity, though not brand-new in industrial experience—technological change had threatened work categories before—could become part, an obviously undesirable part, of the work experience itself. Worry was magnified by the 1990s by new threats to educated service workers, not just to the less-visible blue-collar segments. New machines, like automatic teller systems at banks, unquestionably reduced job opportunities in some white-collar sectors.

There were two complications, however. First, new technologies were not the only threat; increased global competition, including outsourcing of clerical jobs to places like India, might be an even greater menace to job security. This distinction between effects of technology and more varied changes might be lost on an insecure worker, who might not care much what caused the loss of his job, just that he lost it; but it certainly muddies some of the claims of some of the high-tech gurus who preached that work itself might become a thing of the past.

The second complication is that the evidence on unemployment rates was mixed. Certain kinds of jobs, particularly on the factory floor, were gone. But labor demands in some other operations, like clothing manufacture, remained high at the global level, and the service sector might expand rapidly enough to take up the remaining slack. The most troubling statistic came from Western Europe (other than Britain) where, from the late 1980s onward, a number of economies seemed burdened by a 10 to 12 percent unemployment rate that persisted even when the overall economy seemed fairly healthy. This was the situation in France, Italy, and Germany, where unemployment seemed to defy easy remedy, cutting into blue-collar and unskilled (including immigrant) categories particularly. Here, unquestionably, was a chilling change in the work experience of many people. But economies elsewhere did not yet show the same symptoms. Employment rates in the United States and the United Kingdom remained more robust, despite utilization of very similar technologies overall. There was some concern that wages were depressed in the United States—in other words, that workers, in order to keep their jobs, had to reduce salary demands—but jobs themselves were not gone. Japan, with a newly shaky economy, suffered more unemployment than usual in the 1990s, but nothing like the European rates. The employment consequences of the current rounds of technological change are not entirely clear. As birthrates drop in some societies and the population ages, some governments worry about finding more workers, not reducing the labor force. South Korea, for example, early in the twenty-first century embarked on a program to encourage higher birthrates, precisely because of anxieties about labor supply in a highly automated economy.

It was true, however, particularly in Western Europe, that employment concerns did begin to generate proposals and policies aimed at lining up job supply and demand by reducing work. A number of French and Italian leaders in the 1990s came out with proposals for four-day workweeks, and some of these proposals were put into effect. In 1993, Volkswagen, Europe's largest car manufacturer, introduced a four-day workweek designed to save thirty-one thousand jobs that would otherwise be lost to technology-induced per-worker productivity gains and global competition; workers accepted the package even though wages dropped in consequence. A French chemical plant introduced a similar arrangement, but in return for accepting shift work that kept the plant open twenty-four hours a day, seven days a week, pay did not have to be reduced; other savings, plus further improvements in productivity, compensated. Japanese policymakers discussed similar moves in the 1990s, and vacation time did begin to increase. Intriguingly, only American business leaders held out entirely. As one CEO put it, "I cannot imagine a shorter work week. I can imagine a longer one ... if America is to be competitive in the first half of the next century."[4] Yet the notion of reducing work time in favor of assuring greater intensity when on the job—clearly the approach taken by the French chemical company—while also reducing technology's employment impact was hardly a new strategy. Earlier in the industrialization process workdays had dropped from twelve, to ten, to eight hours; and it hardly ushered in workless lives. The degree and impact of change remained to be sorted out, and with it the extent to which older work values would be challenged.

The third major consequence of increasing automation was an intensification of certain aspects of the modern workday, rather than the mitigation of some of the less desirable aspects of modern work that some experts had predicted. A few futurologists argued that computerization would reverse some of the more unpleasant effects of industrialization on the job experience. Work would become more individualized, more creative. And for some computer aficionados, there was change: more work could be done at home (though only a minority took extensive advantage of this possibility by telecommuting entirely); management hierarchies might be flattened when groups of computer experts collaborated on a project. Carefully, casual dress and informality seemed to suggest a new work culture in some high-tech firms. Change was possible, and it might become more extensive in the future.

But against these trends was the obvious fact that most of the new technology made work faster than ever before, and some of it also encouraged new levels of work addiction for a substantial minority of the managerial and professional classes around the world. Computers accelerated the pace of clerical work and allowed new levels of monitoring of job performance in factories and offices alike. Other demands of a modern, high-technology economy, such as the expansion of air traffic control functions, also showed how high-stress jobs might expand, not contract. The Internet and ever more sophisticated portable and handheld devices could almost erase the divide between home and work, and cell phones might have the same effect. Pursuing a job during most of one's waking hours was probably easier than ever before in human history. Vacations took on a new meaning with e-mail at the ready. Only a minority was actively ensnared, of course, but this had always been the case for modern work addiction. The fact remained that modern technology could create a work-ethic dream world in which contact with the demands of the job would never be lost. For some, indeed, the technology itself, and particularly the fascination of the world of computers, might make work more interesting than ever before, feeding a value system that had been born two centuries before.

## Redefining the Labor Force

Industrialization encouraged new decisions about the work of women, children, and the elderly. Developments in the past fifty years have largely confirmed and extended the idea that children should be separated from the labor force, and the results, on a nearly global basis, add to the force of fundamental changes in childhood and the expectations surrounding childhood. In contrast, the same period saw a virtual revolution in women's work roles in mature industrial society (except in regions such as Russia, where women had never been pulled out of the labor force), and women took on new work roles in other areas as well. New questions arose, finally, concerning older workers; many earlier industrial trends were extended, but a few countries began to pull away from these conventions at least in part.

Pressures against child labor increased quite widely. International organizations, including the United Nations after World War II, issued children's rights documents that stressed the importance of freeing young people from work up to at least age fifteen, in order both to avoid exploitation and to facilitate access to education. Standards previously developed in the industrial societies toward redefining childhood were now being projected globally. Disagreements persisted, however. An effort in 1973 to draft an international convention banning work before age sixteen could not win sufficient support because many countries still felt they depended on child labor to some extent. But except in south and Southeast Asia—where child labor actually expanded around 2000, from 6 million to 9 million children—rates of children's work steadily dropped. Children constituted 6 percent of the global workforce in 1950, only 3 percent in 1990. The advent of communism, particularly in China (as in Russia earlier), contributed greatly to a reduction of child labor, because communist leaders were convinced of the importance of education both to produce new work skills and to generate appropriate political attitudes. Some communist youth groups maintained modest work obligations for children. In societies that were still poor, this could ease the transition away from more extensive reliance on child labor, but in general, schooling became the norm for children in these societies, as increasingly in other areas such as Latin America. During the 1950s the number of children in elementary school in China tripled, a huge commitment to the primacy of education over child labor, and the percentage increase in secondary school enrollments was greater still.

Quite widely, though particularly in the mature industrial countries, the withdrawal of children from work was extended into the late teenage years, through the expansion of education requirements. Many European countries moved the school-leaving age from fifteen to sixteen by the 1960s, as most American states had already done. Expansion of college enrollments, to reach over a third of the relevant age groups in Europe, Canada, and Japan and even more in the United States, was a huge development, delaying full work entry for many young adults. In 2003 the Chinese regime committed to placing 15 percent of its older teenagers in universities, moving one of the largest societies in the world in the same direction as the rest of the industrialized countries.

There were some complexities, of course. In the United States a number of high school students, and certainly many college students, took on part-time jobs in order to afford some consumer amenities and/or pay for education. Later childhood could be partially associated with work to this extent, though the primary focus (at least in principle) continued to be education rather than the job. A few countries also introduced modifications of the modern definition of childhood for certain categories of older children. France, for example, encouraged about a quarter of students aged fourteen to fifteen to combine some ongoing study with work apprenticeships; these were adolescents not particularly gifted in school, very unlikely to qualify for higher education, for whom an earlier introduction to work was both practical and motivational.

In general, however, the separation of childhood and work proceeded into the twenty-first century, with one intriguing regional exception in south Asia. There was every reason to believe that this had become a lasting feature of the modern work equation.

The situation at the other end of the age spectrum was somewhat more complicated. Retirement also continued to gain ground, and more older people and more policymakers decided that later age and work should not normally mix. There were a few countercurrents, however, particularly by the 1990s, and certainly a host of new questions as industrial societies faced the rapid aging of their populations and the increase of costs this implied for societies as a whole and for individual families.

Retirement spread in Western Europe and Japan for several reasons. Growing prosperity increased the options of older workers and their families. The rise of the welfare state, particularly in Western Europe, increased the pension funds available to retirees and, in some instances, also facilitated a reduction in the retirement age. In Japan, where welfare programs were somewhat less generous, a veneration of the elderly led to a somewhat similar encouragement to retirement, though more at the family's expense. Companies found that promoting early retirement was a sound, socially acceptable way to respond to economic downturns, when the labor force needed to be cut back. And, without question, more and more individual workers wanted to get out of work at earlier and earlier ages.

Japan and several European countries had already established age sixty as the mandatory retirement age. In Germany and several other places, less formal mechanisms, at least until the 1990s, promoted even earlier retirement by offering partial pension payments. France formally introduced, in 1982, a reduction of the retirement age to fifty-five, mainly in the interest of removing a category of workers from the labor force in order to increase employment opportunities for younger people. In most of these cases, more and more people actually pulled away from work during their fifties: only 22 percent of all Germans between the ages of sixty and sixty-five, for example, remained at work. "Early exit" was an increasingly dominant impulse, responding to ideas about deterioration in old age, corporate interest in removing an expensive labor category, and individual interest in gaining freedom from work. What the balance was between encouragements to retire early and individual preferences was not always clear, but there was little sign that most of the people who left before the mandatory retirement age were compelled to do so. The 1990s brought a demonstration of how deep the retirement habit went: Germany, the Netherlands, and many other countries began to reduce pension payments, particularly for early retirees, as part of a general effort to cut welfare expenses at a time of economic stagnation. But retirement patterns did not change, which meant that many people were so bent on escaping work that they were willing to reduce their living standards to that end. Whether this preference would survive further welfare changes as expenses mounted with the aging of the population, remained to be seen: but for the moment, the retirement option remained deeply entrenched in industrial life.

A few countries, of course, maintained a higher standard retirement age. Canada insisted on mandatory retirement, but at sixty-five, as was the case in the United Kingdom. Scandinavia stood more firmly apart, with its official retirement age of seventy, though Sweden reduced this in the 1980s. Greater life expectancy and a belief that older workers retained considerable health and vitality contributed to this distinctive stance. Some observers argued, in addition, that abundant vacation time earlier in the work cycle reduced the impulse to retire early in Scandinavia by making work seem more palatable, more compatible with rich life experience. In keeping with this tradition, governments like that of Norway tried hard to make sure older workers who wished to work retained that right, as against any age-based discrimination: work could be part of the dignity and meaning of later life. Here too was an attitude different from that of most industrial countries (the United States, as we will see, largely excepted). The government, flush with oil revenue from the North Sea, enjoyed high employment rates that inhibited any interest in using retirement to address larger labor problems. But even in Norway actual trends moved toward earlier retirement beginning in the 1980s. Private employers organized pension funds to facilitate worker departure before the mandatory age, as part of the usual move to create greater flexibility in the size and composition of the labor force. Individual workers sought this option as well, whether because of a sense of personal deterioration, a desire for new experience, a distaste for work, or some combination of factors. A majority of Norwegians were still working at sixty-five, in contrast to patterns in other parts of Western Europe, but after sixty-five the percentage dropped to little more than a quarter. Even a distinctive culture and tradition, then, did not prevent a growing push to retire.

In contrast to substantial continuity concerning retirement trends, the situation of women workers changed dramatically in most industrial countries, and particularly in Western Europe, after the 1950s. In Britain, for example, whereas women's employment as a percentage of the total had increased only 1 percent between 1900 and 1950, it soared from 32 percent to almost 40 percent between 1961 and 1981; women filled 60 percent of the new jobs created in that period. Scandinavian rates were even higher. By the end of the twentieth century well over 40 percent of the labor force in France was female. Germany lagged a bit; by the 1990s only 55 percent of adult women were formally employed, which reflected a more conservative culture and a particularly striking lack of day-care facilities for children; but even here, there was great change. Japan kept more women at home, in contrast to its heavy reliance on female labor during early industrialization. But here, too, large numbers of women moved into service sector occupations, and in the 1990s, when economic conditions worsened, many families relied increasingly on women workers. By 2003 about 60 percent of all adult women were working. Similar trends, of course, developed in the United States.

The following figures give a bit of a thumbnail sketch of women's participation in the formal labor force in 2000[5]:

|                     |                 |
| ------------------- | --------------- |
| United States       | 71.3 percent    |
| Canada              | 67.8 percent    |
| United Kingdom      | 67.5 percent    |
| Japan               | 63.7 percent    |
| Germany             | 61.8 percent    |
| France              | 59.8 percent    |
| Spain               | 47.1 percent    |
| Italy               | 44.1 percent    |
| Bahrain (in 2002)   | 25.8 percent[6] |

The point is clear: industrial societies that had moved women out of the labor force during earlier decades now moved them back in. The change was even more striking than statistics suggest, because young adult women opted for higher education at growing rates, often surpassing men in university attendance. This meant that the previous pattern, where many unmarried women worked but then often pulled out upon marriage, was being reversed. Young women commonly stayed in school, and it was mature, often married, women who now increasingly assumed that they should work.

Two basic factors fueled this historic change, and it is hard to determine priorities. First, changing economies were generating more and more service jobs—in stores and offices and in low-status professions like nursing and teaching school. Women, historically held to be suitable for many of these jobs, and willing (however reluctantly) to work for lower pay than men, constituted an ideal source of labor. At the same time, women from various social classes developed a new desire to work. Education levels had steadily advanced for women in industrial societies. Birthrates, though they blipped upward a bit immediately after World War II in Western Europe, were quite low. European women were also relatively willing to leave children in day-care centers, though in places like Germany there was a lingering uncertainty: many mothers who worked professed to believe that they should be at home with the kids, well into the later twentieth century. Increasing consumer appetites meant that additions to the family wage were most welcome, either for personal purchases by women themselves or for more general goals like a family car. Finally, though to what degree is unclear, a revival of feminism encouraged many women, particularly in the middle classes, to argue that access to work was a vital step toward a greater social and political voice—and toward greater bargaining power with men in the family.

Women's reentry into formal work roles, and their fuller encounter with modern work, did not fully merge them with male workers in the industrial societies. Most obviously, the surge focused very heavily on the service sector, where feminization proceeded very rapidly. Women were concentrated in far fewer occupations than men. Special concerns about family responsibilities also constrained many women; women were more likely to work part-time than men, or to pull out of the labor force for several years of child rearing. They also tended to retire earlier, presumably mainly because they followed their husbands or partners, who were on average a few years older. A combination of gender prejudice, sheer tradition, and the distractions of family roles kept women disproportionately out of higher management slots. In France in 2007, with 46 percent of the labor force made up of females, women held only 17 percent of all managerial positions and a mere 7 percent in the corporate sector. Japanese women even by 2007 faced special prejudice, being required, for example, to serve tea to male colleagues. All this added up, finally, to lower wages for women than for men, both overall and in cases where work was fairly similar. When the female work surge began, women generally earned at best 60 percent of men's wages for roughly comparable jobs.

Gender work issues generated extensive political response, particularly from the 1970s onward. Many European countries passed laws requiring equal pay for equal work, though these proved difficult to enforce fully, in part because of the complexity of defining equal work. Sexual harassment on the job was another issue newly visible as more women joined the workforce, and again legal measures in Europe and Japan gradually provided some protection. Because of their concentration in the service sector, many women were also subject to particularly stringent emotional requirements as part of their modern work experience, being urged to be pleasant with unruly customers or to display maternal attributes in teaching or health care.

By the 1990s, some constraints on women's work had eased a bit. Pay ratios improved. In Japan by the 1990s women's wages had risen to 70 percent of men's, and in parts of Europe the relationship was even better. More women were finding opportunities in management and in many of the professions, based on greater experience and acceptance and on further gains in higher education. On the other hand, other problems became more obvious than before. The combination of work with special responsibilities for child rearing remained difficult, and many countries still provided inadequate day-care facilities. In some countries, such as the United Kingdom, laws pressed employers to provide more flexible hours for working mothers, but response was limited, and the dilemma of whether to single women out for special treatment was not easy to resolve.

For all the difficulties and the undeniably persistent inequalities, industrial societies had effected a historic redefinition of their initial impulse to separate most women from the demands of modern work. The result was a huge change for women, and a huge change in many workplaces.

Patterns globally were more diverse. Communist societies had long depended on the work of most adult women, and a fifty-fifty split in the labor force was common. Women did not have equal access to a full range of jobs, however, and their pay was lower than men's; they also had domestic duties that added greatly to their work day, again in contrast with men. The fall of communism in Eastern Europe led, at least temporarily, to a reduction in job access for many women and also an increase in sexual harassment and exploitation.

Muslim societies in the main were somewhat reluctant to release women into the formal labor force, because of concerns about women in public or women mixing with men. By the 1980s reform-minded countries like Turkey had changed; in these countries women constituted about 35 percent of the formal labor force; but in some other Muslim countries the percentage hovered around 5. Increased entry of women into higher education—where they constituted 55 percent of university populations in places like Iran and the Gulf states by the early twenty-first century—suggested that further change was in the offing.

African societies continued to reflect a gender split. Many women remained in the countryside, in agricultural work; they had less access than men to more modern, urban occupations.

More generally, the spread of manufacturing to many new areas, such as Mexico and Indonesia, offered many factory jobs to women, again partly to take advantage of their lower wages. In some places, women were less likely than men to suffer unemployment because of global competition.

The mixed picture and the complexity of ongoing trends constitute the obvious message. More women were working in factory and office settings than ever before, thanks to the spread of industry and urbanism and the big changes in the industrial world. But gender divisions persisted as well, and there was considerable regional variety based on differences in culture and precise economic situation. It was clear, however, that the implication of initial Western industrialization, that gender might shape entirely different modern work experiences, had been decisively eradicated. Women became a normal or increasingly normal part of the labor force outside the home in most parts of the world.

## Revisiting Modern Work: Efforts at Reform

The most important global changes in work over the past half century have involved variations on already established industrial themes: more technology, with resultant adjustments and insecurities; more commitment to essentially modern work settings, rather than traditional routines; more withdrawal of children from the workforce. Only the dramatic revision in the relationship between women and work set a clearly new tone.

There were, however, two efforts explicitly to modify some of the basic premises of modern work that cut more clearly against established industrial trajectories. One resulted directly from protest, the other from a distinctive Japanese approach to work issues that reflected some elements of older cultural traditions of group solidarity combined with new management ideas and a new estimation of competitive advantage. In both cases, the idea was to confront key aspects and limitations of the modern work paradigm and generate superior alternatives.

The two major reform currents emerged between the 1960s and the 1980s. Both had intriguing implications and some real impact. Both originated outside the United States, which was revealing, and both had at most limited impact in the American context, which continued to seem more systematically devoted to the latest versions of the work ethic and relatively rigorous frameworks for work itself.

Some changes in the setting for work began to develop in Western Europe soon after World War II, with the new political power wielded by socialist and labor parties. Governments nationalized some industries and set up advisory boards with worker representation. France established what they called enterprise committees, again to give worker representatives some contact with policy decisions that might, among other things, affect working conditions; Germany did the same with a system of codetermination, or *Mitbestimmung*. These were not insignificant gestures, but they did not give most workers any real sense of greater participation, and they hardly dented actual experiences on the job.

The uproar of the 1960s, and particularly the massive sit-in strikes in France in 1968, aroused greater concern. There was also a wider sense that worker motivation was deteriorating, that some workers actually preferred taking modest welfare payments to working at all, even for a more generous wage. Productivity itself might require change. A number of companies, for example in Sweden, began to alternate workers in different jobs. While in the short run this might reduce efficiency, over time it reduced boredom and could produce a more flexible labor force, capable of greater teamwork and more stable over the longer term. Thinking of workers in terms of teams rather than individual semiskilled job slots could also increase both workers' social satisfaction and their sense of participating in certain levels of decision making about product lines and working conditions. A French company began to use the same worker groups both on repairs of equipment and on preventive maintenance, rather than dividing them into more specialized categories. Again the result was greater variety for the workers and the emergence of more useful planning: workers who fixed things had better information about how to prevent problems in the first place, and vice versa. Experiments of this sort continued later in the twentieth century, with new management ideas from business schools and the example of Japanese innovation.

The efforts did seem to reduce boredom and job changing in some instances. They did address common complaints about key aspects of modern work. But reforms of this sort were inconsistently introduced; they often did not last, as workers and their unions lost interest or as managers moved on to some newer human resources fad. The basic directions of modern work were not significantly modified. And managers themselves, as one French employer acknowledged, were still more likely to try to stifle worker discontent with a wage raise—an instrumentalist response—than through basic modifications of work systems.

Japanese innovation ran deeper, though its limitations became clear as well. During the 1980s, Japan's soaring international economic success and competitiveness called attention to many distinctive features in the nation's manufacturing and labor policies, including the close collaboration between business and government, a harmonious approach within management ranks that encouraged loyalty, a national tradition of saving, and a corporate willingness to take low profit margins and personal rewards in favor of investments in long-term growth—and a distinctive desire to inculcate worker attachment and devotion to duty by a special rewards system. Many of these characteristics, including the system of lifetime contracts for workers, reflected a national tradition of focus on the group, rather than individualism, derived in turn from adaptations of Confucian and feudal traditions. The results, certainly, contrasted with characteristic approaches in the West, and particularly the United States.

There is some disagreement among scholars as to whether a distinctive labor system operated in the early decades of industrialization in Japan. Some point to the vigorous artisanal tradition in which demonstrations of great skill were rewarded by considerable work security. Most factories, however, offered nothing very different from early industrial work requirements elsewhere, with the result that considerable labor protest emerged, along with high turnover rates. Only in the 1920s and 1930s were alternatives sketched for a few of the most valuable and skilled factory workers. Corporations extended to these workers a lifetime employment guarantee that had originally been reserved for upper management and public servants—a status known as *shokoin*. After World War II, with the economy in shambles and labor agitation rising, the system was extended to assure less turnover and more loyalty from the most valuable segments of the labor force. The system was also encouraged by labor laws.

Under the system, certain workers—never more than half the entire labor force, often less—would be assured of lifetime job security, though they had to be willing to be reassigned as the company might require. Retirement was set, of course, at age sixty. While workers received a payment upon retirement, this aspect of the system depended also on family support for anyone whose longevity extended much beyond retirement—a feature that would raise new issues as family ties weakened and the old-age contingent expanded around 2000. Careful interviewing, along with heavy reliance on school records, determined which workers would initially be offered lifetime guarantees.

This general system was modified further in the 1960s by the quality control movement, which had been devised by American management experts but gained much earlier and more extensive utilization in Japan. (Applications in the United States will be discussed in the next chapter.) In the quality movement, workers were encouraged to make suggestions about products and processes, with quality circles periodically joining small groups of workers and managers to discuss the enterprise. Larger numbers of workers, for example, were asked to contribute ideas about new automobile designs, rather than leaving the process to an isolated engineering department. A sense might develop that employers and workers were part of the same team, and shared dining and other joint activities promoted the same impression. As one manager put it, "One of our most important jobs is to make all of our employees willing to cooperate fully, and to make them want to continually improve themselves. To achieve this, it is necessary for us to provide all kinds of information equally to everyone.... Every employee has the right of access to 'all' computer information within the company."[7]

Finally, by the 1980s Japanese production facilities were increasingly emphasizing "just-in-time" production, reducing backlogs of goods in favor of quick response to new orders. This in turn required emphasis on multifaceted production teams, in which each member had a variety of skills that would promote rapid and flexible reactions.

The Japanese approach seemed to assure relatively high rates of productivity, low rates of strikes and agitation, and a willingness to accept wages lower than those in other industrial countries in the interest of job security. Most important, however, the approach—as least for the workers who had the lifetime assurances—seemed to produce more diligent work and fewer individual lapses and adjustments. Several studies reported that Japanese workers took less time off in sick leave or other types of absence than their counterparts elsewhere. They were less likely to use up all their vacation days, in some instances leaving 60 percent untouched, in favor of spending more time on the job. A 1980 study claimed that Japanese workers viewed it as sinful to miss work—though it also noted that attitudes were changing among the younger generations. Japanese workers were also more willing to put in overtime, even when no extra pay was involved. And of course there was much lower outright turnover, which probably also meant that more Japanese workers developed not only loyalty but also useful work experience and less need for retraining. Workers were more willing to accept changes that streamlined work processes, often proposing them on their own, because they knew that their employment would not suffer and that they would benefit if their company prospered. Above all, some experts argued that the Japanese system generated not only harder work but also more careful and creative effort, which showed up in superior manufactured products. As Japanese automobiles and electronics gained steady ground in world markets, often outcompeting American analogues even within the United States, the argument drew wide attention.

Certainly, Japanese progress attracted increasingly worried commentary within the United States. By the 1980s a number of experts were urging American companies to adopt more Japanese-like policies. The results, however, were mixed at best, particularly among factory workers. American managers showed little interest in offering greater job security, believing that significant swings in employment levels, depending on economic cycles, were more important than another inducement to devoted labor. Japan's experiments with more participation in discussing work systems and products helped generate a somewhat faddish surge of experiments, particularly by the 1990s, but mainly at the white-collar and middle management levels. Particular attention was devoted to the Total Quality Management movement, which built on the quality circles idea. Managers and employees were pushed into training sessions designed to promote better coordination, a willingness to listen to suggestions, and greater utilization of meetings aimed at improving work processes. While the movement aroused great enthusiasm, its impact on actual work patterns was often quite limited. Many participants found that basic decisions still emanated from top management; efforts at coordination could lead to additional efforts to stifle disruptive emotional reactions, continuing this aspect of work discipline that had long characterized the white-collar sector. Process change could lead to a faster work pace—and more dismissals for redundancy, for (to the anguish of many American experts) the notion of exchanging flexibility for security simply did not catch on in the American context.

By the later 1990s, furthermore, the sense of a special Japanese work advantage began to fade somewhat, reducing the power of Japanese example to inspire change elsewhere. Two factors were involved. First, the Japanese economy, though still a powerhouse at number two in the world, began to stagnate. The huge productivity advances now came from places like China, which were using no fancy motivation techniques, just rigorous discipline amid an abundant labor force. Growing economic difficulties caused rising unemployment, and some firms backed away from commitments to lifetime security—the Japanese model receded somewhat in Japan itself. Second, the Japanese began to take longer vacations, soon surpassing American levels, and in general to demonstrate a devotion to consumerism that tended to erode any sense of a massively superior work ethic. The Japanese episode remained revealing, certainly reflecting the relevance of different traditions to the modern work process, but it did not transform either global or American work patterns.

Both European and Japanese examples showed a willingness to take on some of the arguably distressing features of modern work, but they showed also the difficulty of effecting major change or of spreading reforms more widely. The attempts did create greater worker involvement, but they did not reverse concerns about pace and impersonality. The characteristics of modern work could be embellished, but they were hard to unseat.

## Alienation and Addiction

Most workers in the world, save those suffering from outright material misery amid unemployment or underemployment, probably made a complicated if largely implicit bargain with their work experience, particularly in the more modern settings. They looked to work as an instrument of a better life off the job; they found many aspects of work distasteful though not necessarily profoundly disorienting; but they also found ways to identify some personal meaning in their work.

Situations varied greatly, of course. White-collar and blue-collar workers differed in experiences and reactions alike. The unskilled, and the immigrant, had their own liabilities and perspectives. An interesting minority of professionals, intrigued by new knowledge and new technologies, became more work addicted than before. Workers in newly industrializing regions faced challenges of accommodation quite different from those faced by their counterparts in the more mature centers.

Instrumental approaches unquestionably gained ground. For many new workers in China, and the hosts of immigrants, work of almost any sort might seem endurable if it produced money to send back home and if one might hope that it would prove temporary. Individual Chinese workers, proud of their new cars or appliances, showed how quickly new consumer tastes could make demanding work more palatable. In the older industrial centers, rising prosperity since the 1950s rapidly advanced consumer standards, distracting from work concerns in measurable ways. Labor movements in places like Denmark found that workers' interest in attending meetings began to fade when there was work to do on the new motorbike (or the need to put in overtime hours to pay for the first car that would replace the motorbike).

Instrumentalism was greatly enhanced by the extensive gains in vacation time, particularly in Western Europe but, by the 1980s, also in Japan. Workers with five weeks off, as in Germany, had a considerable block of time to explore alternatives to work, and contemplating trips in advance or in retrospect could relieve work directly as well. These were not merely pauses to recharge work zeal, at least for the more affluent, but a basic part of life satisfaction. When retirement came earlier as well, the rebalancing of work advanced even further.

With all this, for a substantial minority, the drawbacks of modern work could not really be redressed by any instrumentalist package. Real alienation persisted. A worker in an American-owned clothing factory in Mexico put it this way:

> We spend ten hours a day in front of a sewing machine to make a man rich and we don't even know him. And the worst of it is that we continue doing it, some not even making the minimum wage, without complaining, asleep at the wheel, watching time go by, years in front of the sewing machine. I recognize the glares. I know how we protest on the inside, because we don't dare say anything to the bosses. We wait for the quitting bell to ring so we can hit the street, believing that it's all a bad dream, and that it's going to change. It's like we put these thoughts aside for a moment and go back to work, without doing anything more about it. At times we forget why the devil we're working, just waiting for a little bit of money so our kids can survive.
>
> You get used to it all, or at least we pretend to. At times we let ourselves be carried away by the noise, or by the radios we all carry. It helps us forget the fatigue and the back pain we all have from working in front of the sewing machine. The moment came when I just couldn't take it any more and I quit, knowing the money my husband makes, together with what our oldest daughter gives us, wasn't going to be enough.[8]

Alienation affected many factory workers in Europe as well, including those with generations of experience in the plant. Thirty-one percent of all blue-collar labor in one survey in the United Kingdom professed no pleasure of any kind in their work. An outright majority said that, if they had to do it all over again, they would choose something else. A majority also recurrently thought of quitting, and a majority also said they had previously had a job they liked better. Most hoped that their children would find something else to do. Obviously, these attitudes might not add up to the kind of despair expressed by the Mexican worker, but they suggested a good bit of pain.

The majority, however, managed to combine these recurrent thoughts with a more routine combination of specific complaints and a sense of reward. The complaints reflected key aspects of the modern work system; many workers could have identified similar concerns in manufacturing centers over a century before. But they also reflected a desire to have work go well, and with this some degree of personal commitment, at least if arrangements were improved. Factory workers wished they had greater variety on the job and that the pace would slacken—basic responses to the modern work pattern. Skilled craftsmen, who were more likely to complain about incompetent management, felt a greater intrinsic pleasure in their work—again, a historically conditioned response. Factory workers were more frankly instrumentalist, like the British machinist who said his wife "wanted income rather than an interesting job for me. I was pushed into the highest-paid work—which means [the automobile factory]." Money clearly drove an increasing number of work decisions, and while this prevented complete alienation, it forced daily compromises as well.[9]

This kind of mixed picture—a minority of work-driven workers, a minority of alienated, a majority with combined reactions—was not in fact new in the history of modern work. It might reflect new technologies, new anxieties about job loss—in the Mexican case the spread of factories to new areas and the growing involvement of women—but fundamentally it was the same pattern that had emerged from the earlier decades of modern work and industrialization. Here was the most important continuity of all, even amid a variety of vital changes in the specifics of the work experience.

# Notes

1. Henri Mendras, *The Vanishing Peasant* (Cambridge, MA: MIT Press, 1971).
2. Maureen Fan, "Rural Chinese Families Feel Migration's Strains: Holiday Underlines Toll of Distant Jobs," *Washington Post*, 18 February 2007, A20.
3. Robert Ayers, *Uncertain Futures* (New York: John Wiley & Sons, 1979).
4. Jeremy Rifkin, *The End of Work* (New York: Penguin, 2004), 227.
5. International Labor Office, ed., *Yearbook of Labour Statistics 2000*.
6. *International Journal of Human Resource Management* 18, no. 1 (January 2007).
7. Rifkin, *End of Work*, 98.
8. Norma Prieto, *Beautiful Flowers of the Maquiladora: Life Histories of Women Workers in Tijuana* (Austin: University of Texas Press, 1997).
9. John H. Goldthorpe et al., *The Affluent Worker: Political Attitudes and Behaviour* (Cambridge: Cambridge University Press, 1968), 22–34.

# Further Reading

## On Japanese Innovations

Tamotsu Sengoku, *Willing Workers: The Work Ethics in Japan, England and the United States* (Westport, CT: Middlebury University Press, 1985); Robert E. Cole, *Japanese Blue Collar: The Changing Tradition* (Berkeley: University of California Press, 1971); Ernest van Helvoort, *The Japanese Working Man: What Choice? What Reward?* (Vancouver: University of British Columbia Press, 1979).

## On Immigrant Workers

Frank D. Bean and Stephanie Bell-Rose, eds., *Immigration and Opportunity: Race, Ethnicity and Employment in the United States* (New York: Russell Sage, 1999). Stephen Castles and Godula Kosack, *Immigrant Workers and the Class Structure in Western Europe* (London: Oxford University Press, 1973); Michael Piore et al., eds., *Asian Migrants and European Labor Markets* (London: Routledge, 2005).

## On Technology

Marco Vivarelli, *The Economics of Technology and Employment* (Brookfield, VT: Edward Elgar, 1995); Jeremy Rifkin, *The End of Work: Technology, Jobs and Your Future* (New York: Putnam's, 1996).

## On the Expansion of Industrialization

Morris Bian, *The Making of the State Enterprise System in Modern China* (Cambridge, MA: Harvard University Press, 2005); Patricia Wilson, *Exports and Local Development in Mexico's New Maquiladoras* (Austin: University of Texas Press, 1992).

## On Retirement

Tony Maltby et al., eds., *Ageing and the Transition to Retirement: A Comparative Analysis of European Welfare States* (London: Ashgate, 2004).

On alienation and instrumentalism: John Goldthorpe et al., *The Affluent Worker: Industrial Attitudes and Behaviour* (Cambridge: Cambridge University Press, 1968).

## On European Labor Reforms and Their Limits

Joseph Melling and Alan McKinlay, eds., *Management, Labour and Industrial Politics in Modern Europe* (Cheltenham, UK: Edward Elgar, 1996); Steve Jefferys, Frederik Beyer, and Christer Thornqvist, eds., *European Working Lives: Continuities and Change in Management and Industrial Relations in France, Scandinavia and the UK* (Cheltenham, UK: Edward Elgar, 2001).

## On Women's Work

Jeanne Gregory, Rosemary Sales, and Ariane Hegewisch, eds., *Women, Work and Inequality* (London: Macmillan, 1999); Marcus Rebick, *The Japanese Employment System* (Oxford: Oxford University Press, 2005); Hilda Kahne and Janet Giele, eds., *Women's Work and Women's Lives: The Continuing Struggle Worldwide* (Boulder, CO: Westview, 1992). Hans-Peter Blossfeld and Sonja Drobnic, *Careers of Couples in Contemporary Societies: From Male Breadwinner to Dual-Earner Families* (Oxford: Oxford University Press, 2001).

# CHAPTER 8

# A Workaholic Nation?
# The Past Half Century

A merican work patterns were in some ways even less distinctive in the later twentieth century than they had been during industrialization. This was not surprising: opportunities for special innovations probably declined as the nation's modern economy matured. Most obviously, the leadership American managers had established through efficiency engineering was not fully repeated after 1945. American firms continued to emphasize productivity, but they offered no fundamental distinctiveness, compared for example to the more self-consciously experimental efforts of the Japanese. U.S. emphasis on personnel research did remain strong, and the nation helped usher in a number of management fads that had some relationship to work experience; but many key fads often basically maintained earlier themes, for example, in the emphasis on emotional control on the job. A high valuation of technology certainly persisted, and this could have major impact on working conditions. Even here, however, the nation had to share leadership. Computerization of office work was featured prominently in the United States, but use of robots lagged behind places like Japan and France.

Real changes, then, often largely involved American participation in trends that were more widely shared among many industrial countries. For instance, the United States shifted increasingly to a service economy, shrinking the blue-collar workforce in favor of occupational sectors like health care, the leisure industry, and so on. But these changes, though extremely significant, largely mirrored patterns visible in Britain, Japan, and elsewhere. American use of automated equipment paralleled innovations in other mature industrial societies. In fact during the past fifty years as a whole, American productivity gains lagged behind several other regions; only in the 1990s, perhaps briefly, did the nation set the global standard in computerization and development of the Internet. Use of immigrant workers was also important, and again there was change involved particularly with growing reliance on an unskilled but hardworking Latino contingent. But Western Europe and areas like the Arab Gulf states relied almost equally on immigrant labor, with south Asians, Africans, and people from the Caribbean taking roles similar to those of Latinos in the United States. Certainly, the United States was powerfully affected by growing competition from newer industrial centers like China. But here, too, Western Europe and Japan faced very similar challenges, which encouraged a further reduction of factory labor, now provided more cheaply elsewhere, in favor of other kinds of work, particularly in the service sector. By the twenty-first century, as a result, the export of high-tech and leisure products (like aircraft, music, videos, and electronic games) became a leading sector in the United States, in exchange for cheaper factory goods produced abroad; but the same was true for Japan and the European Union.

Two areas of distinctiveness did shine through, though they may have been more modest than their earlier-industrial counterparts. First, though this was a partially negative feature, American work highlighted a somewhat greater conservatism than was visible elsewhere. Other advanced industrial countries seemed to be changing more rapidly, pushing out in somewhat newer directions. The kinds of halting experiments in modifying factory labor in favor of greater variety and worker participation won a smaller audience in the United States than in places like Sweden and Japan. American managers—and workers implicitly went along with this—seemed more wedded to older factory methods that had, among other things, produced considerable specialization and regimentation. Of course they modified assembly-line procedures with more automated equipment, and this could be a huge change for the workers involved. But they showed less interest in other kinds of work reforms, including, of course, any significant increase in vacation time. Worker adjustments, as a result, had to focus more on off-the-job rewards than on new qualities within work itself. It was no surprise, then, that American commitment to instrumentalism also ran high, as the nation seemed even more wedded to abundant consumerism than did Western Europe or Japan—which meant that more American workers remained committed to extensive time on the job to pay for consumer items (even as consumer debt mounted to unusual levels) than was true elsewhere. Whether American consumerism simply followed its own dynamic, fueled by particularly clever advertising and unusual interest in training children to be consumers, or whether it also reflected the need to compensate for limitations of the job, can obviously be debated. But work constraints and the widespread intolerance for systematic work grievances (by the general public as well as managers) probably did play a role. The persistence of largely instrumentalist responses offers another suggestion that it was slightly harder to reconsider industrial patterns in the United States than in other advanced industrial regions.

Along with greater conservatism, and in part explaining it, were the unmistakable signs of the particular national commitment to a modern work ethic. Americans did periodically worry that other people in other countries might be working harder. This was a strong theme in the 1980s, when Japanese competition loomed particularly large. This kind of concern also applied to periodic laments that other nations' children were surpassing Americans in school, which in turn prompted pleas that the school year be lengthened to the average in other industrial nations, though in fact little was done as the nation, in this respect, confirmed its earlier anxiety about the need to protect children from too much effort. In fact, while it is not possible to argue that Americans worked harder than other people in advanced industrial societies, given problems of data if nothing else, it is certainly clear that many people in the United States thought about work slightly differently from their counterparts elsewhere. Thus, the length of American vacations remained static, in contrast to patterns in Europe and Japan. Americans took less time off and bragged more about working long hours. American managers were unusually resistant to the idea of cutting the workweek in response to technological change, in contrast to their counterparts in Europe and Japan. Americans uniquely reconsidered retirement at the end of the twentieth century, probably foreshadowing patterns that would emerge later elsewhere, because the dominant national work ethic clashed with the notion that old people should be required to bow out. American feminism reemerged with a special emphasis on work, so though American women shared patterns with their European and Japanese sisters, they argued about work more fiercely.

Thus a society that on the surface seemed addicted to leisure—and the idea of a national leisure ethic predictably emerged in the 1950s—actually worked extremely hard and often thought of leisure in terms of mindless escapism more than an active engagement that could have taken energies away from the job. Even American trade unionism, declining earlier and more substantially than its European counterpart, suggested a particularly pronounced inability to cope with issues of work quality, participating in far fewer experiments to modify the workplace, however modestly, than did unions in postwar Germany or France. On a related note, bitter complaints about work, of the sort evident within a sizable minority of European workers, were simply less present, or harder to voice, in the United States. Finally, a brief national discussion of what got dubbed "workaholic" behavior ended so inconclusively that it was clear that the nation lacked the capacity really to reassess middle-class values in this area. In rhetoric and in many aspects of behavior, the equation of work with special virtue persisted in the national consciousness.

Change in American work, then, involved participation in a host of common trends, from technology to immigration, leavened by a combined conservatism and delight in the work ethic, which continued to make many Americans stand just a bit apart from some wider global trends.

## Limitations on Reforms

The American context for discussions about changes in work systems was different from that of Europe or Japan after World War II. No decisive political change occurred comparable to the new influence of socialist and labor movements in Europe. The American trade union movement remained active, but it reached a peak of membership in the late 1950s and then began to decline. It was unable to attract sufficient numbers of service workers or women workers to keep pace with broader changes in the labor force. Labor movements and strikes continued to have some impact on work experiences, but they could not generate fundamental change. Even at the partially cosmetic level, nothing in the United States rivaled the gestures toward participation in decision making that emerged in places like France and Germany. And workers themselves, even when unionized, disagreed on what kinds of changes were desirable.

A graphic example of the American situation emerged in the later 1960s, a time of protest in the United States as elsewhere. A number of strikes broke out, particularly in automobile factories, involving younger workers who were openly discontent with the quality of their jobs. A particularly bitter conflict erupted in Lordstown, Ohio, as workers protested their lack of control over their daily job conditions and the routine quality of their work. In response, management tried to experiment along lines more common in Europe, assembling worker teams that could discuss work assignments and could trade off jobs in the interest of greater variety and motivation. But the effort did not last long, partly because American managers were unusually hesitant to tamper with the basic parameters of modern work and partly because workers themselves were divided. Some worried that setting aside time for discussion and the challenge of learning more than one job would reduce short-term productivity and so affect pay. And it was more important, for this group, to see jobs as a source of income than to worry about making them more interesting. Without question, innovations in basic work organization were both less common and less extensive in the United States than elsewhere. In many cases, the introduction of Japanese companies—particularly in the auto industry, where major manufacturers set up operations in North America during the 1980s—had greater impact on the structure of work than American initiatives had. To be sure, one industry leader, General Motors, subsequently imitated the Japanese example in setting up a more team-oriented, participatory Saturn plant, but this remained an exception to American industry standards.

There was extensive discussion of innovation, and some real initiatives, at the more strictly managerial level. Here American personnel leaders continued to play a very active role. A whole series of managerial initiatives developed in the United States from the 1950s onward; most of them were American originals, and many of them gained considerable international influence over time. Partly because of the huge importance of business schools, and playing off the expanding profession of business consulting, American management experts had a unique opportunity to spin out theories designed to improve effectiveness. And while a few of the theories were intended to have wider impact on the workforce, the tendency to concentrate primarily within management circles confirmed business conservatism when it came to work settings more generally. Experimentation was fine in the management camp, less acceptable when it spilled beyond these boundaries. And the failure of many of the initiatives after an initial period of enthusiasm confirmed the limitations on the American commitment to innovation even within management ranks. Overall, in other words, unquestionable national inventiveness in management designs from the 1950s onward had relatively modest impact on the modern work experience, partly by intention, partly because a number of promising fads were stillborn.

Some strategies that gained at least brief notice largely confirmed standard practices on work discipline. In the 1950s an MIT professor, Douglas McGregor, introduced Theory X and Theory Y. This divided workers into the self-motivated and those who required direction. Though in principle this might have allowed looser regulation of the first group, in fact most managers assumed the vast majority of workers fell into the second camp so that, if anything, control procedures needed to be tightened. Other approaches, though significant, had little bearing on work. Increasing quantitative sophistication allowed new emphasis on appropriate strategic planning in corporations; while this could affect hiring plans, it had scant impact in the workplace directly. Interest in the qualities of leadership was another recurrent fad that attracted managerial attention but with little spillover for ordinary workers. In the 1960s T-groups surfaced. These groups encouraged managerial teams to meet together to improve their emotional interaction through role-playing and group therapy—again, an interesting notion but without wide impact.

It was in the 1970s that American theories about quality circles began to draw attention, but the domestic audience was limited until Japanese success in using work teams forced some recognition. More important in the United States, from the later 1980s into the following decade, was a larger approach called Total Quality Management, or TQM. This fad, stressing persistent process improvement, also called for more interaction between employees and managers and group discussion of goals and procedures. The concept was to use a wide range of ideas and in the process involve some ordinary workers in decision making, cementing their loyalty and improving their motivation as well. Meetings were to be recast to facilitate the involvement of all parties regardless of rank. At the same time, however, TQM also called for new attention to emotional control on the job—employees at all levels were reminded that anger was never a constructive emotion at work—and for greater sensitivity as well to customer demands. TQM was in this sense double-edged: it involved new constraints as well as greater opportunities for expression, confirming some of the demanding features of white-collar and lower-managerial work.

In point of fact, other aspects of TQM in practice limited its impact, positive or negative, in the workplace. Very few TQM efforts actually spilled beyond middle management. Employees might be asked to respond to surveys, but most realized that nothing would ever change enough for them really to participate in policy discussions, so they largely ignored the questionnaires. Top management might sponsor TQM, but many executives were too authoritarian to yield much ground to group decisions. Middle managers might be retrained, and there was certainly some enthusiasm for the implications of empowerment. But few TQM campaigns lasted more than two or three years, and elements that survived had more to do with benchmarking—carefully studying competitors' practices—or process improvement than with changes in worker involvement.

Management fads, in sum, helped sustain an American reputation for managerial leadership and innovation. They did encourage ongoing attention to greater emotional restraint on the job, so that lower managers, such as foremen, would treat their workers with greater courtesy. Here was a trend with some important implications for job quality. There is every indication that, while bosses might still be resented, petty bickering diminished, even as foremen complained about a loss of authority and a new need to listen to workers vent grievances. This aside, however, American managers probed the workplace only cautiously, often superficially, reserving more attention to relationships within their own ranks. Again, the basic modern model of work was rarely reconsidered in the contemporary American context.[1]

Absence of any major interest in reform—a partial contrast with efforts in Europe and particularly Japan—was the negative side of considerable contentment with established notions of work discipline. It helps explain what did not happen. But there was a positive side as well, which led to some interesting initiatives, particularly in terms of the composition of the contemporary workforce. Large numbers of Americans continued to believe that hard work should be honored, and they expressed this value both in public discussion and in new arguments about including additional categories of people in the modern work experience.

## The Persistence of the Work Ethic

Substantial ongoing support for a strong work ethic showed in many aspects of American life and continued to shape some of the most interesting comparative features of the national experience. To be sure, leisure continued to gain ground, and in the 1950s a perceptive sociologist even wrote of the emergence of a "leisure ethic" that might seem to rival work.[2] Interestingly, personnel forms and interviews for jobs increasingly asked about recreational activities, implying that a well-rounded person needed some hobbies to show energy, balance, and a healthy outlook; as before in American society, leisure continued to be linked to the demands of work.

But work itself continued to command respect and attention. This showed in a variety of specific ways, from clear signs of a work-addicted minority to interesting innovations in retirement policy. However, ordinary people did not seem to move as far as some of the leaders suggested: actual work behavior was less distinctive, where workers had some influence, than policies and discussions were. Here was a crucial dilemma to which we must return in assessing the overall flavor of American work life in the past half century.

## The Workaholic Debate

In the wake of the revival of feminism in the 1960s, a number of observers began to question standard male behavior in the United States. Both feminist leaders and critics of conventional masculinity, who sometimes called themselves male liberationists, argued that men had fallen into behaviors that were unfair to women and families and bad for men themselves. Excessive work sat at the core of the problem. By the 1970s the term "workaholic" emerged, to define men so obsessed with work that they lost all sense of proportion and became essentially as uncontrolled, and as self-damaging, as those addicted to alcohol or drugs.

Two related arguments were involved here. In the first place, men who lived only to work were unfair to women and families. They put women who wanted to rise at work in a difficult competitive position, because it was harder for them to devote the long hours, given their usual family responsibilities. They slighted women as well precisely in forcing wives and mothers to spend a disproportionate amount of time on the family because the workaholic male, though he might take enough time to father a child, simply refused to ease up sufficiently to take on domestic duties.

But second—and this was the more revealing aspect—workaholic males injured themselves. Their hard work took its toll on health, both physical and psychological. It robbed men of the true pleasures of life, which must involve family and leisure as well as work. For their own sake, as well as women's, men must be persuaded to ease up, and the workaholic label was designed to make them see the error of their ways. One liberationist put it succinctly, referring to work-addicted men as "the male machine."

By the early 1980s the male-liberationist critique was joined by a good bit of popularized medical commentary, particularly around the drawbacks of what was called the "type A" personality—hard-driving, competitive, always striving for success, and prone to health problems, particularly heart attacks and strokes. Again, the lesson seemed clear: for your own sake, men, ease up on work.

Undoubtedly, arguments of this sort influenced some men, at least raising some doubts about their own career zeal. Worries about heart attacks were very real among men,[3] and the notion that hard work caused damaging stress won wide attention.

It was revealing, of course, that these critiques of male work behavior advanced particularly in the United States, for they suggested the continuing hold of the older work-is-everything approach. There was less need for commentary elsewhere, because work addiction was less common, or at least less visible, and antidotes like long vacations were more in evidence.

More generally, for a time in the 1960s and 1970s, many Americans discussed the idea of a new breed of worker, no longer motivated by the work ethic and eager to define jobs in terms of personal satisfaction. A 1972 *Time* magazine article, "Is the Work Ethic Going Out Of Style?" captured the mood. Employers, industrial psychologists, and even some union leaders, expressing older work values, tended to bemoan the new worker, who seemed unreliable, self-centered, and undisciplined. Even older workers complained (though with sneaking admiration: "These kids ... don't even know how to take the crap we took."). Many blamed permissive child rearing for this change, and indeed, as we have seen, the American approach to childhood did suggest some difficult connections with the adult work experience. There were some undeniable complexities and tensions in the modern American approach to work.

The basic analysis, though interesting, was flawed. In the first place, most workers had never internalized the middle-class work ethic. Job changing and absenteeism might have been troubling, but they were not new in the industrial world. High wages may have made it easier for some workers to express their ambivalence about work—one automobile factory hand, when asked why he came to work only four days a week, responded that it was because he could not live on what he was paid for three days—but the sentiments were not really new. The notion of a new drive for personal pleasure on the job was extremely attractive, but it proved to be rather fleeting. As we have seen, a brief burst of protest in the period suggested new work goals, but the protest quickly receded in favor of heightened instrumentalism. This brief moment of reconsideration did not lead to durable results in the United States. The quick criticisms of younger workers' carelessness and ingratitude confirmed how older Americans—even workers—thought in work-ethic terms, and this may have been the most consistent result of the episode. Younger workers may have chafed a bit, but they failed to generate durable alternatives.[4]

It was particularly revealing that the various critiques of hard work really did not win out and began in fact to decline by the 1990s. Feminists, for example, either joined in work zeal or adopted a deliberately different agenda; whichever the choice, the popularity of bashing excessive work declined notably. Most men, of course, had never been work addicts, so the liberationist arguments did not appeal to them greatly in the first place. If they worked too hard, it was to maintain a standard of living, not because of an unquenchable zeal. Addicts there were, of course, but they were not persuaded of the error of their ways, because the obsession was so consuming and, for many, the apparent rewards so great. As we have seen, the popularity of long hours and proud claims of working to exhaustion continued to describe an important American minority well into the twenty-first century. The contemporary version of the work ethic defeated its critics. The term "workaholic" either dropped away or became a backhanded form of praise. Related arguments faded as well. It turned out that hard work and a type-A personality were not necessarily damaging to health. Work zealots had lower rates of heart attack than other workers whose stress came, not from work itself, but from a lack of control and self-expression on the job. Zeal itself, to the extent it propelled people to the very top, could actually be a good thing in terms of health. So the debate, briefly confronting the persistent American work ethic directly, virtually disappeared. Excessive work habits, if they constituted a form of insanity, represented a madness that American society cherished.[5]

## Feminism and Work

A second link between an ongoing, somewhat distinctive valuation of work and recent American trends involved feminism. As noted, some feminist leaders were quick to urge revision of excesses in the work ethic, for several reasons. But American feminism, blossoming again in the 1960s, itself reflected a recognition that work had some special meaning in the national context to which women, seeking fairer treatment, needed to connect. Actual trends in women's work—the reentry of married women into the formal labor force, first in the working class in the 1950s, then in the middle class in the following decade—were not too different from developments in Europe and, later, Japan, and the basic causes may have been similar as well. But even at the behavioral level, the process was a bit more demanding in the United States than in other industrial societies, if only because birthrates were higher during the baby boom, so working mothers had more responsibilities to juggle. And at the level of rhetoric, the different valuation of work stood out even more strongly.

Changes in work behavior were striking and fundamental. Women's involvement in the labor force increased 19 percent during the 1950s, so that by 1960 35 percent of all American women were employed at least part-time. Almost a third of these were married, despite ongoing beliefs that women with families should not work outside the home; work commitments were outstripping attitudes. During the 1960s, the pattern continued, with a 50 percent increase in the number of working women with children: in 1960 19 percent of all women with children under six worked, and by 1970 the figure had risen to 28 percent. Some employers continued to refuse to hire such women, and there were many public claims that women were simply working on a "whim," that their commitment to the labor force was temporary. In fact, this was a durable trend; women constituted two-thirds of all new employees, particularly in the service sector, large segments of which became almost entirely female.

These developments were extremely significant, constituting a huge break in American women's history and the history of work alike. As we have seen, however, the same trends were taking shape in Western Europe in the same period, and for essentially the same reasons. Only the higher rates of divorce in the United States, and the resultant abundance of single women absolutely dependent on a job (in 1974, 6.7 million employed women were widowed, divorced, or separated), created an unusual twist. Basic causes, furthermore, were not primarily cultural but rooted in a desire for earnings that would permit a higher standard of living or (an acute factor in the American case) some protection in case of divorce. What was distinctively American was less the shifts in behavior or their motivations and more the ways in which these shifts were discussed, particularly with regard to the middle class.

The first salvo in contemporary American feminism was Betty Friedan's bombshell work, *The Feminine Mystique,* published in 1963. In marked contrast to earlier American feminism, which had a larger political and social focus, and in contrast as well to the more broadly philosophical range of the French intellectual Simone de Beauvoir's *Second Sex* (which considerably influenced Friedan), Friedan's message focused strongly on the need to get women out of the home and into the workplace. Of course the book featured other elements, but the work theme was central, and it surely reflected the continued valuation of work in American society more generally, now translated into a feminist imperative.

Friedan offered two basic, interrelated arguments about shifting middle-class housewives into formal employment. First, she loudly lamented the boredom and lack of status associated with housework; this was simply no undertaking for an educated, alert woman, who would be much more satisfied with a job outside the home. Second, she equally lamented the powerlessness that lack of formal work entailed. Women could not be taken seriously, in politics or society more generally, when they lacked the virtues, and the salaries, associated with formal employment. Both arguments revolved around elements of the work ethic: work is interesting, and its virtues bring power—and women must respond. Friedan's book did not cause the new entry of women into the labor force; the trends had already begun, and they often had more to do with consumer needs than with self-realization. In adding to the trends, however, Friedan's ideas helped create a powerful female constituency for what was, in essence, the old work ethic in a new guise. Work provided meaning and power, and women must assert their work commitments with genuine zeal.

Friedan's work focus was quite explicit throughout her widely popular books. The problem for contemporary women was too little challenge: "As she made the beds, shopped for groceries, matched slipcover material, ate peanut butter sandwiches with her children, chauffeured Cub Scouts and Brownies, lay beside her husband at night—the suburban wife was afraid to ask even of herself the silent question—'Is this all?'" "The only way for a woman, as for a man, to find herself, to know herself as a person, is by creative work of her own." This meant a job, though of course a job up to her capacities, a job that would be taken seriously by herself and others. Formal work was a necessity.[6]

It was thus not surprising that many American feminists, both leadership and rank-and-file, continued to pursue job-related issues, and though feminists in other countries did the same, the work focus in the United States continued to be particularly strong. At the same time, the fierce commitment of many American feminists to a new work identity for women complicated the response to the many real issues that arose, in the United States as elsewhere, as growing numbers of women reentered the labor force.

Problems became evident quite early. As in other industrial societies, women were concentrated in a fairly narrow range of jobs, particularly in the service sector. Feminists easily identified this issue and took pride in calling attention to cases where individual women moved into "male" jobs such as coal mining. But while there was a modest increase in the number of women in factory jobs overall, it was not a major trend. Occupational limitations for women showed up in differential wages, despite passage of the Equal Pay Act of 1963. For a time, the rapid entry of women actually worsened the female-male wage ratio, dropping it to 57 percent; by the 1990s the ratio had improved to a historic high of over 70 percent, but obviously inequalities persisted. Women also found themselves blocked, sometimes by deliberate management policy, from equal access to promotions. American civil rights law, as it developed from the 1960s onward, facilitated the use of lawsuits to protest these inequalities, but an informal "glass ceiling" undoubtedly remained. New work commitments encouraged growing numbers of women to enter professions such as law and medicine, but male-female distinctions persisted.

Concentration in service occupations also subjected women to particular pressures to conform to personality expectations. This had long been a feature of service work, where pleasing bosses and customers was very important, but it could easily take on gendered overtones. Thus in the 1960s American Airlines sought flight attendants (then simply called stewardesses) among "wholesome all-American girl types—single, in excellent health, attractive, and possess[ing] considerable personal charm." Discrimination lawsuits gradually eroded some of these sexist qualifications. It became illegal, for example, to fire flight attendants because of age or marriage (in contrast to societies like China, which retained older gender ideals on airlines), but the problem did not entirely disappear. Growing concern as well about sexual harassment on the job added to women's issues at work.[7]

Another set of problems proved at least as intractable, as ordinary women tried to combine work with family obligations. As in Europe, many new women workers had to cope with their own guilt about being bad wives and mothers as they focused less attention on the household, more on the job. Simply finding enough time could prove a nightmare. Husbands and fathers stepped up their household duties a little bit, but children's work around the American home actually declined, with the result that women saw little relief. Day care was a particular challenge in the United States. Feminists did not pay much attention to the issue: given their work-ethic focus, the family complexities faced by many women workers might draw little sympathy. Betty Friedan herself, in a 1982 book called the *Second Stage*, admitted that she and her colleagues had overdone the emphasis on the primacy of work identities and had neglected family issues, in what she termed "our extreme reaction to the wife-mother role." But American conservatism also discouraged attention to the issue, as many leaders opposed new patterns of women's work in favor of a return to family. Richard Nixon, for example, vetoed a measure to increase day-care facilities in 1971, on grounds of the need to "cement the family in its rightful position as the keystone of our civilization."[8] Not only did day care lag, compared to provisions in most other industrial societies, but also job protection for new mothers remained limited. In contrast to Sweden, where the government insisted on a year's leave for new parents (mainly mothers), American practice often offered only a few weeks.

A combination of a strong work emphasis—the initial feminist contribution, picked up by many women workers—and conservative family values exacerbated, for American women, dilemmas inherent in the new work roles in any society. Women responded variously, particularly as feminist enthusiasm began to cool by the 1980s. Some, as the slogan went, tried to "have it all," blending work zeal with family, though often amid considerable tension. Reductions in the birthrate provided another option, though change was more modest in the United States than in Europe or East Asia. Far more women than men worked part-time or quit work altogether for a family-building period, as in other industrial societies. By the 1990s some women were also discussing a special "mommy track," even at the managerial and professional levels, to permit highly educated women to contribute at the workplace but without the extreme work addiction seemingly essential to full career success.

The change in the relationship between American women and work paralleled developments elsewhere. Issues and compromises were broadly similar as well. Distinctive family values complicated the national picture, however, both in policy and in personal tensions. But the special national commitment to the work ethic factored in as well, reducing feminist attention to the dilemmas of the work-family relationship and putting extra pressure on some women to demonstrate that they could measure up to intense work demands.

## Retirement

In dealing with the spread of retirement during the first periods of industrialization, though after the very earliest decades, we noted that the phenomenon began to generate some concern in the United States. While business and labor leaders largely backed mandatory retirement by the middle of the twentieth century, a growing group of gerontological experts weren't so sure. By the 1950s a number of studies appeared that cast doubt on the beneficence of retirement for the elderly themselves. The argument was simple: in a society where prestige was tied to work, and in which many old people additionally faced unexpected income problems once they lost employment, forced removal from jobs might well be a bad thing. Lack of work risked damage to dignity and voice alike, and gerontologists began to urge that the modern policy be revisited, while of course protecting the interests of those who were explicitly disabled. Early studies of mass retirement, also from the 1950s, confirmed these impressions. Many old people talked of being confused and isolated once they quit work, and a widespread impression developed—although it was not supported by firm data—that retirement often led to death, precisely because of disorientation, separation from colleagues, and sometimes reduction in living standards as well.

This was the context in which new old-age activist groups, using civil rights arguments from the 1960s, began to argue that the elderly deserved to remain on the job if they so chose, as a matter of simple justice. More working elderly would have the dignity and economic clout to insist on proper social respect; loss of work should not add to the other problems of later age in a society that seemed endlessly fascinated with youth. The Gray Panthers, in particular, conceived of an active, and activist, old age in which work could play a central role. Their arguments were bolstered by the late 1970s by growing concerns that the social security system might run into funding problems if the rising number of the elderly were pushed into uniform retirement; more work, by reducing the burdens, could salvage this key welfare program. All of this contrasted vividly with trends in Western Europe and Japan, where discussion during the same period focused on more retirement, not less, to relieve unemployment The American work ethic, because of its association between jobs and moral worth. facilitated an emphasis on reform that went against the global grain.

By the late 1970s, retirement policies began to be revisited, particularly in rulings and legislation that overturned mandatory requirements. Only a few categories of workers—particularly, highly paid corporate executives—could now be forced to retire. All other people should be able to work on if they so chose. Adding to this momentum, a major social security compromise in 1983 moved the full-benefit age (gradually) from age sixty-five to age sixty-seven. At the level of policy, then, the American course began to display clear innovation, based, however, on much older ideas about the validity of work. And individuals in what was now called the "senior citizen" group did begin to work longer, either by remaining in the jobs that they had attained in middle age or by opting for some new line of work. Professional people, particularly, often held on to work as their badge of identity. Many who officially retired, studies showed, did best when they maintained a clear work routine, even when the target was hobbies or volunteerism.

With all this, however, the actual pattern of retirement changed much less than advocates had predicted. As in other industrial societies, many Americans insisted on retirement, even at the expense of full benefits, and they often wanted to retire well before they reached the conventional age. Blue-collar workers, in particular, hoped to retire by their early to mid-fifties, and white-collar workers were only slightly less eager. Hopes could not always be fulfilled, but by the late 1970s workers at companies like General Motors were actually retiring, on average, by the age of fifty-eight.

The gap between rhetoric and reality was fascinating. Advocates, usually of middle-class background, where the work ethic maintained its firmest hold (the Gray Panthers were led by former teachers), saw work as a vital solution for old-age problems, both personal and political. But actual workers, particularly in the lower reaches of the middle class, saw things differently—and very similarly to their counterparts in Germany or France or Japan. For them, it was vital to have a period of life free from normal work. Thinking about retirement, even before achieving it, could help carry people through years of job frustration, and the work ethic in this situation was not really relevant.[9]

In the long run, of course, the reforms introduced in the United States may prove prescient. More elderly in retirement means more social cost, and the trends here are clear as the elderly are the most rapidly growing segment in industrial populations and as baby boomers near sixty-five. Longer life involves personal as well as social expenses, and it is accompanied by improving health, at least for the younger old-age groups. Many societies may face the need to challenge retirement behavior, and the American lead in attacking the justice of mandatory retirement opens the way to revised behavior. But change will be difficult, precisely because so many people have become accustomed to the promise of retirement as one of the ways modern work life can be endured. If studies in the 1950s suggested adjustment difficulties, those by the 1970s showed that most retired people relished their lot, even when their living standards had deteriorated a bit compared to their working years. Again, blue-collar workers were most insistent that they had made a good choice, while upper-middle-class people were most likely to have worklike activities as part of a successful adjustment. But the gerontologists' nightmare that the end of work would produce mass confusion was not borne out by reality. Americans believed the work ethic to an extent; it shaped some of their attitudes to their jobs, but it was not powerful enough to make most people want to keep working indefinitely.

Despite national policy innovations, the preference of most Americans for early retirement—like their counterparts in other industrial societies—raised an obvious question: was optional retirement a quest for new experiences or a reaction to the unpleasantness of modern work? While a bit of both might apply, the escape factor predominated. Many sought to shorten the span of life subjected to the job.

## American Work Adjustments: Accommodations and Addictions

Few signs of massive alienation surfaced in the United States around the turn of the twenty-first century. A popular song in 1977 (composed by "Johnny Paycheck") titled "Take This Job and Shove It" vented some frustration, but more at a nasty boss than at the quality of modern work more generally. Alienation undoubtedly still existed, either with work or with the gap between work and expectations of success and satisfaction (the kind of white-collar alienation discussed earlier), but given the American value system, it was hard to articulate publicly. Insistence on early retirement was about as close as many people could come to expressing these feelings, and obviously a number of factors, not necessarily real alienation at all, entered into this preference.

As a result, it is difficult to characterize complex American attitudes toward work, and particularly hard to identify distinctive features. We know that some national behaviors were unusual—for example, taking less vacation time than workers in other industrial societies—but it is less clear what values supported these behaviors. Work satisfaction may have been no greater in the United States than elsewhere, but high public esteem for the work ethic inhibited certain kinds of expression—except on the positive side, when Americans proudly paraded their work addictions.

Thus, far fewer Americans than Europeans talked about hating their work or finding no meaning in it. Fewer said that they wished that they had chosen a different line of work entirely. Fewer, as we have seen, took all the time off to which they were entitled, and there was simply no huge movement to demand systematic increases in vacation allocations. The vast majority of Americans—85 percent or more—labeled themselves middle class (in contrast to a proud working-class identity in Europe). While this reflected a sense of shared consumer standards, it also mirrored a wide belief that work should be valued, that it was a personal responsibility to commit to the job to at least some degree. The average American worker claimed to like the job either in part or quite well—in contrast to France, where a full 31 percent might dissent. Some improvements in bosses' courtesy may have added to the strength of a positive work ethic. Americans did not differ entirely from other people in industrial societies—a majority in Europe, too, found some meaning in work—but they tended to shave off the negative extreme, at least in public representations, as when pollsters asked generic questions about satisfaction.

The work-addicted extreme, on the other hand, remained particularly visible in the United States. An interview in the mid-1970s captured the work zealot perfectly. A young executive described how he usually left his job at around one in the morning and then went home and made notes to remember for the next day; he claimed to average three to four hours' sleep a night. He complained about welfare recipients and "young people" who did not know how to work properly, but he had no uncertainty about his own life. He normally worked on weekends as well, though occasionally he did something with his wife. He never planned to retire. He regularly took medicine for stomach troubles. He loved to outstrip competitors: "There's a lot of satisfaction in showing up people who thought you'd never amount to anything." As another interviewee put it: "I don't work to live, I live to work.... Working is more fun than fun." The American work addict was not necessarily unique, but his willingness to articulate his values was truly distinctive, a sign of the supportive culture that easily survived the brief attack on workaholism. And while work addiction ran strongest among some executives and professionals, it could crop up in the skilled crafts as well, as with a stonemason who proudly proclaimed that "stone is my life," and who would wake up at night with masonry designs he simply had to put on paper. He remembered, and regretted, every crooked stone he'd ever laid, and he regularly passed houses he had built, recalling the skill he had applied—"That's the work of my hands."[10]

The typical stance, of course, was more nuanced and included individual expressions of what might reasonably be taken as signs of alienation. Some housewives, for example, explicitly argued that keeping house gave them fulfillment and a sense of personal control they could not find in formal jobs. From the 1960s onward, a few professionals dropped out of what was often called the "rat race" outright, moving to the countryside and taking up a more traditional rural or artisanal work pace. But most people mixed some definite grievances—a sense that the job could easily be more rewarding—with an ongoing sense of pride and commitment.

Studs Terkel, an experienced Chicago journalist, caught the American everyman (and everywoman) in his 1970s interviews. A bus driver noted how bad he felt when a supervisor criticized him for running late, for he had pride in the work; but he also admitted he rarely thought about his job and felt, as he went to work, "like a machine, that's about the only way I can feel." A spot welder blasted his foremen for refusing to pay attention to his suggestions about improving equipment; it was hard to feel good about a job when the supervisors did not care; too much complaining and one would be labeled a troublemaker. "So you just go about your work. You have to have pride. So you throw it off to something else. And that's my stamp collection." Other workers complained openly of boredom after a few years on the job, or noted that they survived only because they could get off work in time to "have a lot of the day left." Several women commented that they preferred staying home because they could determine their own pace: they used the word "hectic" frequently in describing their formal work experiences. In contrast, an ironworker loved to look down on the world from his construction heights: "It's a challenge up there, and the work's hardly ever routine.... I'm a good man, and everybody on the job knows it." A former housewife, working-class, "loves" to go to work "because it gets me away from home." She had grown tired of just keeping house, though she also did not mind getting laid off from time to time as a break from what she admitted was a hectic pace. In between the disgruntled and the complacent, a garageman says he can't complain: "You have to work to make a living, so what's the use."[11]

Obviously, ordinary Americans were divided about how much pleasure they found at work, depending on a mixture of type of job and type of personality. It was revealing that, while they were reluctant to slam work entirely in satisfaction polls, many workers were clearly disconnected from their own jobs; in this sense, the range of opinion in the United States was quite similar to that evident in industrial Europe. As in Europe, a wide variety of people were able to find some meaning at work, and extreme grievances were in the minority. Some Americans, at the same time, particularly in the world of management, also talked about the need to conceal honest reactions, about pleasing the boss; here was another component, hard to evaluate precisely, in the relatively mild range of negative work reactions in the United States.

But there was a final factor as well, common in industrial societies but again particularly marked in the United States: the passion for consumerism. "The important thing is to make money," a rather disingenuous businessman, who privately admitted he concealed his distaste for key aspects of work, noted in a leading 1950s novel.[12] Many commentators found the compulsion to maintain or improve standards of living off the job far more important in describing American work habits than any intrinsic work ethic. Americans worked harder or at least longer than counterparts in other industrial societies, in this view, mainly because of their dependence on high wages.

And this dependence, based on an earlier conversion to high-level consumerism, clearly had additional impact from the 1980s onward. For it was at this point that real wages for many middle- and working-class families began to stagnate in the United States, even as the incomes of the wealthiest tenth continued to rise rapidly. Unemployment remained relatively low, in contrast to Europe and even Japan, but at the cost of wage improvements. Many Americans found that they had to rely on some extra earnings either from a spouse or from overtime work by at least one family member just to maintain their current living standards. "Moonlighting," often involving work on weekends, increased by 20 percent in the 1980s alone. A few workers found that they had to think about delaying retirement as well. Credit card debt and other signs of consumer stress mounted at the same time.

The result was another major constraint on options at work. By 2000, American commitment to work, without significant increases in vacation time and amid widespread utilization of overtime arrangements or second jobs, was clearly unusual in the industrial world. It reflected the compulsions of a significant minority who were committed to an unadulterated work ethic. It may have been fed by some valuation of the same work ethic by a larger majority who, at the very least, were influenced by the ethic to the extent that they found it difficult to mount public complaints. But it was also nourished by the extreme version of the instrumentalist trade-off with work.

As with many industrial societies, Americans had learned that modern work could become acceptable if it was compensated by improved wages, and many employers encouraged this bargain. Amid consumer abundance, the lesson may have taken unusually deep root in American soil, to the point of considerable dependence on a demanding earnings standard as opposed to other options such as greater leisure time. When the earnings standard faltered, as in the decades around 2000, work commitments extended in reaction, though of course many workers hoped to find some direct satisfactions in their jobs as well. A minority dedicated to the work ethic and a majority dependent on consumer compensations: this was the complicated American mixture that supported a distinctive national engagement with work.

## American Influence and American Work
## in Comparative Perspective

Developments in American work over the past fifty years have created, or confirmed, something of a national style, which must be assessed comparatively. They
have also contributed to some global discussions about work.

It is true that American influence on work patterns elsewhere has been less
decisive in recent decades than in the days when industrial engineering and the
assembly line were introduced. Japan, with its quality circles, generated wider
discussion about basic work arrangements than the United States did. Often, as
well, American contributions have been part of a larger endeavor involving innovations from many countries, for example, in the technologies that generated
increasing automation and computerization. It would be arrogant to single out a
solely national strand here. On another front, some key developments, like the
modifications of retirement policy, may anticipate wider global debate, but this
has not yet occurred to any great extent.

American impact can be suggested, however, in three respects. First, American
business and political leaders sponsored a number of international projects related
to work. Many Americans have been involved in efforts to improve labor standards
in other countries, out of a mixture of idealism and self-interest in protecting
conditions at home from exploitative competition. Several American groups, for
example, help steer world opinion on sweated labor, including the college-based
Students Against Sweatshops and the more general National Labor Committee,
which sponsors research on working conditions abroad. American representatives
have also been involved at the United Nations and other agencies in some of the
declarations against child labor. American leadership here is not unique: Western
Europe, Japan, and the Pacific Rim contribute strongly, and American administra-
tions have in some cases shied away from too much international standard setting
that might constrain domestic action. But there has been important involvement.
American voices and American consumer pressure have played significant roles
in shaping the public climate in which some leading multinational corporations
evaluate their labor practices.

American managers have also participated directly in setting policies in factories
abroad. We have seen that many Mexican workers point to the evenhandedness
of American managers in across-the-border enterprises, contrasting it with the
harsher policies of local firms.

A second area of impact involves innovations within management itself.
American discussions of management styles and human resources operations continue to reach a global audience through business publications and management
training. American-derived consulting firms (either branch outlets or imitation
foreign models) also play an extensive international role. Individual researchers,
like W. Edwards Deming, contributed extensively in shaping Japanese innovations
such as quality circles. Later management fads, such as Total Quality Management,

also generated wide discussion and considerable imitation. German business leaders, seeing in American research and Japanese example a clear challenge to more hierarchical governance traditions, sent observers to both countries, praising TQM for "creative personnel management and thus the desired innovation." American management terms entered the French language, with odd new verbs such as "empowriser" (to empower). Some of this enthusiasm was only skin deep. One survey suggested that only 9 percent of all French firms really introduced much management change.[13] Outright foot-dragging emerged as well, with calls for resistance to foreign innovation—this was a theme in Britain and Germany—and concerns about the superficiality and oscillations of much American discussion. And while American efforts did, as we have seen, embrace references to empowering employees and diversifying their tasks, the main thrust involved management techniques like strategic planning or just-in-time production, not fundamental reorganizations of the workplace. This was an area of national influence, but its relationship to actual work patterns was not extensive, and again Japan's direct example (however influenced by American research) played a greater global role.

Finally, the American work ethic could spill over into the international arena, at least on occasion. American managers abroad were not always known as hard drivers, but they could be on occasion. An American transportation company bought a French firm in the early 1990s and installed an American director. Immediately the new management began to change the behavior of foremen, reducing their involvement with actual physical labor on the loading docks and increasing their attention to motivating and guiding teams of workers. It seemed imperative to monitor worker behavior more strictly, to ensure higher quality and to attack habits such as smoking on the job. New lower managers were sought, to be trained by the company itself because it distrusted French management experience. Recruitment placed a premium on signs of a good work ethic, such as involvement in extracurricular activities in school. Major emphasis was placed on making sure the new recruits set a good work example. They were expected to arrive on the job a full two hours before the regular labor force, in order fully to plan the day's work activities. Uncompensated overtime was expected after normal hours as well. As a company representative put it, "A team leader is expected to be available to work fifteen hours a day, voluntarily and without pay." The expectation was that work is life, that complete personal investment in the job was essential. Not surprisingly, the enterprise found it increasingly difficult to retain some of its French recruits, who were simply unwilling to define their identities this way.[14]

How often this kind of example was repeated in American efforts abroad is not entirely clear. Certainly many American leaders harbored suspicions about the adequacy of the work ethic in some countries, not only in parts of the "third world" but also now in Europe, given awareness of extensive vacations and elaborate welfare systems. Viewing the world through a national lens could produce some interesting perspectives, and on occasion these could affect actual labor practices. And this, in turn, feeds into the second global vantage point on recent American work experiences, where explicit comparison becomes crucial.

Every specific contemporary work system offers a distinctive mix of advantages and drawbacks, quite apart from an overall assessment of modern work itself. By the early twenty-first century some Europeans worried that they were not working enough, that their vacations were too long, their retirement systems too expensive to keep pace with global competition. New entrants to the industrialization process, like China, had to wonder if their exploitation of labor was too severe, harming population quality and risking social protest.

The American approach to work, fueled particularly by the persistent work ethic, generated several problems of its own. The first, often discussed but hard to evaluate, involved the work-frenzied minority. Were they indeed harming the quality of their lives—and that of their families, when they had them? Were they setting an undesirable standard for other workers, for example, talented women who either could not measure up to the unrealistic levels, given other responsibilities, or who would sacrifice too much if they tried? Some of the cheapest shots about the work addicted—for example, the claims about health damage for type-A personalities—had been partially disproved, but some larger qualitative issues remained.

More broadly, was the rhetoric of the work ethic (even though clearly not fully accepted by the majority of workers in their own lives, as evidenced, for example, by the preferences for early retirement) limiting the capacity to express concerns and grievances? American workers certainly had fewer models available to express anxieties about the basic quality of work than their counterparts in countries with stronger labor movements and more robust traditions of work criticism, and this could frustrate some of them while also limiting the incentive to discuss reforms and alternatives. Alienation undoubtedly persisted for some, but it had to be more silent, more internal, than in some other cultures, and this might be damaging both to individual workers and to the work process itself. Certainly, American work patterns were less susceptible to basic innovation than were those in other industrial societies like Japan, because business and political leaders found it so difficult not to assume that arduous work was not desirable—hence, for example, the unusually uniform rejection of discussions about limiting the workweek in light of the benefits of automation.

Finally, as a number of observers noted, the American penchant for insisting on the validity of modern work patterns, even though the majority of workers harbored some reservations, helped generate a considerable reliance on instrumentalism as a coping mechanism. American dependence on a high consumer standard had several sources, of course, but compensation for work constraints played a role. The result was an obvious irony: workers who were somewhat skeptical about the quality of their jobs worked exceptionally long hours, particularly from the 1980s onward, in order to maintain or increase their earning power—in order partially to justify their work commitments. It might have been better to ease off a bit on the consumer demands in favor of a bit less work—a bit more vacation time, for example—but this was not the American pattern. It was hard to imagine how to break through this distinctive circle.

There is no need to exaggerate. Many Americans were comfortable or fairly comfortable with their work lives, which did indeed help propel a vibrant economy into the early twenty-first century. Distinctive features of the American approach to work involved a few special issues that were worth further consideration; there were some real drawbacks to the model. But the distinctive features also showed how different variants of the basic pattern of modern work could operate successfully. There was no need to insist on a single system, and American work culture could hardly be counted a failure. Furthermore, the nation did participate without particular exception in a number of basic contemporary trends—in women's work involvement, for example, or in the continued quest for more productive technologies.

Comparison sheds revealing light on some American work values, many of them rooted in the nation's earlier history. But comparison must also be subtle. The national model was not dramatically different from other modern work settings; there were some unusual shadings, not a unique American core. The problems embedded in the shadings, around a possibly excessive devotion to a modern work ethic, must be counterbalanced by the advantages this same devotion could generate in economic motivation and in personal efforts to find meaning in work.

# Notes

1. Margaret Brindle and Peter N. Stearns, *Facing Up to Management Faddism* (Westport, CT: Quorum, 2001).
2. Martha Wolfenstein, "The Emergence of Fun Morality," *Journal of Social Issues* 7 (1951).
3. Barbara Ehrenreich, *The Hearts of Men: American Dreams and the Flight from Commitment* (New York: Doubleday, 1987).
4. Natasha Zaretsky, *No Direction Home: The American Family and the Fear of National Decline* (Chapel Hill: University of North Carolina Press, 2007), 114–18.
5. For a typical male liberationist argument, see Herb Goldberg, *The Hazards of Being Male* (New York: Nash, 1976); and Jack Nichols, *Men's Liberation* (New York: Penguin, 1975); Marc Fasteau, *Male Machine* (New York: Delacorte Press/Random House, 1976).
6. Betty Friedan, *The Feminine Mystique* (New York: Dell, 1964), 7, 333.
7. Blanche Linden-Ward and Carol Green, *Changing the Future: American Women in the 1960s* (New York: Twayne, 1993), 97.
8. Linden-Ward and Green, *Changing the Future*, 111.
9. Jill Quadagno, *The Transformation of Old Age Security* (Chicago: University of Chicago Press, 1988); for a typical pro-work gerontological argument, see Zena Blau, *Old Age in a Changing Society* (New York: New Viewpoints, 1973). See also Henry Pratt, *The Gray Lobby* (Chicago: University of Chicago Press, 1976).

10. Studs Terkel, *Working: People Talk about What They Do All Day and How They Feel about What They Do* (New York: Pantheon, 1974), 225.

11. Terkel, *Working*, 10–12, 225, 604–7; Lillian Rubin, *Worlds of Pain* (New York: Basic Books, 1976), 158–59.

12. Sloan Wilson, *The Man in the Gray Flannel Suit* (New York: Simon & Schuster, 1955), 182.

13. Brindle and Stearns, *Facing Up to Management Faddism*, chaps. 7 and 8.

14. Eric Poignant, "U.S. Management in a Transport Company in France," in *European Working Lives*, ed. Steve Jefferys, Frederik Beyer, and Christer Thornqvist (Cheltenham, UK: Edward Elgar, 2001), 74–84.

# Further Reading

## On Retirement

Jill Quadagno, *The Transformation of Old Age Security: Class and Politics in the American Welfare State* (Chicago: University of Chicago Press, 1988).

On women and feminism: Blanche Linden-Ward and Carol Green, *Changing the Future: American Women in the 1960s* (New York: Twayne, 1993); Beth Anne Shelton, *Women, Men and Time: Gender Differences in Paid Work, Housework and Leisure* (New York: Greenwood, 1992).

## On Management Reforms

Margaret Brindle and Peter N. Stearns, *Facing Up to Management Faddism* (Westport, CT: Quorum, 2001).

## On the Leisure Ethic

Martha Wolfenstein, "The Emergence of Fun Morality," *Journal of Social Issues* 7 (1951).

## On Instrumentalism

Gary Cross, *An All-Consuming Century* (New York: Columbia University Press, 2000). Benjamin Hunnicutt, *Work without End: Abandoning Shorter Hours for the Right to Work* (Philadelphia: Temple University Press, 1988) deals with contemporary tension over working hours.

# Recent Studies

Perrons, Diane, ed. *Gender Divisions and Working Time in the New Economy: Changing Patterns of Work, Care and Public Policy in Europe and North America* (Cheltenham, UK: Edward Elgar, 2006).

Cortada, James W. *The Digital Hand: How Computers Changed the Work of American Manufacturing, Transportation, and Retail Industries* (New York: Oxford University Press, 2004).

General Accounting Office. *Women's Earnings: Work Patterns Partially Explain Difference between Men's and Women's Earnings* (Washington, DC: U.S. General Accounting Office, 2003).

Bean, Frank D., and Stephanie Bell-Rose, eds. *Immigration and Opportunity: Race, Ethnicity, and Employment in the United States* (New York: Russell Sage Foundation, 1999).

Neal, Margaret B., and Leslie B. Hammer. *Working Couples Caring for Children and Aging Parents: Effects on Work and Well-Being* (Mahwah, NJ: Lawrence Erlbaum Associates, 2007).

Schneider, Barbara, and Linda J. Waite. *Being Together, Working Apart: Dual-Career Families and the Work-Life Balance* (Cambridge: Cambridge University Press, 2005).

Bailyn, Lotte. *Breaking the Mold: Redesigning Work for Productive and Satisfying Lives* (Ithaca, NY: ILR Press/Cornell University Press, 2006).

Bell, Alice, and Ivana La Valle. *Combining Self-Employment and Family Life* (Bristol, UK: Policy Press, 2003).

Fredriksen-Goldsen, Karen, and Andrew E. Scharlach. *Families and Work: New Directions in the Twenty-First Century* (New York: Oxford University Press, 2001).

Lawler, Edward E., and James O'Toole, eds. *America at Work: Choices and Challenges* (New York: Palgrave Macmillan, 2006).

Karsten, Margaret Foegen. *Management, Gender, and Race in the 21st Century* (Lanham, MD: University Press of America, 2006).

Marchevsky, Alejandra, and Jeanne Theoharis. *Not Working: Latina Immigrants, Low-Wage Jobs, and the Failure of Welfare Reform* (New York: New York University Press, 2006).

Wharton, Amy S. *Working in America: Continuity, Conflict, and Change* (Boston: McGraw-Hill, 2006).

Appelbaum, Eileen, Annette Bernhardt, and Richard J. Murnane, eds. *Low-Wage America: How Employers Are Reshaping Opportunity in the Workplace* (New York: Russell Sage, 2003).

Fraser, Jill Andresky. *White-Collar Sweatshop: The Deterioration of Work and Its Rewards in Corporate America* (New York: W. W. Norton, 2001).

Wheeler, Hoyt N. *The Future of the American Labor Movement* (Cambridge: Cambridge University Press, 2002).

Newman, Katherine S. *Chutes and Ladders: Navigating the Low-Wage Labor Market* (Cambridge, MA: Harvard University Press, 2006).

Fitzgerald, Joan. *Moving Up in the New Economy: Career Ladders for U.S. Workers* (Ithaca, NY: Cornell University Press, 2006).

# CHAPTER 9

# Conclusion: Work Issues in the Present and Future

The modern world of work is barely two centuries old anywhere, though it was foreshadowed by new global trends in the centuries immediately prior to 1800. Given the recency of major change, it is hardly surprising that great discontinuities in work remain around the world, or that even advanced industrial societies are still adjusting and modifying their own arrangements.

Premodern work patterns persist in many places. Many rural workers in India and Africa work without a particularly acute time sense, using technologies and community structures little altered from the preindustrial past. As we have seen, child labor is actually spreading in many parts of South and Southeast Asia, counter to dominant global trends. An Indian reformer, Kailash Satyarthi, tells of going to school and passing daily a cobbler working with his son. He could not understand why the man did not let his boy join him in class, and when he finally managed to ask, the shoemaker replied, "Young man, my father was a cobbler and my grandfather before him, and no one before you has ever asked me that question. We were born to work, and so was my son." Satyarthi would go on to crusade against the use of children in manufacturing, domestic service, and circus performances, rescuing as many as 66,000 youngsters.[1] But in the South and Southeast Asian region as a whole, the number of child workers rose from 6 million to 9 million. Traditional work expectations combined with the need for cheap labor, particularly in crafts and services, to compete against the growing competition from more modern centers.

A key question for the future, then, involves whether, and how rapidly, the still largely premodern areas will move more fully into a modern work mode, in terms of the choices of who works and the type of work performed.

Many parts of the world also are just now entering into intense factory production, often seeking very cheap labor in order to compete with more established centers. China's huge surge into world markets as an industrial power derived in part from the ability to recruit millions of rural workers into factories, where they worked long hours and experienced many of the other changes always associated with the conversion to industrial labor. Multinational corporations established factories in places like Mexico, Indonesia, and Vietnam as well as China, again expecting a rapid pace of work amid relatively sophisticated equipment. Questions arise about whether most of these new industrial centers will make the turn into more fully industrialized societies, and therefore whether the factory labor patterns will become durable parts of the lives of the workers involved. And of course questions arise as well about whether some of the roughest edges, from sheer danger of accidents to long hours, will gradually soften as the societies involved move further into the industrialization process.

White-collar work spread globally as well. Most strikingly, India's rapid economic growth in the early twenty-first century depended extensively on software and service workers. Working in large groups under intense supervision and amid sophisticated equipment and paying careful attention to the clock, workers trained actively not only in accent but also in appropriate emotional expression were moving boldly into the kind of white-collar territory staked out decades earlier in the West.

Modern work patterns, in sum, seemed to be spreading as versions of industrialization fanned out. While factory work was still a centerpiece, broadly modern work conditions—in terms of pace, supervision, dependence on machinery—reached even more widely in new industrial areas and established centers as well. While there could be no certainty about the maintenance of these trends, and no certainty about whether the remaining roughly 40 percent of the world's population would be brought more fully into the industrial orbit, it was probably safe to assume that the spread of modern forms of work was a durable development.

The rise of new industrial regions put pressure on work in some of the older industrial centers. In particular, it was not entirely clear that some of the late twentieth-century efforts to modify or lighten modern work patterns would be able to survive growing competition. There were two obvious examples. As Japan faced stiffer competition from newer industrial regions, many employers cut back on the lifetime-employment system; they thought they needed more flexibility to fire and hire depending on economic circumstances. Many European countries encountered growing doubts about the cost of long vacations, given the fact that so many regions were cutting into industrial markets with far lower-cost labor. And in many regions, of course, questions arose about sheer employment levels: factory jobs retreated in several centers, though they were often replaced by surges of employment in advanced technology or service sectors.

The United States encountered less unemployment and healthier economic growth rates than many industrial regions in Western Europe and Japan. There were important problems, including pockets of employment dislocation and a chronic trade deficit. But it was possible that American work values, less modified than those in other advanced industrial societies, prepared the nation for the new levels of global competition. Certainly, many Americans continued to expect to work hard and wondered if they might have to intensify their efforts in the future.

Established industrial societies, particularly the United States and Western Europe (the issue was less vivid in Japan, where immigration was more limited), also faced interesting questions about immigrant labor. Quite obviously, rapid immigration significantly affected the nature of industrial work in these regions from the 1950s onward. Immigrants did jobs, both in manual labor and in low-paying service categories, that native-born workers now tended to shun. They collected garbage, did unskilled construction work, served as bus conductors. But immigrants could also compete for other jobs, and as they adjusted to their new host societies, gaining better education and language skills, their ability to compete for other jobs was likely to increase. They also posed issues of cultural and political assimilation, though these were more acute in Europe, where the modern phenomenon was newer, than in the United States. For the future, would immigrants continue to supply unskilled labor and would industrial societies want them to? Would greater amalgamation occur throughout the labor force, reducing the dual labor market that tended to concentrate many immigrants only in the least rewarding job slots?

In the 1980s, as computers and other dramatic new technologies gained ground, but before their actual impact was very clear, a number of experts pre-dicted a dramatic transformation in the work experience in the most advanced societies, including the United States. Two major ideas were put forth. First, levels of automation would increase to the point that there would simply be less need to work. This was the context in which one futurologist assumed that people would have to get more accustomed to playing electronic games or doing other things to fill growing leisure hours. The only way for work to be spread around was by cutting back on the work portion of the day. Second, computers would permit more individualized work and less agglomeration into big factories and office complexes. People could introduce more-personalized products and indulge greater creativity. There would be less need for elaborate supervision and regimentation. Without going back to preindustrial patterns—for after all, this depended entirely on advanced technologies—modern work constraints would be eased, perhaps revolutionized.[2]

These images have faded, though not disappeared, as work's future is contem-plated today. Most of the predictions proved to be wrong or greatly exaggerated. In fact, computers today turned out in many ways to extend industrial technology, and while changes in industrial technology have always affected work, they have not necessarily reduced it to the extent many would have anticipated. Computers have allowed a minority of the labor force to work from home rather than the office, at least some of the time. They have allowed some people to shape their schedules more flexibly. To this extent, they have modified industrial constraints on work. But they have often added to the pace of work; because they work so swiftly, they can actually increase the output expected, for example, of clerical personnel. They tie workers to the machine just as determinedly as steam engines ever did, with some new diseases to match, most obviously carpal tunnel syndrome. They obviously cater to work-addicted personalities, enabling them to turn back to work from any location, blurring the boundaries between home and work, even vacation and work. And computers allow rigorous monitoring of the work effort where managers choose to use them for tracking purposes. Unquestionably, thanks to more automated technology, more use of immigrant workers, and global competition, factory settings no longer are the key center of modern work in the oldest industrial economies. But modern work, more broadly defined, persists and expands even so, thanks to the impact of devices like computers on technical, white-collar, and service sectors. Modern work, in sum, has been at most slightly adjusted, not fundamentally reshaped and certainly, to date, not reduced. Indeed, by permitting white-collar competition from foreign sources, computers help keep up the work pressure almost literally around the world. Some further future development may of course produce a more revolutionary turnaround, but it is not clearly in sight.

A more predictable future development, or at least an unavoidable set of future questions, involves older people and work. We have seen that the Industrial Revolution ultimately generated a strong tendency to separate work and older age. This pattern, like the tendency to separate married women from work a few decades ago, must now be rethought, at least to some degree. As a result of the rapid aging of the population in industrial societies, including the United States, for every retired person, only two active workers will be available to provide support for current retirement programs, as opposed to the three or four available when the programs were launched earlier in the twentieth century. This raises the specter of a huge potential social cost. It also means that many older people will have to wonder if enough social and familial support will be available, along with personal savings, to assure their own later age.

There are several possible scenarios. Japan hopes for a dramatic increase in automated processes, including the use of robots, to provide the greater productivity that will sustain its rapidly growing older population. South Korea seeks to encourage a higher birthrate, to modify the percentage of the elderly down the line. Many societies, headed by Western Europe and the United States, rely extensively on immigrants to provide the younger minds and arms needed to help keep the economy going, though amid some uneasiness about immigrant competition. It seems unlikely that these solutions will suffice as the full brunt of aging begins to hit in another decade or so. This is all the more the case in that other societies, such as China, will also encounter the pressures of an aging workforce within a few decades because of the rapid reduction of the birthrate. Already in the 1980s American social security law was modified to encourage (though not require) later retirement; and many individuals, either through interest or necessity, have remained in the workforce, or reentered it, well after what had come to be regarded as normal retirement age.

If retirement is widely challenged, however, further questions arise. What will popular reaction be to older workers in, say, service jobs, given stereotypes of slowness and inefficiency and commitment to outdated technologies? More important, how many people, having counted on retirement as part of the bargain that allowed them to get through unrewarding jobs in middle and later middle age, will feel cheated? How widely will pressures build to provide some other compensations for work pressures—for example, longer vacations—if old age no longer assures a way out? Of course, retirement is not threatened for the really old, those in their eighties and nineties, whose numbers are growing particularly rapidly. Improved health and vigor make it possible for many people to work beyond standard retirement without great difficulty either for themselves or others. Still, some important issues loom, and possibly there will be a significant recasting of one of the most interesting results of industrial work patterns to date.

There is no systematic challenge to the growing separation of children from work, though of course some parts of the world continue to rely extensively on child labor. Global competition did raise issues about children's work habits in school, particularly in the United States, where there was considerable hesitation about demanding too much of children, particularly at the primary and secondary levels. International rankings place American students fairly low in achievements in areas such as mathematics, and many American leaders press for greater rigor. A number of experts have urged longer school days or years, though there has been relatively little response. Many parents, particularly from about 1990 onward, began to expose their children to a variety of lessons and enroll them in more advanced school programs, intending to keep them busy. Whether there would be a wider shift in expectations about the scholastic work habits of American children, however, remained to be seen. Indeed, complaints about an overworked, stressed minority echoed earlier national concerns about children's fragility where work is involved. Even by 2007, some teachers were worrying that American children, and their parents, expected rewards simply for showing up or being bright, rather than any requirements for hard work in the classroom.

Special aspects of the American work experience raise questions for adults as well, beyond American participation in the more global issues including technology and aging. As we have seen, major concerns emerged in the 1970s about the damaging effects of excess work for the work-addicted minority. New technologies, by extending work contacts into private spaces, plus the culture of key law firms, financial houses, and other settings that place a premium on long hours and intensity of work, have probably intensified addiction since that time. The effects on the individuals involved, and their families, are hard to calculate. We know, as against earlier received wisdom, that hard work and high-pressure environments do not necessarily damage health if the individuals enjoy their jobs, feel that they have control over their routines, and participate meaningfully in work decisions. But this does not necessarily cover all the people involved in those situations, and it certainly does not factor in the impacts on families.

Work addiction and the kinds of jobs that depend on it also place pressure on other workers who would like to compete but, for whatever reason, cannot participate at the same level of commitment. Women, particularly with child-rearing responsibilities, have sometimes tried to carve out a special place where they can participate in meaningful jobs at a less frenzied pace. Efforts to define special tracks in management, or simply slightly lower work levels on the part of women physicians, for example, compared to their male counterparts, reflect efforts to compensate in the demanding American context. But issues remain, particularly because the promotion of work addiction shows no signs of abating.

Other questions apply to the larger number of Americans who find some pleasure in work but hardly wish it to define their lives. Have too many Americans, as historian Gary Cross argued, made a fool's bargain in terms of their consumer expectations, forcing themselves to work harder or at least longer than their counterparts in many other industrial societies simply to buy the latest car or electronic gadget? Would it be better to pull back a bit, accepting a slightly lower standard of living in favor of more leisure time?[3] The most recent two decades, certainly, have not been kind in this area: stagnating real wages for many American workers have meant that maintaining or even increasing work time, including taking on deliberate overtime, has become essential simply to make ends meet—as ends are currently defined in a high-pressure consumer society. Material pressures are central here, though the larger work culture provides a nurturing context for the high level of work engagement. The objective trend is clear: Americans enjoy less vacation time than their counterparts in the rest of the industrial world. Whether this should be reviewed, whether it can be reviewed given current American values, is an important issue for the future.

Modern work has always involved mutual influences across geographic boundaries. Early industry began, of course, in Britain, and as societies like France and the United States copied British technology, they imported factory work systems as well. American work patterns became particularly influential in the late nineteenth and early twentieth centuries, especially patterns concerned with the assembly line and also with personnel management more generally. Elements of this influence would continue in the later twentieth century. Briefly, at least, the Japanese work example, and particularly the notion of worker input and job security, held pride of place in the 1980s. In no instance did foreign influence totally displace local cultures, as shown in the impressive continuity of elements of the American middle-class work ethic and its impact on perceptions and policies. With globalization around 2000, no specific model seemed to gain a clear advantage. The sheer pressure of competition from the hothouse factories of China and elsewhere was more important than more subtle national variants in work organization. Is another model in the wings? How will current American practices and values hold up in the global economy?

*    *    *

Modern work almost certainly exposed a growing number of workers to some kind of alienation, and this is still to be the case as new groups of workers face harsh conditions in expanding factories around the world. Almost certainly as well, thanks to the special interest certain modern jobs offer, plus the encouragement of new work ethics, a larger minority of people became addicted to work than had been true before the industrial age. Issues of alienation and addiction continue to influence evaluations of the modern work experience in the United States and elsewhere.

Most people, of course, have skated between the extremes, recognizing the constraints of modern jobs at least to some extent but also finding some degree of satisfaction not just in instrumental earnings but also in a sense of personal contribution. Work interviews in the United States suggest how many different types of workers claim some space in this middle ground. In some ways, this mixture of frustration and reward may have existed before modern work emerged; similar capacities of human adjustment are involved both before and after the Industrial Revolution. But the very real changes must be registered as well: demands on physical strength and also on nervous energy are not the same as before; the familial and community context for work is not the same as before; the sense of participation, barring a few of the bolder modern experiments, is not the same as before. Whether the overall package has improved or deteriorated is obviously an extremely complicated question, but that does not mean that evaluation should be abandoned.

One thing is certain: the pressures of modern work and the distractions of many official work ethics have made it very difficult for many workers to step back and assess this aspect of their quality of life. It is far easier, and far more encouraged, to take stock of earnings and living standards off the job. Even protest movements have found work itself an elusive target. A history of modern work helps establish a framework for assessment both of work in general and of individual work situations. Along with establishing a baseline for key questions about work in the future, this is a vital contribution. There is every reason to use the history of work to think about where we have moved over the past two centuries, and where we are likely to head—and where we should try to head—in the future.

# Notes

1. Kailash Satyarthi, ed., *Globalisation, Development and Child Rights* (Delhi: Shipra, 2006).

2. Robert Ayres, *Uncertain Futures* (New York: John Wiley & Sons, 1979).

3. Gary S. Cross, *An All-Consuming Century* (New York: Columbia University Press, 2000).

# Index

# About the Author

Peter N. Stearns is Provost and Professor of History at George Mason University. He has taught previously at Harvard, the University of Chicago, Rutgers, and Carnegie Mellon; he was trained at Harvard University. He has published widely in modern social history, including the history of emotions, and in world history. Representative works in world history include *World History: A Survey*; *The Industrial Revolution in World History*; *Gender in World History*; *Consumerism in World History*; and *Growing Up: The History of Childhood in Global Context*. His publications in social history include *Old Age in Preindustrial Society*; *Anger: The Struggle for Emotional Control in America's History* (with Carol Stearns); *Anxious Parents: A History of Modern American Childrearing*; *American Cool: Developing the Twentieth-Century Emotional Style*; *Fat History: Bodies and Beauty in Western Society*; *The Battleground of Desire: The Struggle for Self-Control in Modern America*; *American Fear: The Causes and Consequences of High Anxiety*; and *Revolutions in Sorrow: A History of American Experiences and Policies Toward Death in Global Context*. He has also edited encyclopedias of world and social history, and since 1967 has served as editor-in-chief of *The Journal of Social History*.

In most of his research and writing, Dr. Stearns has pursued three main goals. First, as a social historian he is eager to explore aspects of the human experience that are not always thought of in historical terms, and with attention to ordinary people as well as elites. Second, building on this, he seeks to use an understanding of historical change and continuity to explore current patterns of behavior and social issues. Finally, he is concerned with connecting new historical research with wider audiences, including of course classrooms. History must be seen in terms of the expansion of knowledge, not primarily the repetition of familiar topics and materials. As he has worked extensively in world history, Peter Stearns is also eager to promote comparative analysis and the assessment of modern global forces—for their own sake and as they shed light on the American experience and impact. He is deeply interested in using history to illuminate contemporary issues and politics.